Community Service
and
Higher Learning

Community Service and Higher Learning

Explorations of the Caring Self

Robert A. Rhoads

State University of New York Press

Published by
State University of New York Press, Albany

© 1997 State University of New York

For information, address State University of New York
Press, State University Plaza, Albany, N.Y., 12246

Production by E. Moore
Marketing by Nancy Farrell

Library of Congress Cataloging-in-Publication Data

Rhoads, Robert A.
    Community service and higher learning : explorations of the caring
self / Robert A. Rhoads.
        p.   cm.
    Includes bibliographical references and index.
    ISBN 0-7914-3521-0 (hc : alk. paper). — ISBN 0-7914-3522-9 (pb :
alk. paper)
    1. Student service—United States. 2. Student volunteers in
social service—United States. 3. Community and college—United
States. 4. Education, Higher—Aims and objectives—United States.
I. Title.
LC220.5.R56 1997
370.11′5—dc21   96-49881
                                                                              CIP

10 9 8 7 6 5 4 3 2 1

Contents

Acknowledgments   *vii*

Introduction   *1*

1. Situating the Self   *11*

2. Culture and Identity   *41*

3. Thinking about Community   *69*

4. Otherness   *97*

5. Mutuality   *126*

6. Community Building   *152*

7. Action/Reflection   *179*

8. Critical Community Service   *204*

Conclusion   *229*

References   *235*

Index   *247*

Acknowledgments

As with any project the magnitude of writing a book, there are many people to thank. I am grateful to the following individuals who provided feedback on the manuscript in one form or another: Lorrice Bedard, Matt Fifolt, Julie Neururer, Maenette Benham, Dave Guthrie, Scott Dixon, and Sue Cooley Miller. I especially want to thank Yvonna Lincoln and Peter McLaren, not only for their helpful comments, but for their support over the years. Your help has been greatly appreciated.

I also thank my mother, Ruth Carol Filer, and my stepfather, John Filer, for their support and guidance. I thank my brother Gary, and my sisters Michelle, Jamie, and Kim, who all have been a source of inspiration and support throughout my life.

To my nieces and nephews, Amber, Philip, Jessica, Alex, and Samantha, may you be lucky enough to be able to follow your dreams.

And finally, I thank all the student volunteers who have given of themselves to others. May your lives be blessed through your caring.

Introduction

We exist at a time in which a unified sense of identity escapes comprehension. Just when we think we have integrated multiple and complex understandings of our social world and of who we are as people, an event, a feeling, a desire sends all we have worked to unify out an imaginary door that is the threshold between modernity and postmodernity. Modernism calls out to us and speaks a language we comprehend, and yet we suspect it is a language that no longer helps to negotiate the intricate cultural webs of contemporary life. Postmodernism also calls us, and we believe it may enlighten our world; however, because it is a stranger we fear its ever-growing presence. At the center of our passage from modernity to postmodernity stands the self, confused and perplexed by all that was and all that might be.

Postmodernism is characterized by an unabashed questioning of all that we have come to know—this thing we call knowledge. Truth exists in a temporary state suspended by the prevailing discourse of the day. Difference becomes the defining characteristic of social life as a myriad of understandings contribute to an ever-emerging sense of self. Long-established traditions no longer endure; new ways of making sense of the world replace the old and then are replaced themselves by still newer visions. Postmodernity brings a world of multiplicity in which everything, or nearly everything, is brought into question. The margin becomes the center, but the center cannot hold. Conflict and change become the essence of social life as community escapes us, and yet our communal needs remain as strong as ever (Baudrillard, 1994; Benhabib, 1992; Gergen, 1991; Lyotard, 1984).

This brings me to the central problem I face in this work: How do we build community in spite of the cacophonous strains of postmodernity and without resorting to modernist tendencies to silence that which is different? I argue that the struggle to create community is the central challenge of contemporary life and is at the heart of utopian visions of a truly democratic society.

Postmodernism's exhortations for communities to organize around difference come with little substance in terms of how or why people should enter into relationships with diverse others. We are implored to create "dialogue across difference" (Burbules & Rice, 1991), but the basis for conversation and how such interactions might enable community building to occur are like whispers in the wind. A goal of this book is to bring light to the postmodern call for dialogue across difference and the challenge to build communities of difference (Tierney, 1993). I believe higher education must play a crucial role in this struggle.

I argue that fostering a sense of self grounded in an ethic of care is a necessity as our society becomes increasingly diverse and diffuse. By fostering an ethic of care, higher learning encourages the sense of otherness necessary for group actions across difference to occur. I focus on how knowledge of the self derived from students' involvement in community service provides a basis for creating a more democratic and caring form of higher learning. My argument is rather straightforward: Caring is an ethic that can be fostered, and community service is a vehicle for advancing such an ethic. In short, understanding the social processes associated with community service can shed light on how higher learning might be restructured as we struggle to build democratic communities within the tensions and strains of a postmodern world.

But why should we care about caring? In recent years, this question has become a preeminent concern to many scholars of education and society (Coles, 1993; Palmer, 1993; Radest, 1993; Wuthnow, 1995). "Why should we care about caring?" is the central question Joan Lipsitz addressed in the prologue to a special issue of *Phi Delta Kappan* devoted to "youth and caring." Lipsitz offered a response to the question: "Because without caring, individual human beings cannot thrive, communities become violent battlegrounds, the American democratic experiment must ultimately fail, and the planet will not be able to support life" (1995, p. 665). In the same issue, Nel Noddings argued that the fundamental problem of advancing an ethic of care in schools is convincing people that caring is important: "The greatest structural obstacle, however, may simply be legitimizing the inclusion of themes of care in the curriculum. . . . Therefore, it would seem that the most fundamental change required is one of attitude" (1995, p. 679).

This book reflects six years of research on college students' participation in community service. I am greatly indebted to nearly two hundred students who participated in a variety of community service projects and who allowed me to examine their experiences. Many of the student participants in this study were involved in weeklong, highly intensive community service activities that typically took place over winter and spring breaks and were conducted in communities distant from the universities they attended. Additional research was conducted on other kinds of service activities that often occurred in the local communities surrounding the three universities involved in this study: Pennsylvania State University, Michigan State University, and the University of South Carolina. Nearly all of the service projects discussed in this book relate to rural or urban poverty and involve students working to help meet the needs of low-income families and individuals.

A central theoretical aim of this book is to better understand the "self," which has been the subject of much philosophical, psychological, and sociological inquiry. Perhaps one of the curious qualities that modernity set in motion is the fascination we have with understanding who we are as individuals and what it means for us to have a sense of self or an identity (Gleason, 1983; Logan, 1987). Edward Sampson discussed identity and the influence of the modern epoch: "A liberal individualist framework emerged at this time, both to oppose the premodern understanding and to establish the familiar terms of modern life. Individuals were set free from all the ties and attachments that formerly defined them. Individuals, understood as self-determining, autonomous sovereigns, authors in charge of their own life's work, became the central actors on the social stage" (1989, p. 915).

Thus, language and culture have made it possible for humans to situate themselves as objects of their own analysis and inquiry, and a variety of strategies have been employed in pursuit of identity and the self. Most notable, of course, is Sigmund Freud's (1923) work to unravel the essence of the self through his probing of the subconscious. For Freud, the complexities of personality, which arguably is rooted in one's sense of self, come together in the ego through its interaction with the id and superego. Freud's three psychological structures theoretically explain the effort humans make to balance the dynamic tensions among desire, satisfaction, and social constraint. Others, such as Charles Taylor (1989), explored more philosophical analyses, asserting that understandings of the modern self must be historically situated and are inextricably connected to morality. Taylor pursued the self by examining "what makes our lives meaningful or fulfilling" (p. 4) as revealed through the eyes of Western philosophers and social theorists over the ages. Whereas Taylor anchored the self in history, Brian Morris (1994) situated the self in the anthropological context as he examined cross-cultural notions of the self through "cultural paradigms," which, for Morris, are roughly equivalent to worldviews. He argued that cultural paradigms vary from one society to the next and that they emphasize different qualities of the self. The self thus becomes a reflective pond of the larger social body and reveals the essence of what a society values.

There are a multitude of theories of the self, but of particular importance for this book are those theories that explain the self in the context of social interaction. Selecting theoretical treatments of the self grounded in social interactions with others is a logical choice, given the nature of community service to be in Howard Radest's (1993) words "an encounter with strangers" and necessarily then an encounter with otherness. In particular, two streams of thought inform the understanding of the self I adopt throughout this book: (1) symbolic interactionism and discussions of the "social self," and (2) feminism and elaborations of the "relational self." George Herbert Mead (1934) and Carol Gilligan (1982), respectively, are the key theorists representing these two schools of thought.

A central point of both the social self and the relational self is that the nature and context of interactions between the self and the other establishes to a large degree how the self is formed. In other words, the self is inescapably tied to the other. And, perhaps just as important, the social context is the stage upon which the self and the other are framed. There are other complex issues that also relate to this general philosophical view, such as the role of culture in setting the parameters for social interaction, and many of these points will be addressed as the theoretical perspective unfolds in chapters 1, 2, and 3.

Although symbolic interactionism helps to explain fundamental qualities of a socially constructed self, it lacks the visionary component of feminism that aspires for an idealized identity grounded in an "ethic of care." More to the point, feminists not only maintain that people develop through relationships with others, but they go a step further to argue that a sense of connection to others and an attitude of caring ought to be a goal of human development. I embrace this view and argue that a central role of higher learning ought to revolve around the development of an ethic of care among students. I connect a more caring vision of higher learning to democratic views of education such as those embraced by John Dewey (1916) and contemporaries such as bell hooks (1994), Paulo Freire (1970), Henry Giroux (1992), Peter McLaren (1995), and William Tierney (1993). In advancing this vision, I argue that community service can play an integral part in reformulating higher education.

What can we learn from student involvement in community service—which necessarily involves an encounter between the self and the other—that sheds light on how higher learning might be restructured around an ethic of care? Here, I need to distinguish a few terms related to discussions of community service. For example, what is the difference between community service and service learning? Service learning combines community service with a learning component and in the collegiate context typically is supervised by a faculty member or a student affairs professional and often carries with it academic credit or is part of a course requirement or option. Some service learning activities may have prescribed learning objectives as part of the experience and may include students writing a reflection paper describing their experiences. For example, Michigan State University has implemented a service learning curriculum as part of its undergraduate writing initiative. Service and writing activities are intertwined and are used to help foster an educated and socially responsible citizenry. Other educational components of service learning include group reflection as a means of increasing the educational value of the experience. Most of the community service projects discussed in this book have a reflective component built into them and thus may be thought of as service learning. Consequently, sometimes I refer to these activities as "community service," "service learning," or even "community service learning." Eventually, I introduce (in chapter 8) a new conception of service, "critical community service," which is my effort to combine a theory of service with a feminist ethic of care and democratic concerns for social justice and equality. The challenge is to identify key aspects of community service that foster more caring and democratic attitudes among students. In an effort to meet this challenge, I advance a theory of self, other, and community that is highly interdisciplinary and rooted in fields such as social psychology, sociology, feminism, postmodernism, and critical theory.

There is a subtheme to this text as well. Much of my childhood involved a personal struggle with poverty as my family—my mother and four siblings—drifted back and forth between "getting by" and economic hard times. I recall many occasions of going to bed hungry or trying to relieve hunger pains with a ketchup sandwich. The morning strategy (in the summertime) was to sleep in and thereby postpone to a degree a fully conscious awareness of the fact that our cupboards were bare, or barely stocked. One could think of it as a self-imposed hibernation. Although I do not want to dwell on the measure of our struggle at this point in the text, there are sidesteps taken throughout this book in which I share some of my experiences. The personal detours, which are used to connect my own struggle with poverty to issues of student involvement in community service, come at the beginning of chapters 1 through 8 and serve to orient these chapters.

Most of our financial problems were tied to my mother's efforts to raise five children on her own. My father and mother divorced when I was four, and my mother's two subsequent marriages lasted a relatively short period of time (three years and then one year). My mother did the best she could to provide for us by taking factory work whenever possible, but at other times we were dependent on the welfare system. The reason I mention all of this is that my family's struggle with poverty has left an indelible mark on my sense of self and how I approach community service. Experiences with economic marginality, which for me continued into my young adult years, also have influenced how I see myself as an academic and contribute a great deal to how I go about scholarly work. More to the point, this book is based on community service projects designed to better the lives of poor people and it was in their lives that I often saw myself. The experience was and continues to be eye opening and has generated much reflection about my life. Because some of my struggles, my own exploration of the self, are so connected to what I observed among students and those they worked to serve, I include throughout the book thoughts and reflections about my experiences as I move back and forth between a personal and a more theoretic and research-driven narrative. Part of my intention is to demonstrate that within educational settings students are not alone in their quest to explore the self. Indeed, faculty and staff face many struggles that challenge us to think about the moral and ethical ideals we hold dear and what it means to be part of something larger than ourselves.

The decision to weave some of my own experiences and self-reflections into the body of this work reflects a commitment to feminist notions of research and writing, which reject the traditional scientific view that the self can somehow be separated from the object of inquiry. I discuss this in chapter 1 under the rubric of "positionality," which highlights the idea that scholars are neither neutral nor objective, but instead bring to their research biases, subjectivities, and identities, all of which influence the nature of the work. The challenge from a feminist perspective is to clarify as much as possible for the reader how our own sense of self plays a mitigating role throughout the research process and in the narrative structure itself. Thus, as I explore and write about the self-explorations of students through their participation in community service, some of my own explorations are revealed.

THE LAYOUT OF THE BOOK

With a conceptual overview of the book thus provided, I want to delineate more clearly what each chapter offers. In chapter 1, entitled "Situating the Self," I discuss the idea of positionality and the role an author's sense of self plays in shaping the nature of his or her work. I borrow heavily from discussions of feminist standpointism and how such views inform the subjectivity/objectivity debate. I move from a discussion of the author's self to examine how the self in general has been situated by symbolic interactionists. Specifically, I examine Mead's (1934) notion of the social self and how other interactionists such as Herbert Blumer (1969), Gregory Stone (1962), and Norman Denzin (1977) have added to his work. I conclude chapter 1 by discussing the methodology used in conducting this project, where I also focus on the relevance of studying college students.

In chapter 2, entitled "Culture and Identity," I elaborate on the concept of the self by discussing the related conceptual matters of culture and identity. I draw heavily upon feminist notions of the relational self to situate emerging views of gendered identities and the notion of the "relational self." My discussion of feminist notions of the self revolves around the work of Gilligan (1979, 1982) and Nancy Chodorow (1974, 1978). As part of this discussion, I seek to clarify what is meant by an "ethic of care" and caring in general, which arguably is at the heart of feminist conceptions of women's identity and the self. I then move the discussion into the broader arena of identity politics as I explore the oppressive role culture sometimes plays in situating certain identities on the margins of society. Toni Morrison's (1970) *The Bluest Eye* provides insight into the negative self-conceptions often caused by the oppressive constraints of culture. I conclude this chapter by relating the theoretical discussion to the primary scope of this book—the context of higher learning and collegiate identities and selves.

Chapter 3, "Thinking About Community," links theoretical discussions of the self to emerging conceptions of community and how we have come to think about the individual in relation to the larger social body. I review two general epochal understandings of social life: traditional and postmodern perspectives. Within the traditional framework, I discuss three schools of thought: (1) functionalist perspectives, led by the work of Emile Durkheim (1933); (2) conflict perspectives, guided by the work of Karl Marx (1844); and (3) symbolic conceptions, spearheaded by Mead (1934). I then elaborate more contemporary theories framed by postmodernism in which community tends to be conceptualized around difference. After summarizing both traditional and postmodern perspectives, I highlight key aspects of each that may be of help theoretically in the effort to build community within an increasingly diverse and multiplicitous society. I conclude the chapter by offering ten principles that summarize the theoretical stance undergirding this work.

In chapter 4 ("Otherness") I focus on how community service is, by its nature, an encounter with diverse others and thus provides students with valuable opportunities to understand the complexity of postmodern social life. The chapter focuses on a service project involving a group of students from Pennsylvania State University who worked with homeless citizens in Washington, D.C. The focus is on the content of student interactions and the types of understandings students developed in relation to the homeless people they met. The chapter also incorporates findings from other community service projects that have contributed to students' experiences with otherness. One of the more significant findings is that, as a result of their interactions, students are more likely to personalize social concerns and thus more willing to become involved in work for social change. As one student who participated in the D.C. project explained, "Working with the homeless helped me to see that the problems they face are not just their problems." The chapter also reveals a tendency on the part of students to reconcile otherness by situating cultural difference either as irrelevant (as in denying difference) or as something beautiful and exotic (as in essentializing difference).

Chapter 5 is entitled "Mutuality" and focuses on key aspects of the relationship between those involved in doing service and those receiving some form of service. I highlight a service project organized by a group of students from the University of South Carolina, a project that involved working with low-income families on Johns Island, South Carolina. The experiences of these students, as well as additional students involved in different kinds of community service projects, underscore the importance of what Radest (1993) discussed as "mutuality"—a relationship that is based on equality and collaboration between the "doer" (providers of a service) and the "done to" (receivers of a service). From such a perspective, community service is seen more as an act of working with people in need rather than working to serve them. I address the idea of mutuality in two ways. First, mutuality involves the recognition that all parties participating in service that is truly "community" service derive some benefit from the activity. For those in need, the service is designed to help meet those needs. For those who provide a service of some kind, the rewards are more intrinsic and directly relate to one's sense of self. The other aspect of mutuality relates to an idealized vision of community service that entails establishing equal relationships between the service workers and those with a need. The reality is that both the "doers" and the "done to" benefit from the service encounter, and therefore both ought to have say in how service is structured.

Chapter 6 ("Community Building") examines the role community service plays in contributing to the larger problem of building community. I highlight a service project in Yonges Island, South Carolina focused on the learning experiences of a group of Pennsylvania State University students as they worked to renovate a community center and implement an after-school program for local children. Several issues related to community building and community service learning are highlighted in this chapter. For example, the community-building emphasis of community service calls attention to the difference between community service and charity. Students highlighted the power of *community* service by the manner in which they talked about their relationships with the residents of the island. "It was amazing to me how they embraced us as if we were long-lost friends. I didn't know what to make of their warmth." Students also talked about the unique sense of community they witnessed among the residents of the island. As one student explained, "The sense of community here is different from where I grew up. I may not even know my neighbors. But not here. That's the wonderful part of it all. Everyone here is so close." I use students' experiences to highlight some of the theoretical debates about community. In particular, I contrast communitarian with postmodern perspectives and point out how an ethic of care can serve as a connective link among diverse peoples.

Chapter 7 is entitled "Action/Reflection" and focuses on the learning context of community service. This chapter highlights issues related to individual learning and the role that action and reflection play as interactive components of community service as a liberatory educational endeavor. I argue that community service without reflection does not lend itself to challenge students' perceptions of social inequities and therefore is unlikely to achieve far-reaching social change. Community service must be complemented with reflection and the kind of questioning that fosters the critical consciousness (*conscientization*) Freire (1970) discusses as part of a liberatory education. The chapter highlights a Habitat for Humanity trip to Maryland's eastern shore but calls upon a variety of other student experiences in community service to provide insight into the relationship between action and reflection.

In chapter 8, entitled "Critical Community Service," I link some of the key learning experiences derived from my research on student involvement in community service to principles of critical education derived primarily from feminist and critical pedagogy. Namely, I suggest some foundational ideas for creating community service that reflect a commitment to critical consciousness and liberatory practice inherent in the ideals of democratic education as suggested by feminists and critical theorists. I discuss how the work of Dewey (1916) has informed my understanding and in particular how his ideas on democratic education might contribute to how community service is conceptualized. I argue that critical community service is not intended to be a panacea for the many problems associated with higher learning, but instead should be seen as part of a larger effort to foster more caring and democratic citizens. I delineate eight principles that are central to critical community service and go on to discuss specific strategies for advancing community service within academe. I focus on the role of organizational leaders, faculty, student affairs professionals, and student leaders, and then discuss various structural issues to be addressed.

Finally, I offer a brief conclusion in which I seek to bring together the key aspects of my argument and the general challenge to rethink the fundamental goals of academe. As part of the conclusion, I situate this work within the realm of other utopian visions offered over the course of time.

RETHINKING HIGHER LEARNING

This book is about how we might rethink and ultimately restructure higher learning around more caring and democratic forms of education. As a critique of higher education, it contributes to a larger body of scholarly and non-scholarly works that seek to alter the terrain of college and university life. A recent criticism of higher education offered by Benjamin Barber reflects some of the points I make in this book: "There is endless talk today about education, but between the hysteria and the cynicism there seems to be little room for civic learning, hardly any for democracy" (1992, p. 4). Barber goes on to make the point that we are not born free; we are born dependent: "Our dependency is both physical—we need each other and cannot survive alone—and psychological; our identity is forged through a dialectical relationship with others" (p. 4). In this book, I also argue that our existence is one of interdependence and that the struggle to build community reflects the interconnections that we already have but also feel a need to strengthen. It is the communal desire that calls out from one to the other. Yet, at the same time, we experience a social world that is more fragmented and diverse than ever before.

Barber highlights a liberal position on community that reflects the communitarian perspective: "Human association depends on imagination: the capacity to see in other beings like ourselves. It is thus through imagination that we render others sufficiently like ourselves for them to become subjects of tolerance and respect, sometimes even affection" (p. 5). This is where I part company with liberal interpretations of social life and hence some of their primary goals of education; communitarians clearly imply that an individual can care only for someone with whom he or she feels similar. "I am like you; therefore I can care for you." Is it necessary to be like someone in order to care for and respect them? In arguing that likeness is needed, liberals and communitarians intentionally or unintentionally silence difference, which is why their criticisms often focus not only on the conservative right, but also on postmodernists, feminists, and critical theorists, who embrace cultural difference wholeheartedly. Whereas some theorists seek to shroud cultural differences under blankets of commonality as they reach back to preserve the past and modernist conceptions of community, I suggest, as others such as Tierney (1993) have suggested, that we need to move beyond modernist views and seek a sense of connection that does not whitewash our diversity. I believe an ethic of care is necessary for us to embrace such a vision and at the same time share in a common struggle for equality, justice, and a truly democratic society.

A question remains: How do we foster an ethic of care? Throughout this book I suggest that community service, as a learning and liberatory endeavor, provides insights into the question of how caring might be encouraged. These insights converge in chapter 8 as I combine findings obtained from my research with critical views of education to offer some basic principles for using community service as one possible vehicle for transforming higher learning around an ethic-of-care philosophy.

Chapter 1

Situating the Self

*One's sense of self is always mediated by the
image one has of the other.*
　　　　　　　*—Vincent Crapanzano,
　　　　　　　　"A Reporter at Large"*

*When I was a child there were many times when my mom struggled to
provide adequate food and clothing for our family. I especially remember late
August because that is when we had to buy clothes for the upcoming school
year. My mom did the best she could to come up with some extra money so that
we could buy new shirts, pants, or shoes. I remember when I was about to
enter the seventh grade and she gave me ten dollars to get something nice to
wear as I took that big step from elementary school to junior high. I went to a
discount store called Buyers Fair and spent a couple of hours trying to find the
best bargains. The clothes were not the greatest and there certainly weren't
any name brands but after a lot of searching I was able to buy two pairs of bell
bottoms and two shirts for just under ten dollars. That meant four new outfits
for school if I mixed and matched them.*

*The late 1960s and early 1970s were some tough times for my mom, my
brother, my three sisters, and me, but we also had some good times. We weren't
always poor. Sometimes Mom was able to get a good factory job, like the time
she worked at Blazon—the company that used to make those plastic rocking
horses on springs and other large toys for kids. She was able to bring home
some of the broken ones for free. I'll never forget the day she brought home a
toy rickshaw. For hours my older brother and my two younger sisters (my
youngest sister, Michelle, was not born yet), and I would take turns pulling
each other around the projects. We were the only ones in the entire housing
complex with a rickshaw. For once in our lives we felt privileged, and everyone
envied us. These were some of the better times, financially speaking. We even*

had money for school lunches, unlike my high school years when I had to participate in the free lunch program.

Moving was a constant in our lives. By the time I graduated from high school, I could count twenty-seven different houses or apartments that we had lived in, about ten different communities, and five different states, including two moves to California and then back to western Pennsylvania each time. There were a number of reasons for our moves, but the driving force was a desire on my mother's part to make a better life for us, even if that meant moving us to Los Angeles with her third husband, who soon thereafter she discovered was a drug addict. One divorce later and a cross-country trip back to Pennsylvania and we were once again as broke as ever.

During the years that followed our return from California, which were my junior high and high school years, we often were dependent on others for financial help, like when my Aunt Shirley and Uncle Lou let us live with them for a while even though they already had eight children of their own. The government helped too with food stamps, medical assistance, and surplus cheese. I got so sick of the bricklike, dark orange cheese they doled out for free. Members of the community also helped us, especially during the holiday seasons when my mom tried so hard to give us a Thanksgiving or a Christmas like our friends could afford. To buy a few presents or even a turkey or ham for a special dinner drained her monthly budget. I remember men and women from a local church who came to our house with boxes of food: cranberry sauce, pumpkin pie mix, canned yams, pickles, relishes. With all the extra food in the cupboards, Mom was able to spend some of her food budget on a turkey or even a few presents if it was Christmastime. It was also at Christmastime that people from the churches or sometimes one of the local steel unions or community agencies would bring presents that were donated and then gift wrapped. The presents would have labels that read "14 year-old boy"—"That one's for Gary!" one of us would yell. Or "5 year-old girl!"—"That one's for Jamie!"

What weighs on me most when I reflect on the people from the churches or the steel union or the local agencies is not only the gratitude that I certainly felt, but the feelings of shame and even resentment that I experienced at the time. I was ashamed that we were so poor that someone from a local church had to take up a collection for us. I was ashamed that without their help we could not enjoy the same simple pleasure that all my friends' families seemed to take for granted. I was ashamed that we were needy.

At the same time, I resented these people for the knowledge they held about our life, our circumstances. The knowledge that we were poor. Or at least much poorer than they were. I resented them for the power they seemed to have over me and the fear that they might be the fathers or the mothers of my school friends from whom I tried so desperately to hide our poverty. I resented them for having what I did not have—an excess of food, or clothes, or money. I *truly appreciated their assistance, their generosity, their caring; but, at the same time, it was a slap in my pride's face.*

When they came to the door, I would disappear upstairs and either stay in my room or hide at the top of the stairs so I would know when they had left. I felt extremely guilty for accepting their gifts but being unable to look them in the face and thank them. It was more than my pride could bear.

My oldest sister, Kim, who is three years younger than I am, was the same way when it came to protecting her sense of pride. She and I talked some- times about what was worse—going without lunch during the school day or having to use free lunch tickets that told the entire school (or so it seemed to us) that we were on welfare. It's no wonder that I never felt a sense of connection to the guys at my school, some of whom made a habit of mocking those "lazy niggers on welfare" who lived on the other side of town. I identified with the Blacks in my hometown and knew something my White middle-class peers did- n't know: The poor aren't any more lazy than anyone else. They are like my brother and my sisters. They are just poor.

I share a bit of my past as a means of introducing the complex story that lies ahead. We all have a sense of self that we bring to all we do. As we know from our own lived experience, the self is much more than simply a reflection of our present-day circumstances and current feelings. We each have deeply textured social histories, all of which contribute to who we are as a person. For me, the experiences I had with poverty as a child have left an indelible impact on the person I am today and the self I bring to community service and profes- sional tasks such as research and writing.

The college students whose lives and experiences I share throughout this book also have social histories and a sense of self that they bring to their com- munity service work. Carolyn Fisher,* a twenty-two-year-old college student, grew up in a very loving and financially secure family. Her dad is employed as a professor at a major research university, and her mother is actively involved in community concerns. Both her parents play an active and caring role in Carolyn's life. Perhaps it is their influence on Carolyn, their acts of compassion and care directed toward her and her siblings, which contributes to Carolyn's desire to serve the poor and her commitment to social change.

Although Carolyn's commitment to others through social activism has been a source of much passion in her life, it has also produced much confusion. Carolyn is an artist, and for years she has struggled with what she saw as two

---

*The names used for students and community members throughout this text are pseu- donyms.

contradictory pulls in her life: to be an artist or to be an activist. She has gone through an interesting personal struggle, including a cross-country journey to the West Coast, as part of an effort to resolve her identity crisis and make a choice about her future. Carolyn talks about the conflict: "I want to continue with my art, although for a while I pushed that part of me away because all the women in my family are artists and I didn't want to do the same things that they have done. But also, I didn't see the relevance of art in changing the world. I didn't see how art could help solve social problems." Eventually, Carolyn had an epiphany which led to the resolution of her identity struggle. I discuss Carolyn's explorations of the self and how she resolved her personal conflict in detail in chapter 4. Suffice it to say for now, Carolyn Fisher is a good example of how the social histories students bring to their community service contribute to their experience.

Samuel Frias is another student I met through mutual participation in community service. Like Carolyn, he is a college student in his early twenties who is committed to community service and social activism. Samuel strongly identifies with his racial/ethnic heritage and has been deeply touched by the economic suffering of his fellow Puerto Ricans, both in the United States and in his homeland. Samuel's career and personal goal is someday to graduate from seminary (after he gets his bachelor's degree) and return to Puerto Rico to help advance the lives of the poor. In the meantime, Samuel has expanded his commitments beyond his concern for Puerto Ricans and has aligned himself with the plight of all poor people throughout the world. He has worked in poor villages in Mexico to improve educational opportunities and has helped provide food for the homeless of Washington, D.C.

Samuel's sense of self is deeply rooted in his religious convictions and what he considers "the liberatory philosophy of Christ's message." As Samuel explains, "People have forgotten the message of love and empowerment inherent in Christ's teachings. I try to live my life by the message of love, and that means giving a piece of myself to others through service." His commitment to the poor reflects a view that extends beyond merely providing Band-Aids and instead seeks fundamental social change. Samuel cannot see any other way to live his life. I return to Samuel's story in chapter 7 as I discuss a Habitat for Humanity project that he participated in with a group of students from his university.

Both Carolyn and Samuel not only recognize the need to care for others, but they also realize the positive feelings involvement in service offers to them. The feelings reflected back to them are not the reason they give of themselves to others, but the warmth is nonetheless something they very much cherish. Their lives continue to change as they create new social histories, and their service experiences continue to offer them positive sources of the self.

My social history continues to evolve as well. In fact, life has changed dramatically from my childhood days spent on and off of welfare to my current status as a university professor. I no longer participate in community service as a recipient but instead as a giver. Yet, like the students whose lives I reveal throughout this book, I have learned that in giving I receive so much. I recall the comments of a college senior who was taken aback by the good feelings about himself he experienced as a result of his participation in a spring break community service project: "I couldn't believe how moving the whole experience was for me. I mean, I really only went on the trip because it was a cheap way to go south. But once we started working with the kids and helping with home repairs, I found reasons for being there other than my own personal enjoyment. And that's the oddest thing. Even though I started to think about how I could help others and work to improve their lives, it all came back to me and made me feel great. I'm not sure I should feel so good about myself, given the reasons I went."

A second student echoed some of the same sentiments as she discussed an ongoing community service project she became involved with in the community near her school. "What have I learned? Let me think. . . . I have learned so much from working with the kids. I help tutor them in math, and they just continually amaze me with their resiliency. If I had to deal with some of the family problems they deal with, I'm not sure I could make it. They've given me so much strength and energy to do for others. When I get down and think I can't take any more, all I have to do is think of those little girls and the battles they endure every day. They inspire me to be a better person. It's as simple as that, and I guess that's one reason I keep going back."

This book is about some of the complexities and experiences associated with giving and receiving through participation in community service work and how such activities contribute in fundamental ways to one's sense of self. The focus is on the experiences of college students, although as the author, I share aspects of my life as well.

Over the past six years, I have been engaged in a number of community service projects with other university staff and students. Much of our work has involved leaving university communities and traveling to other areas of the country where we have worked with and served people with far less material comfort and wealth than my fellow student and staff volunteers. We prepared and served food in soup kitchens and helped clean homeless shelters in Washington, D.C.; we built houses in the rural areas of Maryland's eastern shore; we restored and repaired homes on two of South Carolina's sea islands; and we worked with low-income families trying to make ends meet in Lansing, New Orleans, Louisville, and New York City. In all the adventures that I share in this book, my experiences with poverty as a child hovered over me like a ghostly specter of a bare Christmas past. It was hard for me to know what kind of attitude, what kind of conversation, what kind of me to bring to interactions with the low-income families and individuals we tried to serve, and who oftentimes, as in our Habitat for Humanity work in Maryland, worked alongside us. At no time in my life can I remember having been so self- and other-oriented at the same time. At no time in my life have I been more aware of how someone else contributes to who I am as a person. It seemed as though my sense of self was changing right before my eyes through someone else's eyes. I was supposed to be doing the giving, and yet I was receiving. I was supposed to be learning about others, and yet I was learning about my self.

Originally, it never occurred to me to connect my sense of self as someone involved in community service to the self I have as a researcher and a writer. When I started participating actively in community service, my understanding of research was different from what it is now. Research was about being disconnected, objective, and neutral. It did not involve the passion, feeling, and concern I brought to many of my community service activities. The kinds of things I associated with community service had no place in research. I had fallen into the trap Parker Palmer (1987) addresses when he argues that traditional modes of research and knowledge production tend to disconnect us from community concerns and caring for others: "Objective, analytic, experimental. . . . This seemingly abstract way of knowing, this seemingly bloodless epistemology, becomes an ethic. It is an ethic of competitive individualism, in the midst of a world fragmented and made exploitable by that very mode of knowing. The mode of knowing itself breeds intellectual habits, indeed spiritual instincts, that destroy community. We make objects of each other and the world to be manipulated for our private ends" (p. 22).

This book represents an attempt to escape from traditional views of research that separate the researcher from the researched, work from play, thought from passion, and neutrality from caring. It is about my life and research of students engaged in service for others and how they come to know themselves through their service experiences and literally understand themselves through the eyes of others. These insights reveal a great deal about how we might create a more caring form of higher learning and thus contribute to building truly democratic communities.

Thus, this book is about how community service work helps us understand others and necessarily the self. I focus on the service explorations of different groups of college students who have given up spring and winter breaks, free time during their busy semesters, and even their summers to serve others. At the heart of my discussion is what I term the "self"—which in part reflects the way we think about who we are as persons. As a social science concept, the self is similar to the idea of identity, although there are subtle differences that I will try to distinguish as the book unfolds.

I have two primary goals in this chapter. The first deals with the self: the relevance of the self the author brings to his or her work, and the sociological roots of the concept. In dealing with the issue of the authorial self, it is important that the reader of this book have a depth of knowledge about the author, especially as the entire research project is rooted in experiences that are emotionally anchored in my own life. Having provided a glimpse into some of my background, I use portions of this first chapter to explore the theoretical rationale for the role I seek to play in this text. Essentially, while I explore college students and their evolving sense of self, I must also acknowledge the self I bring to this work—the self that contributes to the nature of my observations and of my writing, and which is in turn reshaped by these very efforts. This is why I discuss some of my experiences as a child—in particular, my brushes with poverty. Such experiences not only influence how I think about and engage in work to serve the poor, but they also affect how and what I perceive as I observe others serving the poor. In discussing the role of the author's position, or "positionality," I rely on recent feminist discussions of subjectivity and relational standpointism. An explanation of the sociological roots of the concept of the self follow the discussion of positionality. I depend heavily on the work of George Herbert Mead as well as other symbolic interactionists.

The second goal of this chapter is to situate the study. First, I discuss the methodology. I do this by explaining the theoretical rationale for conducting naturalistic inquiry. I go on to discuss the methods of data collection, describe the sample, and discuss the method of analysis and interpretation. I follow a discussion of the methodology by expanding on the general setting in which the study takes place. In so doing, I elaborate many of the cultural intricacies of what has come to be considered the "collegiate context."

POSITIONALITY

Positionality refers to the position of the knower. Questions of positionality are epistemological in nature in that they relate to how knowledge is produced and how the knower comes to an understanding of knowledge. Epistemology involves theorizing about knowledge and exploring the nature, scope, and legitimacy of knowledge claims. Traditional views of epistemology are not concerned with the position of the knower, who more often than not is seen as irrelevant to knowledge itself. More recent epistemological explorations, such as those offered by feminists, postmodernists, and critical theorists, have raised fundamental questions about the position of the knower. For example, in *Social Science and the Self* Susan Krieger (1991) speaks directly to the role of subjectivity and the self in social scientific inquiry when she argues that research findings reflect highly interactive processes between the observer and the observed. Furthermore, the observer is "personally involved": "We bring biases and more than biases. We bring idiosyncratic patterns of recognition. We are not, in fact, ever capable of achieving the analytic 'distance' we have long been schooled to seek. While recognition of the interactional and contextual nature of social research is not new, how we interpret ourselves during this new period of self-examination may, in fact, add something fresh and significant to the development of sophistication in social science" (p. 167).

Krieger's view may be juxtaposed with traditional views of social science, which, as Krieger notes, tend "to view the self of a researcher as a contaminant" and the selves of those under study as irrelevant (p. 43). She argues that, although the self is culturally and socially derived to a large degree, it is essentially "an individual and inner experience" (p. 44). For Krieger, the social scientist studies the social while bringing an individual's subjectivity to the endeavor and thus constructs knowledge that is different from that of anyone else. The knowledge produced is unique because it is relational knowledge tied to the researcher's sense of self, which necessarily is different from all others.

The social construction of knowledge, as advanced by Krieger and others, stands in opposition to traditional social science, which tends to see knowledge as situated within a single reality as if knowledge is "somewhere out there" waiting to be discovered. Knowledge and truth have a quality of permanence to them and are not seen as interactive outcomes resulting from social involvement between the researcher and the researched. From traditional perspectives, knowledge exists independent of the knower; thus, the knower is largely irrelevant. Social science research, if carried out properly, will produce the same results regardless of the identity or sense of self of the researcher. Hence, one concludes that traditional social science operates based on the notion of objectivity and requires that researchers be "impersonal and unbiased because they exclude values, feelings, political intentions, aesthetic preferences, and other 'subjective' states from the conduct of their research" (Messer-Davidow, 1985, p. 12). The objective social scientist speaks authoritatively because *he* has distanced *himself* from any undue personal or political influence.

For feminists such as Sandra Harding (1986, 1987, 1991), traditional views of objectivity are founded in a conception of knowledge disconnected from social experience. Objectivity masks the connections that researchers, scientists, and theoreticians have with their subject matter. In *Whose Science? Whose Knowledge?*, Harding (1991) suggests a view of knowledge grounded in subjectivity and social experience: "A culture's best beliefs—what it calls knowledge—are socially situated" (p. 119). She goes on to discuss "standpoint theorists" who ground research in social values and political agendas but nevertheless produce sound empirical and theoretical work. Feminist standpoint theorists "focus on gender differences, on differences between women's and men's situations which give a scientific advantage to those who can make use of the differences" (p. 120). Harding argues that standpoint theories reject traditional science's claim to objectivity because in a hierarchically organized society, objectivity lends itself to maintenance of the status quo and thus is by no means value neutral. The status quo is reinforced through objectivity by the simple fact that to take no position is to support that which already exists. Desmond Tutu provides a metaphor: "If you are neutral in a situation of injustice, you have chosen the side of the oppressor. If an elephant has his foot on the tail of the mouse, and you say you are neutral, the mouse will not appreciate your neutrality" (Brown, 1984, p. 19). Feminist theorists of the mind of Krieger and Harding would certainly agree with Archbishop Tutu.

For Harding, the unique vantage point from which women view the world offers several advantages in the construction of knowledge. For example, because women's lives traditionally have been devalued, they have had little opportunity to shape knowledge claims that have been put forth. The complexity and diversity of social life and of knowledge itself are therefore undermined, and only when the world is viewed through women's eyes will we begin to approach its complexity. Harding explains, "Using women's lives as grounds to criticize the dominant knowledge claims, which have been based primarily in the lives of men in the dominant races, classes, and cultures, can decrease the partialities and distortions in the picture of nature and social life provided by the natural and social sciences" (1991, p. 121).

Another point made by Harding is that the oppressive conditions that women have faced and continue to face offer them little interest in reproducing the limited and narrow knowledge conceptions offered over the years by male-dominated methodologies. With a healthy skepticism grounded in their own marginality, they may be more likely to pursue new modes of knowledge construction as a means to end oppressive conditions. Again, this suggests that women might be less likely to support the status quo and reflects their lack of investment in the social order as it presently exists. In turn, they may raise important questions that might not otherwise be asked. "They have less to lose by distancing themselves from the social order; thus, the perspective from their lives can more easily generate fresh and critical analyses" (Harding, 1991, p. 126).

A related idea argued by Harding is that women come from the opposite side of the battle of the sexes and that history tends to reveal that "the winner tells the tale." Nancy Hartsock (1987) points out that all knowers reflect, as Karl Marx argued, the material conditions from which they operate. Members of the proletariat experience the world quite differently from the bourgeoisie. Likewise, women experience the world in a different manner than do men, and a feminist historical materialism offers valuable insights: "Like the lives of proletarians according to Marxian theory, women's lives make available a particular and privileged vantage point on male supremacy, a vantage point which can ground a powerful critique of the phallocentric institutions and ideology which constitute the capitalist form of patriarchy" (p. 159). Including women's accounts of social life offers a more complete picture of the struggles any society or group has endured or continues to endure.

In my work with students involved in community service, female students have seemed more likely than their male counterparts to question fundamental aspects about society and social structure. The tendency for women to adopt more liberal or radical views in their criticism of society is a finding supported in Paul Loeb's (1994) analysis of college students. Loeb attributes this difference to the rise in the importance of feminism among college women.

Carolyn Fisher characterizes a group of women volunteers I have encountered over the years who have expressed serious reservations about a number of social and economic policies adopted by our country. Carolyn has grown frustrated with what she sees as a hyperfascination with short-term solutions to some of the lesser problems of our society, all the while big issues that may take years to solve go unaddressed. "There are all these great philosophers and theorists who are hired to advise the government, but all they ever focus on are fixing the immediate problems—the problems that are most visible. They rarely think about the deeper issues that create the problems to begin with. They don't see the lack of love and community that causes people to suffer. They focus on the abortion issue: pro-life or pro-choice. But they never address the fact that no woman wants to have an abortion in the first place. They fail to see the lack of love and caring for one another that leads people to such desperate measures."

Carolyn has plans to finish her undergraduate degree and then perhaps go to law school where she intends to "master the language of politicians" and, she hopes, be able to have an influence on their thinking as well as their actions. Other students also voiced concerns about significant structural issues that they believed warranted major change. The following comments are all from women:

> The fact that there are thousands of people living on the streets in this city—the capital of our country—says something about the priorities we as a society hold. I think it's great that we are here to help prepare meals and serve soup, but much more than that needs to be done. Every time we vote for someone who supports the status quo we guarantee that someone is going to starve and someone else is going to lose their home and have to live on these streets. We all play a part, and we can choose to contribute in a positive way or we can get in the way of progressive change.

> I don't see why so many people are resistant to rethinking what's going on in this country. It seems to me you'd have to be blind and brain dead not to see that something is tragically wrong with the way things are. Then again, maybe people do see it, but since their life is fine and dandy, what's the big deal?

My work with low-income families has left me feeling both angry and sad at the same time. I'm sad that I cannot do more and angry at a country that allows children to live such deplorable lives. Sometimes I have the energy to join the battle to convince people and politicians to reconsider their values. At other times, I'm a weakling and I just want to lie down and go to sleep.

Some of the male students I have worked with in volunteer settings also expressed sentiments about the need for larger societal change. For example, a student from Pennsylvania State University explained some of the activities he has been involved with: "I have been working with the AIDS Project and trying to get the quilt to State College. I think the quilt has a powerful influence on people's attitudes. And we need that. I've also been involved with homeless people and trying to change some of our policies toward the economically disadvantaged in this country. I've written letters to politicians and I've joined various marches and vigils. I'm not sure how much of an impact these things have had, but I feel I got to keep trying." It did not occur to me at the time to delve into the male students' backgrounds to the degree necessary to determine whether there were experiences that might in some way have contributed to their willingness to question the status quo. I am left to ponder whether some of these men may have felt the lack of power of a nonprivileged vantage point at some time during their lives, which may have fostered a greater interest in questioning that which is.

Feminist theorists recognize that the structural arrangements of a given society contribute to the experiences of its members and the way they come to know their social worlds (Cain, 1993; Minnich, 1990). One who assumes that knowledge produced by upper- or middle-class White males is generalizable to all human experience lacks a rigorous understanding of how subjectivity frames social life as well as thought processes. One who assumes that all middle-class White males experience social life in the same manner also lacks an understanding of how varied subjectivity and human experience are. The challenge is to examine social life in light of meaningful categories such as race, class, and gender, while considering in-group differences (and intersecting differences such as race and gender), and confronting one's own subjectivity as researcher or author.

Although one's subjectivity is to be considered and used as part of the research process, this does not mean that the ideals of objectivity are to be tossed aside. Feminist inquiry involves a connective endeavor combining the researcher's subjectivity with the realities of those under study. Feminists recognize that neither objectivism nor subjectivism hold the answers, yet both may contribute to our understanding of the other and of social behavior.

From feminist theorists such as those discussed in this section, we can see that we are all subjective beings striving to understand the other—who is often situated as the object of our inquiry and our work to construct knowledge. Feminism raises our awareness that the subject/object dualism is not so clear in real life—that we are all connected through multiple and complex cultural webs. This is why feminist methods tend to support research strategies that are highly interactive. Strategies such as naturalistic inquiry enable issues involving subjectivity and objectivity to be negotiated through ongoing dialogue between the researcher and the researched.

The point of discussing positionality is that all researchers bring their own social history, economic standing, and cultural background with them to all endeavors—including the writing of a book. For this reason it is important that my own positionality be explained in the context of this first chapter. In the first few pages I provided some insights into the economic problems my family faced when I was a child. We occupied a specific position within the economic hierarchy of our society; most often we were positioned as members of the lower class, although during other periods when my mother found work we might have achieved membership in the working class. In either case, we had little to no control over the means of production, and our material conditions were greatly dictated by others. Obviously, these experiences have shaped to a large degree the way I envision the social world of today.

Perhaps more important is the relation my family and I had to charitable workers. Because of our material conditions, we were positioned on what some might describe as the "receiving end" of charity. There were times as a child when I felt a great degree of humiliation and shame because our family needed help and was assisted by volunteers from a community church or local union. This experience has had a lasting effect on my life and is significant in understanding the sense of self I bring to this work. For example, I am somewhat recalcitrant when I engage in community service work designed to help others who may now be less fortunate than myself, at least economically speaking. It is not a reluctance to serve, but a fear of serving with the wrong attitude or intention. I sometimes ask myself: Is the service I am performing for me more than it is for someone else? Or: Will my service achieve the wrong result? Will I hurt people's feelings by reminding them that others have more material resources?

Throughout this research project I learned that the fears I have about community service are not unique to me. As the following quotations reveal, many students also struggled with mixed feelings and confused attitudes about community service:

> I'm not sure if I'm completely comfortable helping poor families. I mean, who am I that I can help make their lives better? It seems somewhat condescending for me to believe that I can somehow make a difference.

Sometimes I feel like I'm only fooling myself and that I'm really only into service so that I can help myself. I list this stuff on my resume and I feel guilty because I know it will help me get a teaching job. Is that why I do this? I know it makes me feel better about what I do in my spare time, but who am I really serving?

You can say all you want to about why college students get involved in community service and volunteerism, but frankly I think most of them and me included do this for our own benefit. It provides a sense of meaning in our lives. Little else you do in college does. I'm not sure we should feel guilty about it, like I've heard others suggest, but it does make me think twice about who's being served by all of this.

You can't help but wonder what these people [rural families in a South Carolina community] think of us. I mean, they are very grateful that we are here, but maybe they know it would hurt our feelings if they didn't act that way. I'm just not confident, I guess, with my ability to interpret the meaning of it all and whether what we're doing is right.

Involvement in community service sometimes yields more questions than answers about the self and life in general: Is the service I offer desired? How do the people I have volunteered to serve think of me? Am I seen as an intruder in their lives? Am I welcome in their homes? These are all questions that students, as well as I, tended to bring to our community service work. Many of these questions will surface throughout this text as I explore student involvement in various service projects.

In addition to the personal background about my own life that I share in this text is the theoretical and political quality I bring to my research and writing. For me, all writing and theorizing are political. Everything either supports the status quo or suggests some sort of transformation. In this regard, I believe in the classic Marxian imperative: "to understand the world in order to change it." But such a belief implies an overarching philosophical view of what ought to be. An idealized vision of social life is needed. This overarching philosophy will be spelled out more clearly in chapters 2 and 3. For now, I turn to a discussion of the concept of the self as delineated by symbolic interactionists.

SYMBOLIC INTERACTIONISM
AND MEAD'S SOCIAL SELF

The notion of the self discussed in this book is deeply indebted to George Herbert Mead's (1934) social theory of the self, largely expressed in his famous

Social Psychology course taught at the University of Chicago from the early 1900s to 1930. Mead wrote very little but thought very much. If it were not for the foresight of some of his students, who recorded his lectures during the latter half of the 1920s, much of his work might have been lost, except for what was stored in the minds of those students fortunate enough to have had personal contact with Mead and who were enriched by his teachings.

Mead's view reflects the foundations of social psychology in that he explains "the conduct of the individual in terms of the organized conduct of the social group, rather than to account for the organized conduct of the social group in terms of the conduct of the separate individuals belonging to it" (1934, p. 7). Mead does not imply that the internal workings of the mind, of the individual, are not also important to understanding human behavior: "[Social psychology] is not behavioristic in the sense of ignoring the inner experience of the individual—the inner phase of that process or activity. On the contrary, it is particularly concerned with the rise of such experience within the process as a whole. It simply works from the outside to the inside instead of from the inside to the outside . . . in its endeavor to determine how such experience does arise within the process" (pp. 7–8).

Mead's lectures in social psychology inspired the work of sociologists such as Herbert Blumer, Everett Hughes, and William I. Thomas, who went on to become some of the most renowned members of the Chicago school of symbolic interactionism (House, 1977). Later, Norman Denzin played a key role in delineating symbolic interactionism when he outlined three basic assumptions of an interactionist perspective. First, Denzin argued that understanding reality involves a social process because interactions with others are the means by which one makes sense of social life. "Interacting individuals produce and define their own definitions of situations" (1989, p. 5). Second, people engage in self-reflexive behavior and are capable of guiding their own behavior and the behavior of others. Third, to create their own definitions of the situation and to align self-definitions with those of others requires people to interact with one another in an ongoing basis. Denzin described ongoing social interaction as "emergent, negotiated, often unpredictable . . . [and] symbolic because it involves the manipulation of symbols, words, meanings, and languages" (p. 5).

How individuals interpret events and interactions with others as part of the process of creating meaning and constructing the self is central to the work of symbolic interactionists (Blumer, 1962, 1969). As Denzin noted, "Any theory of society must ultimately answer the question, 'How do selves develop out of the interaction process?'" (1977, p. 114). The *process* of interaction is key. For Denzin, the self is "not a thing, but a process, the self is consciousness conscious of itself" (1987, p. 289). An action taken by another, or something indicated in the context of a discussion, in many respects is not as important as is how another individual gives meaning to that action or indication. The importance the individual plays in the process of sense making within a social context calls attention to the classic proposition framing much of symbolic interactionism and known as the Thomas Theorem: "Situations defined as real are real in their consequences," or as William I. Thomas and Dorothy Swaine Thomas originally noted in their classic sociological work *The Child in America*, "If men define situations as real, they are real in their consequences" (1928, p. 572).

Let us return to Mead and his notion of the self. Mead argued that the self forms out of the interaction between the "I" and the "me." The "I" is the individual acting out some sort of behavior: the individual doing something such as talking, listening, interacting with others, expressing an idea. Language is essential to the development of the self as it serves as the central vehicle for communication within the interactional context. The "me" relates to the sense one has about the "I" who is acting out a behavior or set of behaviors. The sense we develop about the "I" derives from the interpretations we suspect that others have of us. We cannot develop an initial sense about ourselves without the help of others who provide feedback and interact with the behaving "I." Through the imagined thoughts of others, we envision ourselves as a "me," which becomes the object of our thoughts. As Mead noted in his lectures of 1914: "The self that answers to the 'me' arises out of the attitude of others toward the individual. Our view of the self, so far as the form is concerned, is the individual as we conceive him to exist in the minds of other members of the group. This is the 'me.' The 'I' is the speaker over against the one spoken to, but the attention is given to the other. If we cannot turn the attention back to the self without taking the attitude of the other, we cannot immediately view ourselves" (1982, p. 92).

The interaction between the "I" and the "me" is fluid and ongoing. Mead argued that the "I" is the response of the individual (as part of an action or a thought) to the attitudes of others. The "me" reflects the thoughts of others towards the individual, which in turn guide the action of the "I," which subsequently creates new reflections of the "me." It is a highly interactive process that is dependent on the use and interpretation of the symbols of language in particular and communication in general.

The idea of the "I" and the "me" interacting to form the self, which is processual in nature, can be confusing yet at the same time is so basic to our nature as users of symbols. Allow me to offer an example. When I make a joke at a dinner party, I can imagine myself through others' eyes. I might even say to myself: "That is 'me,' whom I envision in my mind's eye, making a fool of myself at dinner." Thus, observing the "me" of the self involves taking the role of the other and imagining how I might appear, be interpreted, or be understood by someone else. As Mead explained, "We are continually following up our own address to other persons by an understanding of what we are saying, and using that understanding in the direction of our continued speech. We are finding out what we are going to say, what we are going to do, by saying and doing, and in the process we are continually controlling the process itself" (1934, p. 140).

Oftentimes, the other is imagined in our minds as the "generalized other," projecting general cultural understandings of a society or social group with sets of expectations for behavior. Once the generalized other becomes part of one's repertoire, we can envision someone in solitary confinement further developing a sense of self as the individual is now able to imagine himself or herself in interaction with others, and able to continually take the role of the other by carrying on a personal conversation in one's mind.

At other times, however, the other is a specific individual (a particular other) with whom we may be interacting or with whom we imagine ourselves to be interacting. Obviously, social interaction is crucial to Mead's view of the development of the self: "It is impossible for the self to develop outside of social experience" (1934, p. 140). As Michael Schwalbe elaborated, "The thinking individual is thus thoroughly social; in fact, there could be no individual thought at all if not for the existence of communal life based on the creation and use of symbols" (1991, p. 283). Unless we can take the role of the other and view the "I" who is behaving as the "me" once it becomes the object of our examination, we cannot develop a sense of self. Otherwise, we are only organisms acting without reflection.

Mead's view of the self is indebted to the early psychological writings of William James (1890) and the "looking glass self" delineated by Charles Horton Cooley (1902), who suggested that an individual's self-conception derives from the responses of others mirrored back to the individual. Cooley stated, "As we see our face, figure, and dress in the glass, and are interested in them because they are ours, and pleased or otherwise with them according as they do or do not answer to what we should like them to be; so in imagination we perceive in another's mind some thought of our appearance, manners, aims, deeds, character, friends, and so on, and are variously affected by it" (p. 184). This is the same general perspective brought to bear on the work of Erving Goffman (1959) when he described social life as a series of theatrical performances involving impression management through a reflective "presentation of the self." One cannot help but think of William Shakespeare's oft-quoted passage from *As You Like It* (Act V): "All the world's a stage, and all the men and women are merely players."

A symbolic interactionist conceptualization of the self has much utility for making sense of students' self-explorations through community service. First, service involves a great deal of interaction between the self and the other. Service demands that students meet community members as part of identifying various needs and actions to be taken. Second, because of the caring context of community service, students often get positive feelings reflected back to them that intuition tells us ought to have an effect on students' sense of self. For example, two students discussed their involvement in service and the positive feelings derived from their interactions with community members: "I didn't feel that what I did was that big a deal, but the woman whose house we painted sure did. She was so gracious and thankful to us. I couldn't help but feel very good about the whole experience." And a second student commented, "Volunteer work is great. You get so much back from the people you help. To see kids smile at me and look up to me because I've helped them in some small way is an incredible feeling."

A rather philosophical student named George Watkins, who was interviewed as part of my research, offered some insights that tend to support interactionist conceptions of the self and the other. George talked about the week he spent on Johns Island, South Carolina, doing community service work and what he learned about and from others: "I realized how much people learn by interpreting signals from others. It's so obvious in a situation like this—where you're working with people you hardly know. People learn so much without decisively learning it. Most of what I learned about people is obscure and circuitous. . . . People hide things from people, but they see through the masks. They see things you don't want them to see. And I learned about initiation and taking a first step. There's this understood fakeness. You're supposed to be nice. When you're getting to know someone. You're not supposed to barge right up to someone. But, by making the first step obtrusively, you by-pass a lot of the crap. It seems unnatural, but it's efficient. It's not good or bad, just efficient. I never thought I'd learn about thirty people this way in my normal life. Living with people has something to do with it. There's the 'fronts thing' that is difficult to maintain when you live with people. They get dirty and grungy. You get a much broader perspective of a person."

The comments from George appear to be those of a symbolic interactionist in the making. He alludes to the importance symbols play and the need to interpret or "read" others. He also mentions the games individuals enact as part of meeting new people when he discusses the "fronts thing." Although he suggests that a more obtrusive style involving less managed behaviors may be more efficient, he nonetheless highlights the reality that many of us find ourselves existing within as we give thought to how we might appear or desire to appear to others. This is the sort of behavior and thinking that Goffman (1959) devoted much of his analyses to and which he discussed in terms of a theory of dramaturgy. In the conclusion to his book *The Presentation of Self in Everyday Life*, Goffman summarized his perspective:

> In this [book], the individual was divided by implication into two basic parts: he was viewed as a performer, a harried fabricator of impressions

involved in the all-too-human task of staging a performance; he was viewed as a character, a figure, typically a fine one, whose spirit, strength, and other sterling qualities the performance was designed to evoke. The attributes of a performer and the attributes of a character are of a different order, quite basically so, yet both sets have their meaning in terms of the show that must go on. (p. 252)

Goffman went on to add, "The self, then, as performed character, is not an organic thing that has a specific location, whose fundamental fate is to be born, to mature, and to die; it is a dramatic effect arising diffusely from a scene that is presented, and the characteristic issue, the crucial concern, is whether it will be credited or discredited" (pp. 252–53).

Although Goffman's theory of dramaturgy tends to portray people as somewhat contrived—through his depiction of individuals engaged in interaction as preoccupied with impression management—his perspective taken as a whole offers some basic insights about how the self is formed and reformed within the social context that to Goffman parallels the stage.

The work of Goffman, as well as the comments from George Watkins, reinforces Mead's contention that the self is best explained not as a structure (which tends to be the Freudian position), but as a process. Mead rejected the views of scholars who identify the self with the ego, or with an organized body of needs or motives. For Mead, the self is not an extension or part of one's personality. Nor is it the internalized norms and values one holds. To think of the self in a structural manner is to miss the ongoing and reflexive process involved in constituting the self. Blumer (1969) offered clarification when he argued that for a psychological structure to be a self it must be able to act upon and respond to itself. "Otherwise, it is merely an organization awaiting activation and release without exercising any effect on itself or on its operation. This marks the crucial weakness or inadequacy of the many schemes . . . which misguidingly associate the self with some kind of psychological or personality structure. For example, the ego, as such, is not a self; it would be a self only by becoming reflexive, that is to say, acting toward or on itself" (p. 63).

As I have already noted, Mead's conception of the self is tied to the acquisition and management of language and meaning. Gregory Stone elaborated on Mead's position: "The emergence of the self in society is inextricably linked to the expansion and consolidation of personal communication as the child participates in and successively generalizes an ever widening universe of discourse—that set of social relations that is mobilized by the symbols the child acquires" (1962, p. 104). The process for Mead involves two stages beginning in early childhood: the play stage and the game stage. Stone later suggested a third stage called "pre-play"—the phase involving rudimentary language acquisition.

There are some significant similarities in how symbolic interactionists and feminists treat the self. Both tend to see the self as a "social self" strongly bound to others and forming through social relations. However, there are some major differences as well. For example, in his analysis of games and how the self develops from such activities, Mead pointed out that the child begins to develop a sense of rules and learns how such rules shape social relations. He cited the example of a baseball game in which the developing child must learn to take the role of various "others" (both teammates and opponents) involved in the complex drama that is baseball. Here perhaps Mead fails to take into account that boys and girls often play different types of games and that boys' games may be more competitive and last significantly longer than games adopted by girls. This and other related ideas have been pointed out by Janet Lever, who also noted the different manner in which girls and boys handle disputes during games: "In the gravest debates, the final word was always to 'repeat the play,' generally followed by a chorus of 'cheaters proof'. . . . Boys seemed to enjoy the legal debates every bit as much as the game itself. Even players who were marginal because of lesser skills or size took equal part in these recurring squabbles" (1976, p. 482). By contrast, conflict among girls usually means that "the game breaks up, and little effort is made to resolve the problem" (p. 483). It seems that girls would rather maintain positive feelings for one another than enter into heated debate to resolve disputes. This finding is compatible with the research of Nancy Chodorow (1974, 1978) and Carol Gilligan (1979, 1982) who argued that interactions among girls (and women) tend to focus more on maintaining relationships than settling disputes by appealing to issues of justice or fairness (as boys and men tend to do). The work of feminists suggests that symbolic interactionists may have overgeneralized the development of the self across both genders, when in fact men and women develop a sense of self through slightly different routes. I return to this issue in chapter 2.

Although there are many appealing aspects to Mead's explanation of the social self, there are some shortcomings as well. First, whereas Mead and symbolic interactionists in general highlight the self as a process, it also seems logical at times to speak of the self as a structure—as something that exists and has a remote degree of permanence attached to a complex social history. Otherwise, how can I speak of having a sense of self if it is entirely a process? I like to think of the self as something I can discuss as an object of a conversation (albeit a moving object), while at the same time recognizing that the self is formed through a dynamic, highly interactive process.

A second shortcoming of Mead's theory is the apparent lack of agency or individuation of the self. The social context seems so powerful from Mead's perspective that one is left to wonder what makes us each unique. Denzin spoke to this issue: "Many sociological descriptions of the self are inherently debunking. They foster a view of self as being totally socially constructed. The self is viewed as a precarious entity fashioned through social discourse. There is no face behind its various masks. So too, morals are seen relativistically and ritualistically. They are reduced to roles and performances and the institutions wherein they take place" (1985, p. 233). Denzin's point is well taken. How can the self be socially constructed and at the same have some psychologically oriented qualities that make individuality possible? The solution lies in how the "I" of Mead's theory is to be understood. We not only must envision the "I" as a response to reflections derived from situating oneself as the object (the "me"), but we should also understand the "I" as representing some of those complex, difficult-to-explain aspects of personality that make one's actions different from another's despite similar social histories. In this way, we can envision the self as having agency and thus being capable of breaking away from social norms and customs. In other words, we are capable of removing the masks at times and stepping away from a socially staged drama in an effort to write our own script. This is important in understanding the lives of community activists such as Carolyn Fisher and Samuel Frias, as well as other student volunteers we will meet throughout this text.

Up to this point, I have spent a good deal of time situating the self and discussing the role this concept plays as I seek to make sense of students' lives. What might be helpful at this point is to explain my study in greater detail and outline some of the primary methods used for collecting data about students.

THE METHODOLOGY

This book represents my effort to break away from the traditional strategies of research and data presentation. As an academic who is fully socialized to the boredom that sometimes is academe, I often fall back on numerous strategies for putting readers to sleep. I, like others before me, tend to rely on traditional antiquated structures that organize our narratives into neat compartments labeled with such terms as "the review of literature," or "research design," or "findings." As much as possible, I want to avoid compartmentalizing this text as I attempt to create a more integrated narrative. By the same token, I understand that some readers have a desire to review a clearly articulated discussion of how the data were collected and analyzed.

The data for this book were derived from six years of research and participation in community service projects conducted in conjunction with three universities: Pennsylvania State University, the University of South Carolina, and Michigan State University. Community service projects range from week-long intensive experiences requiring travel to distant out-of-state communities to ongoing student service projects in the local communities or states in which these universities are situated. I participated as a volunteer in many of the service projects described throughout this book. My role ranged from a staff supervisor in a few cases, to that of a graduate student volunteer with limited responsibility in other instances. In every case my primary objective was as a "volunteer" and not as a "researcher"; the data I collected was more or less an outgrowth of the community service experience and was not the central objective. My comments here are not meant to shortchange the research strategy employed, but are intended simply to clarify for the reader the context of my interactions and involvement with the student volunteers.

The research methodology used in this study borrows to a large degree from what is generally described as "naturalistic inquiry." Yvonna Lincoln and Egon Guba used several axioms to describe the naturalistic paradigm: (1) reality is multiplicitous and socially constructed and therefore must be examined holistically; (2) the researcher and the research subject interact to influence one another; hence, the knower and known are inseparable; (3) the aim of inquiry is to develop an interpretive understanding of social experience; (4) because social phenomena are highly interactive, cause and effect are difficult to ascertain; and (5) the various choices made by researchers reflect the values they hold (1985, pp. 37–38).

Lincoln and Guba went on to argue that the naturalistic paradigm strongly leans toward qualitative methods because they are more flexible in addressing multiple realities, offer greater insight into the transaction between the inquirer and the object(s) of study, and make assessing the mitigating role of the inquirer easier. From their perspective, the researcher is far from a mere bystander and instead actively engages research participants in the creation of meaning.

The naturalistic setting also has been discussed by Norman Denzin who described "naturalistic interactionism" and suggested that such a method "involves the studied commitment to actively enter the worlds of interacting individuals" (1989, p. 7). Additionally, Denzin emphasized that "because symbols, meaning, and definitions are forged into self-definitions and attitudes, the reflective nature of selfhood must be captured" (p. 8). Denzin's points are central concerns of my study as I seek to understand students' explorations of the self in the social context of community service.

Based on the methodological strategies of qualitative inquiry, data were collected using a variety of techniques, including formal and informal interviews, surveys, participant observation, and document analysis. The principal documents used as a source of data were journals students kept as part of their community service experience. In the six-year period (1991–1996) in which data were collected, 108 students participated in interviews, 66 students completed open-ended surveys, and more than 200 students were observed at various project sites in which participant observation was central. Approximately 90 percent of the students involved in the community service projects were undergraduates, and about 10 percent were graduate students. The vast majority (approximately 80 percent) of the undergraduates were traditional-aged students in the range of 18 to 23 years old. Females represented approximately 60 percent of the sample, and in terms of race, the vast majority were Caucasian students (roughly 85 percent), with African Americans constituting the largest minority group—about 8 to 10 percent of the overall group.

The small percentage of African American student volunteers reflects the fact that all three universities from which the students came have rather small percentages of African American students. A second factor is the tendency for many African American students to get involved in volunteer work through service-oriented Black fraternities and sororities. This may limit African American student participation in campus-wide service projects (Bulger, 1995). In any case, the fact that the students participating in the service activities examined in this study were predominantly White, combined with the fact that the majority of community members whom they served were African Americans, raises an important concern about how racial differences might influence the nature of community service interactions. This concern will be addressed at various points throughout this text.

Interview transcripts (from both formal and informal interviews), field notes from participant observation, student journals, and documents collected in conjunction with various service projects form the entire data base for the study. Once collected, the data were analyzed using the kind of cultural analysis suggested in the work of Renato Rosaldo (1989) and Clifford Geertz (1973), involving a systematic interrogation of textual data that seeks to understand how research participants create meaning. Geertz maintained that cultural analysis is not a scientific strategy designed to discover some ultimate schema of facts, but instead is more of an interpretive adventure in search of meaning. Such a process involves "guessing at meanings, assessing the guesses, and drawing explanatory conclusions from the better guesses" (p. 20). And Rosaldo argued that cultural study (ethnography) is more about "making the familiar strange and the strange familiar" than it is about uncovering the "brute timeless facts of nature" (p. 39). Viewed in this light, cultural analysis may be seen as a process of making sense of how others make sense, a process that necessarily involves the researcher as an active participant in the construction of meaning. This is compatible with my earlier discussion of positionality and feminist contentions arguing that the researcher or author is an integral part of knowledge construction.

Cultural or interpretive analysis involves identifying themes around which data may be organized and rejects the type of quantification of textual data often associated with content analysis. To count the number of times an action was taken or the number of times a comment was made is antithetical to an interpretive process. For an interpretivist, understanding the context of behavior is just as important as understanding what specifically was said or done. In other words, meaning is created through both the content and the context. For example, a lover may say to his or her partner a thousand times "I love you" as they embrace. However, that same lover may say "I'm leaving you" only one time as he or she walks out the door, forever. Clearly, both phrases have meaning, but if we depend on a strict quantified analysis, the "I love you's" count one thousand and the "I'm leaving you's" are counted only once. Obviously, there is more to making sense of social interaction than counting the "I love you's."

Based on an interpretive analysis of the data, several key themes were identified. These themes form the basis for chapters 4 through 7 and relate to the following general topics: the implications of working with and in service to others ("Otherness"—chapter 4), a need to understand community service as a mutual activity between the "doer" and the "done to" ("Mutuality"—chapter 5), the central role that community plays in students' experiences of community service ("Community Building"—chapter 6), and the significance of combining action and reflection as part of community service efforts ("Action/Reflection"—chapter 7).

This work suggests a moral dimension in that it supports a perspective that community service is something that *ought* to be considered as a fundamental aspect of higher learning. Such a view rejects the traditional positivists' claim that true social science is a neutral activity and is apolitical. Mary Savage elaborated, "The positivist tradition of research is often supported by conventions that border on 'scientism' and that obscure the fact that research, like all social life, is a kind of praxis, action with a political moral dimension" (1988, p. 6). By "scientism," Savage referred to the notion that formalized method exemplified by the classic experimental design "yields truth or verifiable fact, that reality may be described objectively" (p. 6). As I discussed at the beginning of this chapter, this book involves positioning the author within the research and the writing. From such a perspective, knowledge is seen to be relationally situated within the experiences of the observer and the individuals under study. Hence, any discussion of reality must involve some type of interactional process between the researcher and the researched. Lincoln and Guba discussed such an attempt as "member checks," which they defined as, "the process of continuous, informal testing of information by soliciting reactions of respondents to the investigator's reconstruction of what he or she has been told or otherwise found out" (1986, p. 77). In the case of this study, a concern for adequate member checks involved two processes. First, the data collection itself was a participatory and highly interactive endeavor involving students' reflection and discussion about their experiences working in community settings. Second, several students acted as readers of significant portions of this text and in turn provided feedback about its content. This feedback formed the basis for a dialogue between the researcher and research participants and served to reshape both the findings and the narrative.

THE COLLEGIATE CONTEXT

The college years are key times for the development of a sense of self because so many decisions about one's future and past come together and so much thought and learning typically are given to identity matters. For example, a student I met on a service project in South Carolina talked about why she chose to participate: "I've always done service work. During my freshman year at the University of South Carolina, I worked on the City Year project and the Serv-a-thon. I believe service is an important part of leadership. It's important to give back to the community. The last four weeks I've been totally into myself. . . . Like running for vice president of the student body. This project was a chance for me to get outside myself for awhile." This student saw the service project as an opportunity to connect with others and in her words "get outside" herself. For her, community service provides an opportunity to become more other-focused and examine her life from a reflective, external position, through the eyes of another. In many ways, she highlights the kinds of developmental struggles students often face during the college years—developmental outcomes that have attracted a great deal of attention over the past twenty-five years (Astin, 1979, 1993; Feldman, 1972; Feldman & Newcomb, 1970; Pascarella & Terenzini, 1991).

A set of outcomes that has long concerned higher education faculty and practitioners is the idea of developing students as whole persons. A more holistic view of students is rooted in the long history of liberal education and the role of schools and universities in preparing citizens. John Dewey (1916) spoke to this concern when he argued that a democratic society is dependent upon an educated citizenry capable of making informed choices and actively participating in community, regional, and national governance. Schools have a key role to play in the development of students as citizens who are able to make such informed choices. And, of course, many of the choices that an educated citizenry must make involve matters of moral significance and hence necessitate moral education of some sort. Dewey's point is taken up by Pearl Oliner and Samuel Oliner in *Toward a Caring Society* when they highlight the innovative quality of Dewey's thinking:

> That virtue was complex and required thoughtful consideration was not a new idea, of course; philosophers had so argued for centuries. What *was* new was the idea that the 'common man' could think in this way; if that

were not the case, then democracy itself seemed doomed to failure. As many prominent thinkers interpreted it, authorities had the responsibility to provide a social climate where reasoning and reflecting about democratic community life could occur, and the place to begin was in the schools. (1995, p. 55)

Whereas liberal views of higher learning and the curriculum have long stressed the development of students as whole persons, the specific field of student affairs has been primarily charged with this massive undertaking, and a whole body of literature has sprung up around the developmental challenges college students face (Chickering, 1969; Erikson, 1968; Kohlberg, 1975; Perry, 1970; Sanford, 1956, 1967; Strange, 1994; Upcraft & Moore, 1990). Oftentimes, however, issues of vocational, intellectual, and emotional development have taken precedence over concerns associated with developing a sense of community- or civic-mindedness. Somewhere in the chasm between faculty work and student affairs practice, encouraging students to develop the sense of community-mindedness necessary for democracy to thrive has been lost. A goal of this book is to speak to this issue and to how higher learning might reconsider the development of students as caring and community-oriented citizens. Part of the solution clearly involves not only closing the chasm between faculty and student affairs professionals, but also the division between "in-class" and "out-of-class" student experiences, as well as the separation of practical and academic knowledge. One presumption behind this book is that involving students in community service work ought to be a concern of both faculty and student affairs professionals, and that such activities should be situated not simply as out-of-class learning but as an extension of the classroom into the "real world." In this light, academic and practical knowledge may be integrated as students struggle to solve important social problems through action and reflection.

Understanding the unique qualities and social dynamics of the college student experience (often described as the "collegiate experience") is helpful in making sense of this text and the role community service plays in the broader goals of higher learning. Consequently, various aspects of the college student experience need to be addressed.

The vast majority of students in this study are of traditional college-going age (18 to 23). For many traditional-age students, the college years are a rite of passage to adulthood. They are a time of great decision making and personal change. Freedom from parents and high school social networks not only brings about increased autonomy, it also results in many responsibilities and personal decisions that must be weighed (Chickering, 1969). In some cases, students consider relationships for the first time in a serious manner (Moffatt, 1989). Career decisions also weigh heavily on the minds of most traditional-age college students (Erikson, 1968). Notions of a personal philosophy, religion, and lifestyle all come to the forefront (Parks, 1986; Perry, 1970). Many students deal squarely with issues of sexual identity during their college attendance (D'Augelli, 1991; Rhoads, 1994). Arguably, nearly every decision faced during the college years pertains in one way or another to issues of identity. Although identity is constantly changing, there is perhaps no other period of time when it is challenged to a greater degree.

In Michael Moffatt's anthropological account of undergraduate life at Rutgers University, "College as the students saw it was . . . about coming of age. It was where you went to break away from home, to learn responsibility and maturity, and to do some growing up. College was about being on your own, about autonomy, about freedom from the authority of adults, however benign their intentions" (1989, p. 28). But, as Moffatt noted, college was about having fun, too—"unique forms of peer-group fun—before, in student conceptions, the grayer actualities of adult life in the real world begin to close in on you" (pp. 28–29). Moffatt's portrait of students "coming of age" is insightful but at the same time raises the issue of how college students should be classified in terms of their maturity level. I do not care to enter the debate about whether traditional-age college students are adults or are "coming of age" as adults; like nearly all linear conceptions of development, the category of "adult" obscures the reality that change often varies dramatically across individuals. What is important here is that both traditional and nontraditional students face many crossroads during the college years. And, as individuals at significant decision-making points in their lives, they make for interesting observation and analysis.

But college life is much more than the fun and silliness often depicted in Moffatt's portrait of college students and American culture. For example, Sharon Parks discussed the serious challenge students often face in developing their own faith understandings and a spiritual sense of self: "Young adults in higher education quickly don the trappings of adulthood—an aura of independence, a measure of responsibility for self, and cultural permission for participation in all adult behaviors. But the young adult is still in formation, still engaged in the activity of composing a self, world, and 'God'. . . . The young adult is searching for a worthy faith" (1986, p. 133). As the musicians Crosby, Stills, Nash, and Young once wrote, it seems "everyone must have a code they live by." Developing a clearer sense of one's spirituality or a philosophy about life—a code to live by—is another of those challenges that seem to be more psychologically salient during the college years. My contention throughout this work is that community service is an activity that brings students into a direct and significant relationship with others, and thus challenges students to consider a variety of significant issues about the self, such as a code to live by. And, although a number of researchers and authors, such as Moffatt and Parks, situate the emerging sense of self college students reveal at the transition between immaturity and maturity, or adolescence and adulthood, it is hard for me to envision many of the serious-minded students who commit to serving others as anything but mature adults. After all, if change is a lifelong process, it seems to me that complete maturity occurs only when we are six feet under.

In *Generation at the Crossroads*, Paul Loeb (1994) discussed the much maligned students of the late 1970s through the early 1990s, often described as the "me" generation or more recently a generation of "slackers." As Loeb pointed out, these students have been attacked on many fronts. From Allan Bloom's (1987) suggestion that students are self-indulgent, isolated, ignorant, and in need of, as Loeb stated in summarizing Bloom's point, "a stiff dose of the classics" (p. 2), to E. D. Hirsch's (1987) criticism of their cultural knowledge and ability to communicate effectively in today's world, to Dinesh D'Souza's (1991) warnings about zealous campus radicals whose commitments to equal opportunity threaten academic excellence, today's students clearly have attracted the wrath of many a writer. However, Loeb was quick to point out that these students have "come of age under the sway of political, cultural, and economic currents that convinced citizens in general to seek personal well-being over a common social good" (p. 3). Additionally, Loeb maintained that today's students work more hours, graduate with greater debts, and are less likely to find employment related to their major than students of twenty years ago. It is hardly surprising that many of today's students are oriented toward their own career concerns and getting ahead in the world or, to the contrary, have become disenchanted and tuned out.

Nonetheless, many students, often marginalized on their own campuses, have heeded the call to broader social concerns and have become involved in campus activism and community service. Loeb described a number of student groups who have become actively engaged in national, regional, and local concerns. For example, he discussed the Greeks for Peace movement at the University of Michigan, in which students organized protests over United States interference in foreign countries. He also called attention to the student strikes at City University of New York over tuition hikes that threatened educational accessibility for low-income students. And the work of students involved in volunteerism in conjunction with the Campus Opportunity Outreach League has grown significantly over the past ten years. The questioning, protests, and community service commitments of students described by Loeb challenge those who envision students as immature, apathetic, uninvolved, and disengaged slackers. As Loeb argued, the activists pose a direct challenge to traditional sources of power within American society. It is not surprising that they have faced so much resistance.

As students have begun to question, they've also challenged deeply rooted institutions of power. It is for this reason, I believe, that they have been so vehemently attacked and baited with labels like "politically correct," that their opponents have denied their right to speak out about the world they will inherit and sought to drive them back to passive silence. Yet I believe these attacks will ultimately fail. The crises in American life are too grave, the shifts in the student population too profound, the growing commitments of a significant minority too strong. (1994, p. 366)

A good deal of optimism is conveyed in Loeb's treatment of contemporary student culture. Similar optimism is inherent in the work of Robert Coles, who discussed his years of involvement with college students and the idealism that strongly flows through many of the current generation: "Today's students are likely to express their lofty political and social impulses and practical desires to change the world through community service, even if in limited or modest ways. . . . They tutor the young, keep company with the elderly, visit the sick, run summer camps, design and implement educational programs in prisons, help the medically needy and indigent get hospital care, and argue in the courts on behalf of tenants or workers" (1993, p. 40).

A student who participated in my research supports Coles's depiction of today's students: "There is an incredible movement promoting social justice and peace issues in this country, and I am excited that there are opportunities for me to contribute to social change." And a second student mentioned the importance of action among his peers as he discussed the ideal of community: "I define community as my peers, my social strata. And I know now that we aren't a bunch of do-nothing twenty year olds. Many are capable and willing to give part of themselves. They want to help." George Watkins, whom we heard from earlier in this chapter, highlights the kind of commitment many of today's students exhibit: "I worked at a camp for handicapped kids for two summers. I'd never worked with handicapped kids before. The first day the kids came, they checked in and then we went to lunch. I was grossed out. I was in shock. I wanted to leave. But an older person showed me what to do; I really needed that. I was so scared. I just wanted to leave. I'd never changed a diaper before. But I knew I couldn't leave. I'd signed a contract and everything. . . . And then amazingly I started to love it. I loved the kids. I went back the next summer and did it again."

Much of the work that today's students do goes unnoticed by the media, their professors, and even their fellow students. I recall a colleague of mine—a political science professor—commenting recently on how disinterested his students are with politics and social issues. "I can't get the students in my classes excited about anything. They are just completely removed from present-day social and political concerns. Their apathy is rampant." I was quick to point out to him that his experiences were not reflective of my community service work, in which the greatest source of help was students from the same university at which he taught. It occurred to me that perhaps we were talking about two different groups of students, and then on second thought, two different aspects of students' lives: the classroom and the world beyond the classroom. Perhaps where we have failed the most in helping students make the connection between academic work (theorizing in its broadest sense) and action such as community service is that we have too narrowly defined the classroom as "that place with desks, walls, and a teacher." I tend to think of activities such as community service projects as "classrooms without walls." This is different from the traditional notion of the out-of-class experience of students, which is typically seen as secondary to formal classroom learning. A point I hope to make throughout this book is that community service and the learning that comes with it deserve better than a marginal identity within academe.

SUMMARY

One goal of this chapter is to offer a feminist perspective on the role of subjectivity in shaping social science inquiry and in creating narrative. To accomplish this, I introduced a variety of feminist writings about the self and inquiry, as well as revealing some significant aspects about my own life that I hope will aid the reader in understanding the positionality that I bring to this work.

Another goal of this chapter is to advance a sociological view of the self framed by Mead's notion of the "social self." Mead's work and that of other symbolic interactionists is critical for making sense of the kinds of self-explorations students exhibit through their experience with the other in the contexts of community and community service.

I also spent some time explaining the appropriateness of naturalistic inquiry for a study of students' lives. A central component of this discussion focused on the use of qualitative methods and the role of cultural analysis in making sense of complex and highly interactive social experiences. Finally, I concluded this chapter by discussing the relevance of college students as a population worthy of cultural inquiry. Simply stated, the collegiate context fosters a unique set of developmental challenges that makes analysis of the self perhaps more revealing than at other stages of life.

In chapter 2, I focus on issues of culture and identity and expand on some of the feminist conceptions of identity and the self that were briefly alluded to in this chapter. The work of Gilligan is central to my discussion. I also talk about the changing nature of identity in today's postmodern world and how such changes may influence how the self evolves in a culturally diverse society. Central to my discussion is what may be termed the "politics of identity" as I point out the role education plays in legitimizing or delegitimizing various identities. I conclude the chapter by offering in-depth profiles of two students who highlight how educational contexts might contribute to the development of the self.

Chapter 2

Culture and Identity

*The person is embedded in a society that
anchors and sponsors identity. Different societies and cultures forge, within their citizens, a
unique way of shaping and sensing reality.*
   *—Carol Hoare, "Psychosocial Identity
    Development and Cultural Others"*

*I experienced a lot of pain in high school that no one ever knew about.
My pride prohibited me from sharing those experiences with anyone, although
every now and then my sister Kim or I would let out a few words that offered a
glimpse into the depths of our souls that each of us recognized in the other. I
never could understand why people in our society humiliate the poor. If there is
some kind of service, or food, or medical assistance we give to someone in
need, it seems we have to make sure the entire world knows "these people"
have not earned whatever it is they have been provided. The best example I can
think of is the "free lunch" tickets I received in high school.*

*Each day, on the way to the cafeteria, I had to stop at the principal's
office to pick up my little red ticket. I remember the strange looks I got from my
classmates as they passed by the office on their way down the hall to the cafeteria, only to see me disappear like some apparition into an office that few
students ventured into voluntarily. I was with them one moment, gone the next.
I developed a number of clever tactics in the hopes of their not noticing my
daily visits, but I'm not sure whether I was fooling them or fooling myself. I
would terminate conversations at least three or four doors away from the
office, turn the joke or conversation on someone else just in time to vanish, or
be so far ahead or behind so as to attract minimal attention. The real craft,
though, was passing the ticket to the lunch lady without anyone noticing that it
wasn't money. I would always wait for her to extend her hand, palm up, and*

then I would place my clenched fist on top of her palm, quickly releasing that little red ticket of shame and humiliation. I hoped that she would pull away instantly and deposit it in the cash register, which is exactly what she usually did. I will never forget Mrs. Moore for understanding my pain. She was the exception, though, and not the rule.

Of all the lunch line horror stories I could tell, like dropping my ticket in front of a group of friends, or forgetting to stop and pick one up at the office and not having a cent to pay for my lunch, none of them compares to the time the prettiest girl in the school got in line behind me and started talking to me as if I was someone who mattered. She was a senior and I was just a sophomore, and yet she knew my name and was even saying nice things to me. She told me that her boyfriend thought I was the best athlete in my class, and my face must have turned as red as that damned little ticket in my clenched fist. I wanted so desperately to talk to her, to say nice things to her, but I was afraid she would continue to talk to me all the way right up to the lunch lady and then she would see the truth—that I wasn't so nice after all.

I offer the preceding narrative because it highlights how the cultural experiences we have throughout our lifetimes contribute to our identities. Such experiences become our social histories, which, in part, define who we are as people. As a child I experienced what may be called the "culture of welfare." The oppressiveness of this aspect of my life is epitomized by the free lunch tickets my siblings and I received when we were in school. The handouts and the manner in which they were disbursed left a lasting impression on my sense of self. As a child, part of my identity was rooted in being poor, and in our society being poor means you are a second-class citizen, perhaps something less than human. Against this childhood backdrop I struggle to this day with feelings of inadequacy. Am I really intelligent enough to be a college professor? Am I a good enough person to someday have a wonderful and caring partner? Do I deserve to have close and intimate friends? These are just a few of the questions that are so connected to my present-day identity, which is so tied to the past and the complex maze of social interactions I had growing up.

Related to my experiences, past and present, is a battle inside of me that seems to get waged daily. On the one hand, there are a whole host of social experiences that speak to my sense of self and are best termed negative and dysfunctional. On the other hand, I have a collection of warm and positive feelings offered by my family, former coaches and teachers, colleagues, and others who at one time played or still play a key role in my life. These two sides of my life's experiences battle for supremacy and for the right to determine the kind of person I am and the kind of self I have. Of course, there is this unexplainable piece, too, that is unique to me. I certainly have some power over this war that wages inside me, and I know that my attitude can affect which side wins on certain days. It is clear to me that my sense of self, which is constantly evolving, is the by-product of all that I have experienced, and at the same time there is an individualized quality that I bring to the interpretation of my experiences and interactions.

My goal in this chapter is to explore issues of the self in terms of culture and identity. I begin by situating the concept of identity within the work of Erik Erikson. I use his work to lead into a discussion of feminist explanations of gendered identities and how women may develop different conceptions of the self. In essence, through early childhood and later socialization, women are more likely than men to develop relational ways of knowing, which foster a strong sense of caring. I then highlight how various feminist theorists have discussed an ethic of care and its place in women's and men's development. I go on to discuss the interaction among culture, identity, and schooling in which I include a discussion of what may be termed the "politics of identity." The politics of identity underscores the notion that, despite how we may be situated within culture, there are opportunities for us to play a role in shaping our own place in the social world—we have a degree of "agency" in our lives. I then highlight key aspects of what has come to be considered "postmodern culture," which leads me to address the need to transform education and the role community service can play in fostering more caring selves. Finally, I conclude the chapter by focusing on collegiate culture and identity, where I introduce two students as examples of how educational contexts contribute to one's sense of self. I use these two examples to return to the central concern of this book—students and their involvement in community service. I maintain that fostering an ethic of care ought to be an educational concern applied to both male and female students and that colleges and universities can play a crucial role in this process.

SITUATING IDENTITY

When one discusses identity, the work of Erik Erikson (1950, 1968) must be addressed. Erikson is the first significant identity theorist to ground the process of identity development in both the psychological and social contexts. Not surprisingly, his view has been termed a psychosocial perspective and rests on the *epigenetic principle*. Simply stated, epigenesis suggests that certain psychological characteristics (related to biological forces) must be in place before the individual can move to higher levels of development, which for Erikson involves eight stages in the human life cycle: trust versus mistrust, autonomy versus shame and doubt, initiative versus guilt, industry versus inferiority, identity versus identity confusion, intimacy versus isolation, generativity versus stagnation, and integrity versus despair. Although there is a psychological "readiness" that must be present before an individual can begin to face the developmental challenge of the next stage, certain social and cultural factors must exist as well. Erikson explained,

> It is important to realize that in the sequence of his most personal experiences the healthy child, given a reasonable amount of proper guidance, can be trusted to obey inner laws of development, laws which create a succession of potentialities for significant interaction with those persons who tend and respond to him and those institutions which are ready for him. While such interaction varies from culture to culture, it must remain within "the proper rate and the proper sequence" which governs all epigenesis. (1968, p. 93)

Erikson is credited with coining the phrase "identity crisis" (seen as a turning point for Erikson). He described a period in the life cycle, roughly coinciding with adolescence and young adulthood, in which an individual seeks to resolve important aspects of his or her life. Issues such as identifying a vocation and developing a general outlook about life are central to resolving the identity crisis. Because the majority of students in this study were of traditional college age, many were in the midst of serious identity exploration. For example, a college sophomore discussed how his involvement in community service was part of an effort to identify a career: "Volunteering to help tutor kids is something I do to see if I can be a teacher or not. I don't want to spend four years as an education major and then get a job, only to find out I can't handle it. My hope is that this kind of work will help tell me that." A second student, a junior, talked about her participation in a community service project: "This is all part of an adventure for me. I haven't quite figured things out yet. What kind of person do I want to be? What do I want from life? I know this trip won't provide any concrete answers, but it's a start."

Another student, who has been involved in community service since she was a sophomore in high school, saw her involvement as part of a process of building character: "In high school I joined a club that was committed to doing community service. You had to do so many hours each week. I think it was four or five. I mostly worked with kids from a very poor neighborhood. Tutoring and just being a friend to them . . . to me, it was an opportunity to do something to help others, but it also helped me a great deal. Some of the work I did with low-income families was difficult, and I think it helped build character. Maybe that's my mother talking. She used to always say, 'Stick with it. It builds character.' I think she was right because now I can't imagine going through life without doing some kind of community service. It's become part of who I am." This student, like the other two students, has used her involvement in community service to fill in another piece of the identity puzzle.

Successful resolution of a developmental challenge, such as the identity stage, makes it more likely that an individual will resolve the next crisis. For example, a child who develops a sense of trust is more likely than a mistrustful child to later develop a sense of autonomy. Likewise, someone who achieves a stable sense of identity is more likely later to achieve intimacy in his relationships. I intentionally use the pronoun "his" in this case because, in fact, Erikson seems to be speaking primarily of males' development. He acknowledges this when he points out that women's development may follow a somewhat different trajectory, in which their sense of identity is strongly linked with establishing intimacy, whereas for men, identity seems to precede intimacy. Despite suggesting that women develop along different lines from men, Erikson presents his life cycle model as if it were generalizable to everyone. In part, this is the criticism feminist scholars such as Carol Gilligan offer as they seek to expand and clarify a women-centered view of identity development. The "inner space" that Erikson wrote about in relation to women's lives reverberates with the echoes of what today's feminists describe as a "different voice."

FEMINIST CONCEPTIONS
OF GENDERED IDENTITIES

Trinh Minh-ha (1991) argues that if you cannot understand the other, then you will not be able to understand yourself. For Minh-ha and other feminist scholars such as Gilligan, the self and the other are inextricably intertwined in the webs of social life and sense making. The relationship between the self and the other is a vital aspect of understanding issues of women's identity.

Gilligan was one of the first theorists to point out that women often make decisions based on a sense of connection with others. Nona Plessner Lyons claimed that "to her [Gilligan] women's concerns centered on care and response to others. Noting too that women often felt caught between caring for themselves and caring for others, and characterized their failures to care as failures to be 'good' women, Gilligan suggested that conceptions of self and morality might be intricately linked" (1988, p. 23). Lyons summarizes three central tenets of Gilligan's theorizing: (1) two distinct modes of moral reasoning exist, based on either justice or caring; (2) men tend to make moral decisions based on justice, and women tend to make moral decisions based on caring; and (3) the modes of moral judgement are linked to definitions of the self.

Gilligan's work is partially grounded in the research of Nancy Chodorow, who examined the significance of the child-mother relationship in terms of the child's gendered identity. Chodorow (1974, 1978) argued that separation and individuation are associated with the identity of boys because they must learn to distance themselves from their mothers as adult models in order to establish a masculine sense of self. Girls, on the other hand, can continue to build a sense of attachment to their mothers.

> Because all children identify first with their mother, a girl's gender and gender role identification processes are continuous with her earliest identifications and a boy's are not. A girl's oedipal identification with her mother, for instance, is continuous with her earliest primary identification (and also in the context of her early dependence and attachment). The boy's oedipal crisis, however, is supposed to enable him to shift in favor of an identification with his father. He gives up, in addition to his oedipal and preoedipal attachment to his mother, his primary identification with her. (1978, p. 174)

As Gilligan explains, "They [girls] do not depend on the achievement of separation from the mother or on the progress of individuation. Since, in Chodorow's analysis, masculinity is defined through separation while femininity is defined through attachment, male gender identity will be threatened by intimacy while female gender identity will be threatened by individuation" (1979, p. 434). The development of the self for females may be characterized by connectedness. Male development may be characterized by individuation. This difference has significant implications for how males and females relate to others and how they understand themselves in the context of the other.

Chodorow argues, "Girls emerge with a stronger basis for experiencing another's needs or feelings as one's own. . . . From very early, then, because they are parented by a person of the same gender, girls come to experience themselves as less differentiated than boys, as more continuous with and related to the external object-world and as differently oriented to their inner object-world as well" (1978, p. 167). Relationships become central to the social world of women. For men, the relational quality of social life is often replaced by a strong sense of individualism. The other is fundamentally a part of women's experience and kept at somewhat of a distance for men.

Recall from chapter 1 that symbolic interactionists theorize that the self is essentially a social self: An individual comes to know herself or himself through social interactions and taking the role of the other. In their conceptualization of the self, traditional interactionists tend to group men and women together, as if there are no gendered patterns to identity development. Yet we see in the work of feminists that men and women may develop self-conceptions through different routes, with women seeking greater connectedness and men seeking greater autonomy. This raises an interesting dilemma. If interactionists are correct when they argue that the self evolves primarily through social interactions and hence social relations, and if feminists are correct that women tend to develop a stronger sense of relatedness, it seems logical to conclude that women may develop a clearer sense of self. Women, through the development of a sense of connectedness, may be more adept in taking the role of the other (the particular other as opposed to the generalized other), and hence better suited for understanding one's self through the reflections of the other. If social relations are central to the development of the self and men tend to be more individualistic in their social orientation, then developing a sense of self rooted in caring is problematic for men. Pearl Oliner and Samuel Oliner considered this point when they wrote, "If Gilligan and others . . . are right, then the environments in which men in particular spend most of their childhood and adult years need to encourage affiliative bonding" (1995, p. 25). That is, if one accepts the philosophical and practical goal of Oliner and Oliner—the movement toward a more caring society—then creating learning contexts in which men have the opportunity to develop in a more relational manner is imperative. As they went on to explain: "If schools and the workplace, as well as other social institutions, eschew such responsibilities, empathy will continue to be primarily women's work to the detriment of men and social life generally" (p. 48).

Based on the contrasting images of the relational self (connected knowing) and the autonomous self (separated or objective knowing), we can project two different images of social life and of community. For example, Iris Marion Young discusses Gilligan's conception of the feminine self grounded in an ethics of care (and oriented to the other) with the masculine self grounded in an ethics of rights or justice (and oriented toward autonomy).

> The "ethic of rights" that Gilligan takes to be typical of masculine thinking emphasizes the separation of selves and the sense of fair play necessary to mediate the competition among such separated selves. The "ethic of care," on the other hand, which she takes to be typical of feminine thinking, emphasizes relatedness among persons and is an ethic of sympathy and affective attention to particular needs, rather than formal measuring of each according to universal rules. This ethic of care expresses the relatedness of the ideal of community as opposed to the atomistic formalism of liberal individualism. (1990, p. 306)

Young makes clear that how the self gets situated has significant implications for how we think about society, community, and social life in general. If women's ways of knowing the self and the other are to be considered, then how organizations are structured must be reexamined because prevailing conceptions of organizational life have been grounded in male-oriented views stressing an ethic of justice and an orientation toward competition and autonomy (Ferguson, 1984; Ianello, 1992). Furthermore, if we accept the feminist interpretations offered in this section, then one would have to conclude that educational structures reflect mostly individualistic perspectives as men have been the dominant architects of educational processes and structures. Research and theories about gender-related differences in educational contexts, such as differences in learning styles, suggest that male-oriented perspectives do in fact reflect the dominant modality (Baxter Magolda, 1992; Belenky et al., 1986; Cully et al., 1985).

In my work as part of a research team that explored the experiences of women in engineering as part of a five-year National Science Foundation grant, we found evidence of the difficulties women face in educational contexts favoring competition over cooperation and individualism over collaboration (Paulson, Rhoads, Campbell, & Millar, 1994). For example, one of the findings from our research was that there existed a general feeling of frustration and ambivalence among women toward the predominant modes of evaluation pitting students against each other for grades. The women engineering students participating in this research project, which involved seven nationally ranked engineering programs, often talked about their desire to "work together" rather than compete against fellow students. When one department of engineering adopted a more team-oriented approach to teaching and learning in which students worked cooperatively in groups, women engineering students were described as being much more involved in the class than they were under previous instructional strategies.

In addition to a preference for collaboration and cooperation, women engineering students exhibited other qualities different from their male peers. A number of the faculty (most of whom were male) reported that women seemed to be more intimidated by engineering than were men. Women students also gave indications that they were less confident than their male counterparts. There was a tendency for women to internalize a poor grade and allow the feedback to have a negative effect on their sense of self. The men were more likely to blame the instructor or the test instead of internalizing their poor performance, thus protecting their sense of self. Given the relational orientation of women's identities, it is hardly surprising that feedback from the other, in this case a professor, might have a significant influence on a female engineering student's sense of self.

Other concerns about the experiences of women in engineering were tied to the overall culture of academic engineering and its deeply entrenched male-centered views. For example, when women performed well and received outstanding grades, their abilities and intelligence often were called into question. It seemed easier for male engineering students to denigrate the performance of women by making derogatory comments such as "You did the professor" or "You're sleeping with him during office hours," than it was to acknowledge their hard work and intelligence. In addition, even when less competitive instructional modes were used and women became more involved in the class, other problems surfaced. When they participated in group design projects, women often were marginalized by their male peers and assigned demeaning roles. One woman complained about being relegated to the task of painting the final design project that her group developed, while the men took on the more serious tasks of design and testing. Other women reported "being ignored" or "not listened to" by members of their groups, which were composed predominantly of men.

Engineering education furnishes perhaps the ideal case study (in a negative sense) of male domination in that it provides extensive insight into how male perspectives have shaped and continue to shape the teaching and learning process and how women's ways of knowing have been marginalized. Gender-oriented research and feminist theorists speak to many of the problems made evident by the field of engineering, which are pervasive throughout other fields of study as well. Clearly, creating and understanding knowledge in a relational and caring sense is subordinated to individualism and competition. Educational institutions need to do a much better job of including women-centered perspectives into the structure of teaching and learning, but to do so requires a depth of understanding about feminist advances associated with women's ways of knowing and the role of caring. Feminist views of the self, combined with what can be learned from observations of community service, can contribute significantly to the restructuring of higher learning around an ethic-of-care philosophy and a commitment to more democratic forms of education.

AN ETHIC OF CARE

The topic of caring has become a central concern to many feminist theorists. Feminist theories of moral reasoning tend to argue that men and women think differently when weighing decisions about moral dilemmas. Theories advancing gender-related patterns of moral reasoning, and reasoning in general, have largely been based on a critique of the work of Lawrence Kohlberg (1975, 1980) and his stages of moral development.

Kohlberg argued that there are six stages of moral development and that the sixth stage—the universal-ethical principle orientation—represents the highest level of moral reasoning. Not everyone reaches the sixth stage, but one of the goals of what Kohlberg describes as the "cognitive-developmental approach" is to stimulate students' movement to higher levels of reasoning by fostering open peer discussion of value dilemmas. Such discussions enable students to challenge one another and to consider alternative modes of reasoning. Because the cognitive-developmental approach seeks movement to higher levels of reasoning, it differs from traditional values-clarification activities that merely seek clarity as an end.

When women's moral reasoning is evaluated using methods of analyses based on Kohlberg's work, they tend to exhibit lower levels of reasoning as defined by his stage theory. Of course, Gilligan (1982) pointed out the gender bias in Kohlberg's work and challenged the belief that men and women follow similar moral reasoning paths. In this regard, it appears that Kohlberg is a victim of his own male-centered reasoning, as well as the fact that his research itself is entirely based on studies of males. Although his theory captures the tendency for some males to evaluate moral dilemmas based on principles of justice (which Kohlberg defines as the highest level of moral reasoning), it fails to capture possible differences between male and female reasoning patterns.

In contrast to a male-oriented focus on justice, females tend to depend on issues of caring in weighing moral dilemmas. By caring, feminists typically talk about the importance women place on establishing and maintaining a sense of connection with others. The ethic of care highlighted by Gilligan's work is "distinguished by an emphasis on attachments, issues of self-sacrifice and selfishness, and consideration of relationships as primary. . . . For Gilligan an ethic of care is achieved through perception of one's self as connected to others" (Brabeck, 1993, p. 36). Gilligan and Jane Attanucci differentiate between the justice orientation inherent in Kohlberg's work and the care orientation of Gilligan and other feminists: "A justice perspective draws attention to problems of inequality and oppression and holds up an ideal of reciprocity and equal respect. A care perspective draws attention to problems of detachment or abandonment and holds up an ideal of attention and response to need. Two moral injunctions—not to treat others unfairly and not to turn away from someone in need—capture these different concerns" (1988, p. 73). In short, a women-centered view of moral reasoning emphasizes building and maintaining connections with others and thus may be considered as relational or "connected knowing" (Belenky et al., 1986).

Relational ways of knowing involve developing and maintaining caring relations with others. But what does it mean to care for someone else? This is the essential question Nel Noddings asks in her work *Caring: A Feminine Approach to Ethics and Moral Education.* "When we see the other's reality as a possibility for us, we must act to eliminate the intolerable, to reduce the pain, to fill the need, to actualize the dream. When I am in this sort of relationship with another, when the other's reality becomes a real possibility for me, I care" (1984, p. 14). Noddings does not suggest that we walk in the other's shoes. Nor does she imply the notion of empathy in its strictest sense—the power of projecting oneself to another so fully as to understand one's object of contemplation. Instead, for Noddings, caring involves *feeling with* someone else. Her notion of "feeling with" does not suggest projection of oneself but reception of the other. She calls this process "engrossment." Noddings explains, "I do not 'put myself in the other's shoes,' so to speak, by analyzing his reality as objective data and then asking, 'How would I feel in such a situation?' On the contrary, I set aside my temptation to analyze and to plan. I do not project; I receive the other into myself, and I see and feel with the other" (p. 30). Minh-ha offers a poetic parallel: "You and I are close, we intertwine; you may stand on the other side of the hill once in a while, but you may also be me, while remaining what you are and what i am not" (1989, p. 90).

Engrossment is different from the symbolic interactionist idea of "taking the role of the other," which has the purpose of more clearly perceiving the self. For Noddings and other feminists, the self may more fully emerge as a caring being by "feeling with" the other. Feeling with the other is not a means to an end; it is an end in itself. Furthermore, engrossment is hardly a reasoned approached to caring for the other, but instead reflects more of an emotional appeal to another. Noddings provides an example of engrossment: "Mothers quite naturally feel with their infants. We do not project ourselves into our infants and ask, 'How would I feel if I were wet to the ribs?' We do this only when the natural impulse fails. Naturally, when an infant cries, we react with the infant and feel that something is wrong. *Something is wrong*. This is the infant's feeling, and it is ours. We receive it and share it" (p. 31).

It is important to keep in mind the subtle differences between Noddings's view of engrossment and interactionist thoughts about taking the role of the other as we explore students' experiences in community service. I believe that Noddings has captured, in essence, the difference between a rational act—taking the role of the other—and an affectional act of caring for or loving another—engrossment. The need to examine the affectional domain is something Iris Murdoch also alludes to when she discusses the need to conceptualize the self as something more than a purely philosophical agent: "We need a moral philosophy in which the concept of love, so rarely mentioned now by philosophers [as well as educators], can once again be made central" (1970, p. 46). Although one of the goals of this text is to advance the idea of the "caring self," Murdoch reminds me that part of what I am really writing about is *love* and what it means to be a loving community member or citizen.

I believe that both rational (the reasoned act of taking the role of the other) and affectional (the caring for another as part of engrossment) qualities of human experience are helpful in the development of the self and in understanding the other through community service activities. Through the work of feminists such as Gilligan and Noddings, we can envision the development of the self along both affectional and rational dimensions, in which the driving moral conviction concerns building and maintaining a sense of connection. In other words, a desire to care for others has both an emotional and a moral appeal to it. One could say that feminism adds an affectional dimension to the traditional interactionist emphasis on the reasoned act of taking the role of the other (an act tied to morality).

What I suggest here is that acts of service to another vary considerably from context to context, from individual to individual. Sometimes service to another reflects a reasoned concern for someone else in which we imagine ourselves in that person's shoes and find their situation so deplorable that we must try to alter their circumstances. We believe in this instance that we have a moral obligation to the other. Listen to the following two students, one male and one female, explain why they engage in community service. Both of these students participated in community service work with homeless citizens in Washington, D.C.:

> [College Male]: I can't stand the thought of people going hungry or freezing in the streets. I imagine what my life would be like if I had to live that way, and it forces me to want to do something to change things.

> [College Female]: The other day I saw a homeless man who I had seen a few days before at one of the soup kitchens we worked at. He looked so lonely. I don't know how I could handle living like that. I don't think I could. . . . The whole thing makes me angry. I feel like there are so many people in our country who just turn their backs on others. Working with the homeless has helped me to see what it's like to have to live on the streets, and it helps me to be even more committed.

Other students expressed a more affective dimension of engagement and tended to reflect the engrossment idea that Noddings highlights. Whereas theoretically one might expect engrossment to be more a part of a woman's repertoire, I did not observe any significant differences between male and female students. Of course, it is also quite likely that the men who choose to participate in community service may be more inclined to relational ways of knowing (and thus may express a greater capacity for engrossment-type behaviors than other men). Once again, I offer two examples, one from a college male and one from a college female, both of whom discuss their experiences working with low-income families.

> [College male]: It hurts me to see people living in such poor conditions. One of the houses we worked on was so badly constructed that you could hear the wind whistling through the cracks around the windows. It must have been about 50 degrees in the kids' bedroom. It's no wonder why they all had colds. I spent the entire day in that room trying to fix the windows and the leaks in the ceiling, but I don't know how much I actually accomplished.

[College Female]: I have never had to go to bed hungry one day during my entire twenty-one years on this earth, and I have never had to worry about whether or not my family will be kicked out of their home. These kids face those kinds of fears every day. It's just not right that children have to think about such things. I can see the pain in their eyes and I just want to take that pain away, put it in a ball of newspaper, and throw it out the window. But I don't know how to do that.

The differences between taking the role of the other out of a concern for justice and doing the right thing, and the idea of walking with someone as an act of engrossment in which the other is seen to be fundamentally connected to the self are subtle. I do not wish to create a hierarchy of one over the other but merely want to point out that these differences do in fact exist. Whether such differences are gender related is not clear from the data I have obtained, although previous research strongly suggests that gender is a key variable (Gilligan, 1982; Belenky et al., 1986). What is clear, however, is that many of the men and women involved in this research offered a variety of complex explanations designed to reconcile their own sense of self with that of the other. Sometimes, students reflected a justice-oriented perspective. At other times, they seemed to express more of an emotional appeal reflective of engrossment. I offer one more example of a student whose narrative has both a rational and an emotive quality to it.

[College female]: The work I've been doing with inner-city kids hasn't been as rewarding as I had hoped. It's very painful at times to witness some of the poverty they face. I don't know if I'll volunteer again next year, but for this semester I need to distance myself as much as possible and just plug away. That's where I've been lately. Do what I can do to help and then put it behind me. It's hard but it's the only way I can continue giving.

One can sense the emotive quality of this student's experience and the personal struggle to distance herself from her volunteer work. Her desire to continue despite her effort to disconnect demonstrates a commitment to service and social justice. Otherwise, one would expect that she would simply withdraw completely and go about her own life separated from those with serious needs.

Symbolic interactionists offer no rationale for elevating an ethic of care to our acts of taking the role of the other. Feminists do, however, and I believe their discussion of caring as a fundamental aspect of the self is helpful in thinking about community service and involvement with diverse others. If one accepts the idea that fostering an ethic of care in students is a relevant educational goal, then learning to take the role of the other and learning to walk with the other ought to be central pedagogical challenges established within the higher learning context. Community service offers one such vehicle for exploration of the self through role taking and walking with the other. In essence, *students explore the self while learning about and experiencing the other.* Gilligan's research supports the idea that experiences gained through different kinds of relationships are linked to changes in one's conception of responsibility and thus may influence the development of an ethic of care.

A subtheme throughout this book is the idea that the sense of self women bring to the educational context has been undervalued and that one of the central challenges we face in our society and in our educational settings is embracing an ethic of care along with the already prevailing ethic of justice associated with male development. I am not saying that only women can care and that only men can be just. Whereas women's socialization tends to foster an ethic of care, this does not mean that men cannot also care. And, likewise, women also develop conceptions of justice that shape their sense of self. But the ideals (not actualities) of justice are pervasive throughout our society because male-centered perspectives are solidly interwoven into the very fabric of social life. One of the central questions embedded in this work is: How do we go about encouraging an ethic of care to a greater degree throughout our society in general and within our educational settings in particular? The idea of an ethic of care as fundamental to *human* development (not just women's development) is a concern addressed by Edward Sampson several years ago. "The feminist perspective should no longer be understood as developing a psychology of women but, I believe, is better seen as developing a psychology of humanity tomorrow. The real issue, therefore, does not involve gender differences per se, as much as it speaks to an emerging theory of the person that is appropriate to the newly emerging shape of a globally linked world system" (1989, p. 920).

The fact that male perspectives tend to dominate our social and educational structures highlights how certain identities—in this case, the identities of men—get situated by our culture as superior. Because people interact with one another based on their positionality and how they perceive the other to be situated by the culture within which they exist, the positioning of identities has significant implications for how the self gets defined. For example, the interactions I have with my mountain-biking friends involve certain language and communicative styles that are different from those I use in communicating with my department chair. Because culture and identity play major parts in shaping interactions and in contributing to one's sense of self, this means that particular attention must be paid to these concepts.

CULTURE, IDENTITY, AND SCHOOLING

Over the years, issues of culture and identity have become increasingly relevant to educational theory and research (Giroux, 1992, 1993). This has been true for research on K through 12 settings (Eckert, 1989; Fine, 1991; MacLeod, 1987; McLaren, 1986, 1989; McRobbie, 1978; Willis, 1977), as well as in postsecondary contexts (Holland & Eisenhart, 1990; London, 1978; Rhoads, 1994; Rhoads & Valadez, 1996; Tierney, 1992; Weis, 1985). Emerging from this body of research and corresponding to notions generated largely by critical postmodernism and feminism is a heightened awareness of how culturally diverse people are situated within educational institutions and subsequently depicted in research and writing (Rhoads, 1997; Tierney & Rhoads, 1993). Just as feminism and critical postmodernism have challenged what gets defined as knowledge and as truth, they also have raised concerns about how cultural identities get situated within social hierarchies that assign some superior and others subordinate status (Foucault, 1978, 1980; Lyotard, 1984; Minh-ha, 1991; Nicholson, 1990; Ramazanoğlu, 1993). A concern for social hierarchies and inequalities surrounding cultural identities has led many scholars to discuss the "politics of identity" or the "politics of difference" (Hall, 1990; West, 1993; Young, 1990).

To understand the politics of identity in relation to schooling, one must make sense of culture. Culture is an often used expression that conveys the values, beliefs, norms, and attitudes understood by a group of people. It is a concept that can be applied to a wide array of human groups, as large as whole societies, as small as dyads. Culture provides a framework for interaction within social groups and at the same time is continuously revised through those same interactions (Geertz, 1973). And here is why culture and identity may be thought of in terms of a polity. Since culture and social interaction have a reciprocal relationship, it is possible through contestation and struggle to engage culture with the hope of transformation.

Culture not only establishes the parameters for our social interactions, it provides a framework for how we define ourselves in relation to others. This is the point Carol Hoare made in her discussion of psychosocial identity development: "As is true for knowledge, identity is constructed from within the person and culture in which it is forged" (1991, p. 48). Definitions of the self and the other contribute to how identities are represented and understood through a process that is dialectical and interactive. The politics of identity involves raising questions about how people are represented through culture and, of course, through language. Such questions in the end serve as challenges to the very means our society has used to define knowledge and truth. As Minh-ha (1991) opined, "To raise the question of representing the Other is . . . to reopen endlessly the fundamental issue of science and art; documentary and fiction; masculine and feminine; outsider and insider" (p. 65).

"The self is always in the making" (Minh-ha, 1991, p. 113). A sense of self is continually modified through social interactions that occur throughout one's lifetime. But the self does not form in a vacuum. I have already pointed out how social interaction provides the vehicle for the formation of the self. Without social interaction there can be no self. However, social interaction itself is dependent on a larger source for its own structure. One might say that the parameters of social interaction are established by culture. And again, social interaction reshapes culture. This is the dialectical view of culture that Clifford Geertz stresses throughout his work and that is captured to a degree in his oft-cited passage: "Believing, with Max Weber, that man is an animal suspended in webs of significance he himself has spun, I take culture to be those webs, and the analysis of it to be therefore not an experimental science in search of law but an interpretive one in search of meaning" (1973, p. 5).

To be clear, culture pertains to the norms, values, beliefs, and attitudes that guide social interactions and are re-created by such interactions. Cultural codes such as dress, table manners, and how one presents oneself in various settings such as weddings, funerals, or college classes, provide the cues around which people organize their actions. The cues, however, are not static but continuously change as innovative ideas or behaviors enter, emerge, or are discovered within a society or social group. Hence, culture provides the parameters for social interaction, as well as the formation of the self, and is fundamentally tied to notions of identity.

Hoare (1991) maintained that the idea of the self may be understood as a "personal sense of identity." One's personal sense of identity, however, is linked to one's public identity, which is rooted in one's positioning within the larger culture. The opening quotation to this chapter (from Hoare) highlights how individuals and their sense of identity is rooted within the larger culture: "The person is embedded in a society that anchors and sponsors identity. Different societies and cultures forge, within their citizens, a unique way of shaping and sensing reality" (1991, p. 45) But Hoare also pointed out that people are "embedded" or situated within society in different ways and that some, such as African Americans and women, are positioned on the margins. "It would be remiss to fail to include a commentary that, just as there are diverse cultural realities with multiple possible images of self and identity embedded therein, a heterogeneous society such as America includes the experiences of many who do not fit the mold of dominant White, middle-class man" (p. 49). Being situated on the margins of society has significant implications for one's sense of self as one must battle the negative cultural messages. Hoare discussed the problem that many African Americans face in their identity development: "There is the immutable experience of posing, believing one cannot escape a skin color that is equated with being less than. This reality places the identity of many Blacks at developmental odds with mainstream American society, one in which Blacks forfeit rewards, absorb loss, and experience anger and depression" (pp. 49–50).

Hoare calls attention to the struggle marginalized people face in reconciling their public identities with their sense of self. And again, identity and self are highly interactive concepts. In many ways, identity is, as Don McAdams argued, "an autobiographical story of the self, complete with setting, scene, character, plot, and theme" (1990, p. 151). Seen in this light, "Identity is a quality of the self . . . a particular way in which the self may be arranged, constructed, and eventually told (McAdams, 1995, p. 385). Identity links the self to the social structure in suggesting various roles one may assume, which in turn provide the context for interaction (Kuhn, 1964; Stone, 1962; Stryker, 1991; Turner, 1987). In the case of members of underrepresented groups, such as African Americans, the social structure limits their roles and quite often produces disempowering interactive contexts.

From Hoare's perspective, the larger social world sends a pervasive message of inferiority and exteriority assigned to one's identity as a minority that must somehow be cast aside as irrelevant, and yet one's sense of self forms from such social interactions and the identity narrative one seeks to weave is caught within this pernicious attack. This is the same identity and self-struggle that I highlight in previous work concerned with gay and bisexual college men and the challenges they face in seeking to establish a positive sense of self, despite a culture that situates their lives on the margins (Rhoads, 1994, 1995a).

Allow me to ground this discussion in a literary example from Toni Morrison's (1970) *The Bluest Eye*. In this work, Morrison describes the psychological consequences of an African American child having to deal with notions of beauty based on White European models. Morrison centers her story on Pecola Breedlove, who grew up facing the harsh social norms prescribing that blond-haired, blue-eyed White girls were beautiful and that dark-skinned, dark-eyed African American girls were ugly. The attacks on Pecola's sense of self included not only the many times she was ignored or not chosen for a class activity, but also the glowing looks her classmates and teacher reserved for the blond-haired, blue-eyed, Shirley-Temple-look-alike Maureen Peal, who at one point in the narrative offers an example of the pain Pecola endured: "I am cute! And you ugly! Black and ugly" (p. 73).

Throughout her social interactions, Pecola learned to despise her own physical appearance. She was a Black girl in a world where white-skinned, blue-eyed blonds were held up as the epitome of beauty. Her identity as a Black girl framed many of her interactions and her sense of self. She saw her self reflected in the eyes and words of others (both Blacks and Whites) and came to despise what she saw, because they despised what they saw. Her identity as an African American in a racist society situated her life within certain cultural parameters that shaped the interactions she had with others—interactions that often involved depreciation and denigration of her own beauty. Such interactions did not change her public identity as an African American, but they dramatically influenced her sense of self. Feelings of inferiority, hatred, and resentment were reflected back to her every time she looked at herself in the mirror, both literally and figuratively. The following passage from Morrison highlights Pecola's pain:

> It had occurred to Pecola some time ago that if her eyes, those eyes that held the pictures, and knew the sights—if those eyes of hers were different, that is to say, beautiful, she herself would be different. . . . If she looked different, beautiful, maybe Cholly [Pecola's father] would be different, and Mrs. Breedlove too [Pecola's mother]. "Why, look at pretty-eyed Pecola. We mustn't do bad things in front of those pretty eyes." (p. 46)

Morrison makes an important point and offers insight into the sense of self I write about in this book. Her first sentence in this passage bears repeating: "It had occurred to Pecola some time ago that if her eyes, those eyes that held the pictures, and knew the sights—if those eyes of hers were different, that is to say, beautiful, she herself would be different." It was not just that a new pair of eyes would make Pecola different, and become suddenly beautiful, but the images that her eyes held—the images of her self—would be replaced as well. With a new pair of eyes would come a new vision—a new vision of Pecola as beautiful.

As the book progresses, Pecola's actions become even more tragic as her sense of self erodes a little bit each day. But clearly, not everyone internalizes the reflections others offer of the self in the same manner. Listen to the sense of self reflected by the narrator of Morrison's work—Claudia, who also is an African American girl and a friend to Pecola—as she describes her Christmas memories.

> It had begun with Christmas and the gift of dolls. The big, the special, the loving gift was always a big, blue-eyed Baby Doll. From the clucking sounds of adults I knew that the doll represented what they thought was my fondest wish. I was bemused with the thing itself, and the way it looked. . . . "Here," they said, "this is beautiful, and if you are on this day 'worthy' you may have it." I fingered the face, wondering at the single-stroke eyebrows; picked at the pearly teeth stuck like two piano keys between red bowline lips. Traced the turned-up nose, poked the glassy blue eyeballs, twisted the yellow hair. I could not love it. (pp. 20–21)

Why some people take to heart the interactions they experience in different ways is perhaps an unanswerable question. We have all known people who, in crossing our lives, have amazed us with their ability to grow and remain, in Erikson's (1968) words, "vital" despite numerous hardships and setbacks. And despite everything, they always seem to remain positive about themselves and others. It is a mystery. Yet it does not dismiss the significance our interactions have for us and for the development of our sense of self—as Pecola Breedlove and many others clearly reveal. Why and how some individuals develop a critical consciousness capable of filtering certain interactions and interpreting others in a manner that protects a strong and enduring sense of self is not within the domain of this work but is certainly a question to pursue in the future.

The point of introducing Morrison's work is that identity, whether it be related to one's race, gender, sexual orientation, age, occupation, or other significant characteristic, obviously influences how social interactions are structured and how we are framed by them. One does not typically have the same conversations with one's supervisor at work as one would with his or her two-year-old daughter. In many ways, identities correspond with all the roles adopted throughout our lives, which form a story about who we are as individuals. These roles shape the interactions we have and thus influence the development of the self. The roles we enact are not the self, but shape the types of interactions we have through which the self becomes, which is a process that never ends.

Symbolic interactionists are guilty at times of understating the role of culture in contributing to social life and the kinds of roles we have available to us. Indeed, until language names something as real—such as the self—we have a difficult time experiencing that something. As Hoare argued, "Languages do not merely voice ideas; they shape and guide concepts and cognition itself" (1991, p. 48). Kenneth Burke echoed this thought when he noted the importance of the symbolic: "However important to us is the tiny sliver of reality each of us has experienced firsthand, the whole overall 'picture' is but a construct of our symbol systems" (1989, p. 58).

The politics of identity moves beyond merely understanding how different forms of culture have named and situated individuals and groups through language and discourse. It also interrogates the intention behind representations and attempts to create newer self-representations (Hall, 1990). For people who exist on the margins of society—culture's borders, so to speak—the struggle to create one's own representations is necessarily a struggle to seize power. Cornell West (1993) dealt with this issue in his discussion of the "new cultural politics of difference," primarily in reference to Black struggle: "The intellectual challenge . . . is how to think about representational practices in terms of history, culture and society. How does one understand, analyze and enact such practices today?" (p. 5). For West, this question cannot be answered unless one first comes to terms with previous struggles to create more honest and empowering self-representations. Understanding the role history, culture, and society have played in shaping people's lives is crucial to moving toward newer forms of representation.

But history, culture, and society are not static concepts; they are theoretical constructs that serve as vehicles to engage oneself and others in the process of constructing, deconstructing, and reconstructing knowledge and truth. The goal, as West (1993) explains, involves more than merely expanding access and contesting stereotypes: "Black cultural workers must constitute and sustain discursive and institutional networks that deconstruct earlier modern black strategies for identity-formation, demystify power relations that incorporate class, patriarchal and homophobic biases, and construct more multivalent and multidimensional responses that articulate the complexity and diversity of black practices in the modern and postmodern world" (p. 20).

West has helped to raise awareness about the notion that ongoing agency—social action grounded in emancipatory theory and critical reflection—is crucial to successful engagement in the politics of culture and identity. Agency is grounded in the hope of a more just and equitable society in which those currently situated on society's borders have a voice in a truly democratic process. As bell hooks (1992) highlighted in her work, the emancipatory vision that calls for social transformation involves much more than merely criticizing the status quo: "It is also about transforming the image, creating alternatives, asking ourselves questions about what types of images subvert, pose critical alternatives, and transform our world views and move us away from dualistic thinking about good and bad" (p. 4).

Colleges and universities are composed of faculty and administrators who make representations of others to themselves, to colleagues, to the public, and to students. When institutions favor competition over cooperation, individualism over collaboration, and an ethic of justice over an ethic of care, a representation that male-oriented perspectives are superior to women's ways of knowing gets produced and in turn reproduced. The challenge we face in terms of education is developing a more relational curriculum and an educational experience that combines women's ways of knowing with the already pervasive structures favoring male-oriented modalities. Hooks (1992) challenges us to transform our worldview and move away from dualistic thinking. With this in mind, one might envision a society in which multiple and diverse ways of knowing are brought to a variety of contexts by both men and women. Identity as multiplicitous thus becomes the essence of social life and the development of the self.

An emphasis on the multiplicity of culture and identity helps us to face the challenge of a postmodern society characterized by difference and fragmentation. Difference displaces universality, and local narratives replace grand narratives. This is one of the points Jean-François Lyotard (1984) made in *The Postmodern Condition* as identity and the development of the self become even more complex: The self "exists in a fabric of relations that is now more complex and mobile than ever before" (p. 15). In postmodern societies, efforts to explain social life in any kind of overarching manner become inadequate in their ability to make sense of localized experiences. The idea of a common culture or common experience becomes some past horizon seen from the back seat of a junked 1963 Chevrolet Impala.

Jean Baudrillard (1994) discusses postmodernity in terms of a culture of simulation in which the real and the unreal become fused together into a confused mosaic of the hyper-real and the quest for a concrete sense of identity is problematic. A culture of simulation bordering on the surreal is the focus of Sherry Turkle's work *Life on the Screen*, in which she examines the postmodern dilemma of "identity in the age of the internet." Although she described the multiplicity of a computerized and technologically rooted identity, she also explained how internet interaction may lead to an Eriksonian developmental journey: "Once we put aside the idea that Erikson's stages describe rigid sequences, we can look at the stages as modes of experience that people work on throughout their lives. Thus, the adolescent moratorium is not something people pass through but a mode of experience necessary throughout functional and creative adulthoods. . . . Time in cyberspace reshapes the notion of vacations and moratoria, because they may now exist in always-available windows. . . . We enter another reality and have the opportunity to develop new dimensions of self-mastery" (1995, p. 204). Turkel argued that whereas "dreams and beasts" were the intellectual objects for Freud and Darwin and represented modernism, "the computer has become the test object for postmodernism" (p. 22).

A more differentiated and complex society has resulted in a changing view of culture and identity; overarching truths are unlikely in such a diverse and technologically oriented culture. As a result, social scientists increasingly have called on local narratives in their effort to understand and create meaning (Geertz, 1983). These changing circumstances, both in society and in how we envision culture, have altered and continue to alter how we think about the self, community, and necessarily the role of education in a postmodern society.

EDUCATIONAL TRANSFORMATION

A postmodern politics of identity highlights how educational practices and processes may be understood in terms of their support of or opposition to culturally diverse peoples and perspectives. Specifically, educational practices may be examined in terms of how they foster male-centered or female-centered ways of understanding. Typically, it is the individualistic and competitive characteristics most often associated with men that are encouraged throughout the schooling process. Thus, education plays a profound role in the shaping of identity and in the way the self gets defined by students.

One of the challenges taken on in this book is framed by Hoare (1991) when she argued that the struggle posed by a postmodern order is to develop a "constitutive" idea of the self—"one in which persons are defined through their attachments, relationships, and common purpose with others in community" (p. 46). The challenge to develop a constitutive idea of the self suggests that there are many possible conceptions of the self (or many "possible selves") that one might develop (which is especially true in postmodern times). "Possible selves are the ideal selves that we would very much like to become. They are also the selves we could become, and the selves we are afraid of becoming. The possible selves that are hoped for might include the successful self, the creative self, the rich self, the thin self, or the loved and admired self, whereas the dreaded possible selves could be the alone self, the depressed self, the incompetent self, the alcoholic self, the unemployed self, or the bag lady self" (Markus & Nurius, 1986, p. 954).

The idealized self at the heart of this book is the caring self. But the caring self is one of many possible selves that might emerge within an individual's overall sense of who she or he is as a person. Listen to the following student discuss her journey to achieve a certain "hoped for" self against the pressure of another possible self that she fears: "Volunteer work is one of the things I've made time for as part of my own struggle to figure out what's important to me. It helps me to figure out the kind of person I am going to be. I don't want to do things only for me. I want to help others and contribute to someone else's life if I can. My siblings are all very successful and so there's an incredible weight on me to achieve. 'Achieve, achieve, achieve.' That's all I ever hear when I'm at home. I love my family but I'm not sure their definition of success fits me. I'm not sure I want the same things as my brothers and sisters. Maybe there's more to my life than making a lot of money. Maybe I want to put people at the center of my life. Not just my own family either. But people in general. That's why I do volunteer work. It brings me closer to what seems important to me."

For this student, developing a sense of self committed to others is important to her, and yet she faces family pressures that pull her in different directions. Her struggle is one of reconciling the possible selves her future holds and the decisions she must make about present-day choices, such as whether service work will remain a priority in her life, whether it will be replaced with more career-oriented interests, or whether the two can somehow be combined.

The struggle exhibited by the aforementioned student is not limited to women, however. Many men with whom I have interacted over the years in community service settings also struggle between the pursuit of more individualistic career orientations or service to others. The following comments from two male students are examples: "I spend a lot of time on homework and schoolwork in general because I want to have a successful career in business. But sometimes I wonder, especially after spending a week like this [working with low-income rural families], if a great job is really what will make me happy." And a second student commented, "I get a lot out of community service. Maybe more than I should. I find this kind of work far more enjoyable and rewarding than the summer jobs I've had. And they're the kinds of jobs I'll get when I have my degree. I think if service-type professions paid better I might choose something like that over engineering."

What gets emphasized throughout the schooling process contributes to the possible selves envisioned by students as they anticipate their futures and the kinds of persons they desire to become. Community service is one educational activity that may be used to foster a caring self in that it is grounded in an ethic of care and involves more connected ways of knowing. In turn, higher learning may be reconstituted around an ethic of care in which activities such as community service become central processes rather than peripheral activities. Such a goal is not intended as resistance to the technologically grounded self highlighted by Turkle (1995). Instead, community service may be seen as a complementary objective to a more technologically advanced educational experience. While students become increasingly engaged with computers, there is no reason they cannot also engage with others on a caring and personal level through acts of compassion and service.

In chapter 1, I discussed how Mead and other symbolic interactionists have conceptualized the self. Their thinking clearly points to a social self dependent on relations with others. In this chapter, I have explored feminist contributions and discussed what some have termed the "relational self," suggesting that women tend to develop in more connected ways whereas men tend to be more individualistic. I situated the development of the self within the context of culture and identity in which I highlighted what has been termed the "politics of identity." The politics of identity underscores the potential for reshaping culture and thus re-situating identities and reconstituting selves through the educational process. In what follows, I offer two examples of students whose identities have been strongly influenced by the collegiate context. Their lives highlight the transformative power of educational settings.

COLLEGIATE CULTURE AND IDENTITY

Educational settings play an active and fundamental role in how one's sense of self is formed. Social interactions are key to this process. In ethnographic studies I have conducted of the collegiate context, I have witnessed the power of the group to shape the individual. Greg Ward was a senior and heavily involved in his fraternity when I met him in the fall of 1990. My idea at the time was to conduct an ethnographic case study of his fraternity as a means of identifying the organization's culture—the values and beliefs evident in its ceremonies, rituals, and social interactions. One thing that struck me then and continues to fascinate me to this day is the way in which the fraternity becomes an all-encompassing source of identification for young men. The social life of the brothers I studied revolved almost entirely around the fraternity and the relationships among the brothers. Greg had always been close to his family and called them several times a week. This all changed, however, during his sophomore year when he became a member of the Alpha Beta (pseudonym) fraternity. He described the closeness that grew from his relationships with the brothers: "The most significant thing about fraternity life is that we all have a house to live in. We're all together. It's like a family. As a family you always want each other to share friendships, memories, parties. It's really hard to contribute to college life as an individual, whereas with a group of guys you can do this and that. . . . At parties we get to reminisce about pledging and the good times. Alumni come back and it's like you know them even though you've never met. It's like you have much of the same things in common. . . . It's hanging around together on Sunday mornings talking about the weekend—the parties, sports, just about anything we did over the weekend. It helps adapt to living on your own away from your parents. And if you have problems with a class or something, you can always find someone who can help you. It's different being in a fraternity from being an independent. When I walk from a class I might see 20 to 30 people I know. Maybe not by their first names, but at least I recognize them."

When I interviewed Greg, it seemed as though his membership in the fraternity had become the center of his life and that the "brotherhood" had become vital to his sense of self. "I would do anything for the brotherhood. You want to do anything you can to show respect and commitment to the brothers." According to Greg, his view of himself changed dramatically during the two years of his involvement in the brotherhood: "I was a big athlete in high school, but when I got to college I couldn't relate that well. Fraternity life has given me opportunities to socialize and to improve my social skills. I'm much more self-confident." Greg no longer considered himself to be shy, or unattractive to women. He believed himself to be a good and dependable brother and friend. The support offered by his brothers and the brotherhood in general became a source of positive affirmation for Greg. His sense of self changed over the years, and he was pleased with the person he had become and was satisfied with his life in the brotherhood.

In my research of Greg's fraternity, one of the more significant aspects of the organization was the oppressive attitudes toward women that were promoted by the social and cultural context of Alpha Beta (Rhoads, 1995c). Part of the brothers' self-affirmation as men came at the expense of women. For example, many of the brothers in Greg's fraternity spoke of women as sexual objects. One brother even described some of the women who associated with the brothers on an ongoing basis as "creatures who were not worthy of wearing the fraternity's letters." There is research to suggest that the identity of young men that is perpetuated by fraternities reflects a narrow conception of masculinity and involves the degradation of women and traits typically associated with feminine identities, such as sensitivity and caring. My research tended to reinforce the earlier findings of Peggy Sanday (1990), who described the culture of fraternity life as a contributing force in the ongoing victimization of women in collegiate settings. One's identity as a member of a fraternity and the related social interactions contribute in significant ways to a student's sense of self. Unfortunately, many of the contributions foster negative and oppressive attitudes toward women, which then are enacted with women. Such interactions may, in turn, contribute negatively to women's self-conceptions.

Other collegiate experiences also play a pivotal role in identity formation. Another study I conducted focused on the coming-out experiences of gay and bisexual college men, most of whom were involved in the Lesbian, Gay, and Bisexual Student Alliance at Pennsylvania State University (Rhoads, 1994, 1995a, 1995b). Benjamin Rogers was one of forty students who participated in interviews and served as a key informant in a two-year ethnographic study conducted in the early 1990s. Benjamin struggled for years with his sense of self as a sexual person, and only after coming out and becoming actively involved in the gay student community at Penn State could he understand significant aspects about his life and his childhood. "I came out when I got to college. I think that it was one of the most positive things that ever happened to me. It gave me a sense of identity. Finally, there was something I could call my own—my gayness. Being gay was something that I knew for sure."

For Benjamin, the internal struggle he went through for years in trying to establish a sense of his own sexual identity never fully made sense to him until he began to meet other lesbian, gay, and bisexual students at the university. It was through his interactions with these students and the gay community in general that he finally came to realize and face the idea that he was gay. Benjamin explains, "Coming to college was an opportunity to be independent and have the advantage of a university community for support. It's a safe space where other supportive people are and where there are resources and opportunities to learn."

In discovering the gay student community at Penn State, Benjamin found an aspect of the collegiate context to be empowering. His interactions with other gay and bisexual men helped him to deal with years of repression and self-hatred. As Benjamin became more knowledgeable of gay identity and the years of struggle for equality, his passion and commitment to the gay community grew and he took on increasingly important roles in gay student organizations. Benjamin's identity as a gay activist was being forged and his once shaky self-concept was gradually replaced by a gay-affirming sense of self. His emerging sense of self was strongly tied to the larger gay community and his desire to change social conditions so that other lesbian, gay, and bisexual people would be free to come out.

Both Greg Ward and Benjamin Rogers experienced numerous social interactions during their college years that provided a cultural context from which to grow and develop a sense of self. From my work with students such as Greg and Benjamin, I have witnessed the utility of Mead's theory of the social self. Also, throughout my research on students involved in community service, the significance of students' interactions with others is readily apparent; their emerging self is strongly influenced by these interactions.

However, the development of the self should not be a neutral process as classic symbolic interactionists imply, as evidenced by their lack of commitment to an idealized view of the self and a utopian vision of community. Some collegiate experiences contribute negatively to the development of a caring sense of self; many of the interactions I observed at the Alpha Beta fraternity come to mind. Although the interactionist perspective may prove insightful in unraveling how the self is shaped and reshaped through fraternity interactions, it has little to say about whether fraternity life ought to be transformed to foster more sensitive and caring attitudes. This is the strength of feminism and other critical perspectives that argue that research and theorizing ought to seek social transformation by enhancing the struggle for democracy and a more caring social world. Do we really want to promote educational contexts that foster oppressive attitudes toward others? The fraternity offers a good example of how some of the more oppressive aspects of a male-oriented culture get reproduced and in turn contribute to the continued marginality of women. The point is that collegiate contexts need to be carefully analyzed for the subtle and not-so-subtle cultural messages they send to college students. If caring is to become central to the educational mission of colleges and universities, then aspects of the collegiate experience contributing to inequality and oppression need to be altered or eliminated. Merely to examine student identity without a critical vision of the kind of social life we might hope to create is inadequate.

The question that feminism and other critical perspectives such as postmodernism and critical theory pose is this: How do we structure educational settings so that an orientation toward caring for others and the driving concerns for democracy inform the developing self? Furthermore, how do we construct learning environments in which a relational or caring self might be fostered? One argument framing this book is that college students who participate in community service have unique opportunities to explore the relational self. Specifically, they come into contact with diverse others within the context of what we typically think of as a caring encounter. The following students offer comments about their experiences and interactions with homeless citizens. These students allude to the kind of learning that often occurs when students are challenged to interact with diverse others:

> We pass the time without really questioning our lives. The people of the streets have challenged me.

> Going into this project, I had many assumptions about the homeless. They have been shattered by this experience. I have a much deeper understanding of their struggles.

> Working with the people of the streets has transformed 'those people' into real faces, real lives, and real friends. I can no longer confront the issue without seeing the faces of my new friends. This has an incredible effect on my impetus to help.

> The statistics about homeless people and the stories of people freezing to death in the winter never really hit home until I made friends with Harry and Reggie.

Based on the preceding comments, as well as the theoretical arguments offered in this section, it seems logical to conclude that there are valuable lessons to be learned from students' community service experiences that might inform educational practices.

SUMMARY

It seems safe to assume that if part of our understanding of the self derives from taking the role of others or walking with others (as in the case of engrossment), and that if such role taking occurs within the context of community service, then positive feelings and attitudes from others are likely to be reflected back to students as a result of their service encounters. Logically, it also follows that positive reflections about the self occurring through community service interactions ought to contribute to a positive sense of the relational self. Hence, it is no stretch of the imagination to presume that participation in community service reinforces a student's relational or caring self. This is the central presumption I examine throughout this book as I seek to unravel its validity and use such knowledge to inform higher learning.

Before I delve into my findings in greater detail and begin addressing the questions and issues raised in chapters 1 and 2, a final concern must be addressed. Because the self is a social self and develops in the context of social interaction, it is imperative that we come to terms with what constitutes social life in general and the ideal of community in particular. With this in mind, I turn now to discuss issues related to the self by delineating diverse perspectives of social life and what it might mean to examine community service and explorations of the self within the context of a postmodern vision of community. This is the central concern of chapter 3.

Chapter 3

Thinking about Community

*Selves are constituted within culture, and cul-
ture is maintained by the community of selves.
—Andrew Lock, "Universals
in Human Cognition"*

*As a child I spent a great deal of time by myself. I enjoyed being left
alone and having a chance to create my own forms of entertainment. I played
army with my mother's clothespins for hours, using blankets and bedspreads to
create mountains around which the generals had to mobilize and then deploy
their troops. Another of my pastimes was bouncing rubber balls off the bedroom
or basement walls and practicing catch with my baseball glove. I came up
with intricate ways of actually playing games with batters and fielders all having their own names, which were either fictitious or the real names of the players whose team they represented. Of course, it was always the Pittsburgh
Pirates versus some other team. Roberto Clemente was the usual hero of the
imaginary games I played unless I installed myself into a situation here or
there.*

*Perhaps my greatest private passion as a child was playing the Strat-O-
Matic Baseball game I received on Christmas morning in 1967. I was ten years
old, and I must have played more than one thousand games by the same day
one year later. I became the full-time manager of the 1966 Pittsburgh Pirates
(the games are based on statistics achieved by players from the previous year).
Matty Alou led off and played centerfield. He hit .342 that year and won the
batting crown. I had Manny Mota hitting second and put him at third base,
where he was a terrible fielder but with his .332 batting average I could afford
his weak glovework. And then came Bobby Clemente, or the "Great One" as
the "Gunner," Bob Prince, the Pirates' announcer, called him from time to
time. I can hear Bob Prince to this day with that gravelly voice of his: "Batting*

third and playing right field, Bobby Clemente." Roberto did not like the name "Bobby" because it seemed too Americanized, and he was proud of his Puerto Rican heritage. Roberto was the league's most valuable player in 1966, and he hit .317 with 29 home runs and 119 runs batted in. Willie Stargell followed Clemente in the batting order. He had a great year as well. Then came Donn Clendenon at first base, Gene Alley at shortstop, Bill Mazeroski at second base, and Jim Pagliaroni at catcher. The best pitcher on the Pirate team that year was Bob Veale. He won sixteen games and lost twelve. I played so many games between the Pirates and the rest of the teams (there were twenty teams in Major League Baseball in 1966) that at one time I could recite the batting order of every team, along with the names of the reserve players. It's almost embarrassing to admit, but I also knew nearly every statistic for each player.

The game was my escape. My fantasy world. A victory by the Pirates and a good game by Clemente meant a good day for me, and greater excitement and energy directed at my own ball playing in Little League or with friends. I don't think it's unusual for young kids to have such extensive fantasy worlds, and in many ways it can be a healthy way to develop one's imagination. But many of my baseball fantasies died on New Years Day, 1973, as did the dreams of a lot of other kids and even adults who grew up with Roberto Clemente as their idol.

It must have been around noon, and I was camped out in front of the television like all the other football fanatics around the country. I was pre-pared for my yearly overdose of college football as the bowl games began to kick off. All that changed, though, when my mother came into the living room and informed me that Roberto Clemente had been killed in a plane crash some-where off the coast of Puerto Rico. There had been an earthquake in Nicaragua, and Clemente had collected goods and supplies from fellow Puerto Ricans and had chartered a private plane to deliver the supplies. He decided to travel with the supplies in order to ensure that everything would be properly delivered. The plane went down just off the coast near San Juan. His body was never found.

At first when she told me I thought she was only joking. I was in denial. But then a news flash came on the television and it was confirmed. Roberto Clemente was dead. I pretended not to be too bothered by it all but soon snuck up to the private world of my bedroom and cried for hours. I played a few games of Strat-O-Matic, as if to offer my own tribute to my fallen hero. But it was never the same.

All the time I spent by myself playing imaginary games of one sort or another should have told me something back then—that I should someday become a writer since so much of what we do is spent within the confines of our own minds. My isolationist tendencies still prevail to a great deal, and sometimes I have to force myself simply to socialize with the rest of the world.

But I have found some vehicles for building connections, and one of them is involvement in community service. Perhaps it is because I am kept busy by the physical work that comes with repairing a house or preparing meals that the interactions seem more enjoyable. It seems so stereotypically male to socialize around a common task, as if enjoying the company of others requires some kind of overarching objective. Community service has enabled me from time to time to feel the sense of community that I long for so deeply but have failed to achieve through so many other efforts. Service work seems to balance my life as an individual and my desire to connect in some deeper way to others. Despite my isolationist tendencies, I know that I am nothing without others to care for and to care for me.

My intention in this chapter is to examine some of the tension that is played out within the social drama encompassing individualism and the struggle for community. I use my own story to introduce the topic, but I know I am by no means alone in working through such issues. I begin by using the work of Robert Bellah, Richard Madsen, William Sullivan, Ann Swidler, and Steven Tipton (1985) to frame a discussion of individualism and community and to highlight how tensions between the two often are revealed through acts of service and volunteerism. I go on to present varying perspectives of communal life, in which I discuss functional, conflict, and symbolic views. As I will point out, the way we think about social life creates a variety of possibilities that may foster or inhibit our ability to build community. I then discuss postmodern conceptions of community. I argue that the perspective we adopt is particularly relevant as we move further and further into a postmodern world in which new and innovative ways of thinking are needed to make sense of life. I relate the changing context of society to the role that community service and caring might play as innovative educational programs. I highlight the idea of community service as a classroom in which colleges and universities seek to foster the kinds of caring citizens who are needed in a postmodern democracy. Finally, I conclude the chapter by offering ten propositions that summarize the theoretical perspective introduced in chapters 1, 2, and 3 and that undergird the presentation of data in the remaining chapters.

INDIVIDUALISM AND COMMUNITY

In *Habits of the Heart*, Robert Bellah (1985) and associates discussed how Americans pursue happiness in a variety of ways. Bellah pointed out that, despite the pervasiveness of a language of individualism, many people have sought public and community commitments as a source of peace and content-ment with life. "Many Americans are concerned to find meaning in life not pri-marily through self-cultivation but through intense relations with others. . . . There is in the desire for intense relationships with others an attempt to move beyond the isolated self, even though the language of individualism makes that sometimes hard to articulate" (p. 291). Robert Wuthnow conveyed a sim-ilar point in his analysis of how Americans make commitments to caring for others, despite a culture that seemingly fosters the rugged individualist. As Wuthnow explained, "For all the talk about a 'me generation' and who can accumulate the most toys before we die, most of us recognize the importance of caring for others and many of us put that value into practice. At the same time, few of us want to be Mother Teresa . . . few of us are willing to give up any of the intense individualism we have inherited from our culture" (1991, p. 28).

Although a commitment to compassion and a concern for others, as dis-cussed by Wuthnow, may be strongly rooted in some members of our society, nonetheless many place individualism at the center of the self. Listen to the fol-lowing student introduced by Paul Loeb in *Generation at the Crossroads*: "Maybe I don't put my first priority on larger issues because I'm concerned with me first. It's going to sound really cold, but that's the way I am. I still feel God helps those who help themselves, and maybe we'd be better off if everyone else admitted that too, instead of using excuses for not making it. Or maybe I'm just selfish. I want to have a family, people I love. I want to do what I can for them" (1994, p. 122).

The tension between a commitment to individualism and a commitment to community was evident throughout my research on students' involvement in community service. Students struggled with their desire to help others and a concomitant belief that anyone can become successful if he or she is just willing to work hard enough. The "God helps those who help themselves" philosophy was ingrained in the students' thinking. This created incongruence among some students who found themselves caught in a double bind: If the poor can be suc-cessful if they just work harder, then am I hindering their chances by helping them? A student commented: "I don't mind helping the poor who really need help. But I do mind helping those who are just soaking the system for all they can get. I mean, how can you be sure if someone really needs help or if they are just lazy and want to take advantage of someone else's kindness? Part of me wonders if what we're doing is helpful or not. I mean providing free meals." And a second student added, "It's kind of a dilemma. I mean you want to help someone but at the same time you can't help but think if we weren't here to provide handouts wouldn't they find some other way to survive? Perhaps that might provide the ini-tiative to get a job. I know it sounds kind of crass and I also know there aren't a whole lot of jobs out there. And if I truly felt that way I wouldn't be here to help. It's just something that I think about from time to time."

Questions about one's commitment to community also surfaced when students gave serious thought to being in community with other volunteers. Students struggled to contribute to group solidarity despite strong tendencies toward individualism. One student in particular recognized this source of tension and articulated her dilemma: "The community service project I participated in really forced me to think about the tension between individual interests and group or community interests. I brought some frozen yogurt on the trip and I was really intent on not sharing it with other people. But after I thought about it, I wondered how that would contribute to the group. I had to decide between what's best for me and what's best for the group. . . . This whole experience has been an eye opener in that it reminds me of how every little effort can contribute to the good of an entire community and how little things can serve to tear down communities too." This student felt the strain between the ideals of the caring self and those often encouraged by a society centered on competition and a survival-of-the-fittest mentality. Individualism is so pervasive that, even in the context of community service projects, some students still wrestled with whether it was helpful or not to make connections with others.

Bellah (1985) and his coauthors offer a portrait of Wayne Bauer, a Californian actively engaged in the Campaign for Economic Democracy. Wayne was in his middle thirties at the time of the book's publication and was very much influenced by the activism of the 1960s. Wayne explained: "During the sixties we saw a dream, we had a vision. And we had a belief that things could be much better, on many levels. I mean, it was a time of personal growth as well as political change. And what was exciting about that is that the personal change was what would be leading into a very significant political change in the country" (p. 17). Wayne went through his own changes in the 1960s. He joined the Marine Corps when he was only seventeen and professed that he had always bought into the John Wayne image of an American and what it means to be patriotic. Not long after completing basic training, Wayne began spending time on leave in New York City, where he met up with some of his old friends who were now attending college in the city. It was 1965, and students at New York University were protesting the Vietnam War by marching and burning their draft cards. His friends opposed the war and engaged in extended arguments with Wayne about his involvement in the military. Wayne's view of the war, the world, and his own identity were being challenged for the first time in his life. He described the challenge as being like looking in a mirror and seeing a reflection that was not himself, and yet it was him. He could almost see himself changing before his own eyes as friends were successfully challenging long-held values and beliefs.

Wayne went AWOL and spent several years traveling around the country, trying to maintain a quiet and anonymous life. Finally, in 1972, he turned himself in to the military. After spending four months in a stockade, he was given a general discharge. The commitment to serving his country that had led him to join the Marine Corps in the first place had not left Wayne; it became translated into a new vision of life and a commitment to others.

Wayne moved to Southern California and became actively involved in helping Spanish-speaking residents resolve disputes with their landlords. This helped lead him to his involvement with the Campaign for Economic Democracy. Wayne talked about his work: "I feel good about what I do. I feel that the work I'm involved in is directly affecting other people in beneficial ways. . . . You can spend all your time in seeing how many material goods you can get together and how much money you can make or you can spend it helping one another and working together. You know, we can adopt any type of system we want, let's say it was socialism, communism, or what have you, but the system that we adopt isn't going to mean anything unless we can educate the people to think differently and to be different. And I see what I do as sort of an educational thing in the community, that what I do when I organize tenants is to take care of an immediate crisis that they have. But really what I do is give them a sense of power about their own lives" (Bellah et al., 1985, pp. 18–19).

Bellah went on to point out that Wayne had embraced a commitment to working for social justice for economically disadvantaged people and communities. However, when pressed to explain the meaning of concepts such as "justice" and "community," Wayne stumbled for the appropriate words to provide insight into his personal vision. Bellah explained that Wayne's conception of justice, which offered such a powerful force in his life, was limited in substantive content. Wayne spoke of justice in terms of individual rights but had little conception of how to create greater equity in the distribution of resources and opportunities. In his struggle to move beyond the isolated self, Wayne's embeddedness in the language of individualism made it difficult for him to articulate a sense of self committed to community and an ethic of care. Throughout *Habits of the Heart*, Bellah focused on the following paradox: Americans desire to connect with others through community building and acts of caring, while at the same time they exist within a culture that linguistically and conceptually limits the accessibility of such a vision.

Providing a frame of reference for Bellah's portrait of American life is the work of French social philosopher Alexis de Tocqueville, who examined the social fabric of the United States in the mid-1800s. In *Democracy in America*, Tocqueville (1945) argued that it is the moral and intellectual condition of a people that makes democracy possible or not.

> I have previously remarked that the manners of the people may be considered as one of the great general causes to which the maintenance of a democratic republic in the United States is attributable. I here use the

word *customs* with the meaning which the ancients attached to the word *mores*; for I apply it not only to manners properly so called—that is, to what might be termed *habits of the heart*—but to the various notions and opinions current among men and to the mass of those ideas which constitute their character of mind. I comprise under this term, therefore, the whole moral and intellectual condition of a people. (p. 299)

Tocqueville's "habits of the heart" are what Bellah sought to uncover as he examined a range of American identities. And, of course, what he found is a fundamental tension between a culture of individualism and a quest for community.

As the social world changes, our views and theories about social life also need to change. Bellah's portrait of social life offers few theoretical insights to explain the rise of an "internet community," exemplified by Multi-User Domains (MUDs), or to make sense of an "internet identity," two relatively emergent ideas conveyed in the work of Sherry Turkle (1995). Of course, how could Bellah have anticipated the incredible technological changes occurring over the past ten to fifteen years? Criticizing Bellah for his lack of foresight would be akin to attacking Tocqueville for his inability to anticipate the role of American professional sports in supplanting religion as the number one cultural force in the production of zealots.

Socially, we have arrived at the postmodern turn. But theoretically, we have fallen behind. In making sense of community and caring and their role in a society, we must understand the ways in which social life is conceptualized, past and present. Furthermore, we cannot separate a vision of social life—in its most utopian form—from our understanding of the role of education. Tocqueville commented on this very idea when he wrote, "It cannot be doubted that in the United States the instruction of the people powerfully contributes to the support of the democratic republic; and such must always be the case, I believe, where the instruction which enlightens the understanding is not separated from the moral education which amends the heart" (1945, p. 317).

How do we desire to amend the heart? And how does a vision of democracy get reflected in theorizing about social life? With the preceding questions charting the course, I briefly trace some of the major streams of theorizing about social life, leading up to a discussion of the postmodern condition. I pick up the story not long after Tocqueville returned to France from America. This was the same general period in which Ferdinand Tönnies developed his thoughts on the changing face of social life in light of industrialization and what has come to be termed "modernity." The point of all this is that the way we think about social life and community in turn influences to a great degree the possibilities that may be imagined. Relatedly, the way people have viewed social life throughout modernity offers insight into how we might conceive of societies and communities existing within postmodern times. Throughout my theoretical discussion I offer student comments as a means to ground theory in the real life experiences of people involved in this project.

TRADITIONAL CONCEPTIONS OF SOCIAL LIFE

In examining how traditional theorists have framed the idea of social life it is helpful to discuss three differing schools of thought: organic/functional, conflict, and symbolic perspectives. Within the organic/functional framework I highlight the works of Ferdinand Tönnies, Emile Durkheim, Talcott Parsons, and Robert Merton. The works of Karl Marx and Georg Lukács frame a discussion of conflict perspectives. And finally, the works of George Herbert Mead, Herbert Blumer, and Kenneth Burke guide a discussion of symbolic perspectives.

Organic/Functional Perspectives

Emile Durkheim framed social organization around functional and organic propositions. Durkheim (1933) argued that two predominant forms of society exist, based on different types of solidarity: mechanical and organic. Mechanical solidarity represents the earliest forms of society, where bloodlines and clanship are prominent and is akin to Tönnies's (1957) idea of *gemeinschaft*. Organic solidarity is a more advanced stage of social organization and tends to assimilate mechanical solidarity and redirect social structure along functional lines. At the center of Durkheim's notion of organic solidarity is, of course, the division of labor. "The ideal of human fraternity can be realized only in proportion to the progress of the division of labor" (p. 405). Solidarity is achieved by one's assimilation into a functional role within society.

In Durkheim's thinking, the diversity of cultural experience eventually and inevitably becomes assimilated. "It is a general law that partial aggregates which participate in a larger aggregate see their individuality becoming less and less distinct" (1933, p. 185). Discord, although it may exist for a period of time, must ultimately give way to the influences of the larger body. "It is . . . a leveling analogous to that which is produced between liquid masses put into communication" (p. 185).

The division of labor stressed in Durkheim's functional analysis reflected the changing face of Western civilization in the nineteenth century and the steady progress of industrialization and modernity. For Tönnies, this marked a change in social relations from *gemienschaft* to *gesellschaft*, in which Western societies moved from personal and familial ties to impersonal and labor-related social bonds. The United States exhibited its own take on industrialization and the advanced stages of capitalism as new forms of anomie and alienation emerged along with urban expansion and population growth. Indeed, the book *The Lonely Crowd* was not an oxymoron but the reality of modern life amidst a social world turned impersonal (Riesman, Glazer, & Denney, 1950). As functional connectedness steadily replaced personal connections, individuals sought solace in a variety of ways, including the pursuit of materialism. A mentality of "whoever has the most toys wins" was taking root. Something was surely missing, and Americans in particular seemed determined to fill this social void.

From the works of Durkheim and Tönnies, among others, the functionalist approach became the principal lens for understanding social life. American sociologist Talcott Parsons (1961) elaborated the classic functionalist position as he theorized about social control and the need to maintain stability in social systems. Parsons explained that the internalization of norms ensures the stability of institutionalized values. Values are articulated through various belief systems such as religion and ideology. Discord can be seen as either a failure to become socially integrated into the normative value system or a choice on the part of the individual to reject social and cultural influences. The idea of individual choice is captured in Parsons's discussion of motivation, in which the level of commitment to values plays a role in the adherence to certain norms. For instance, an individual may have internalized a certain set of values through the process of socialization, but may decide to reject those values at any given time based on motivational factors. Thus, although Parsons's theory has a functionalist vent, it is not a deterministic theory. Individuals, because of personality (the psychological force), may choose means to ends that do not fit normative patterns.

Another functionalist perspective of society was offered by Robert Merton, who delineated three fundamental postulates associated with functional analysis: (1) cultural items or elements are functional for the entire social or cultural system, (2) all social and cultural elements fulfill sociological functions, and (3) cultural items are indispensable. The first postulate—the postulate of functional unity—relates to the conception of society as a system in which maintenance requires various subsystems to work together to produce social harmony. The second postulate—the postulate of universal functionalism—holds that all cultural forms have positive functions. Merton went on to qualify this postulate by noting that a more useful interpretation of universalism is to say that "persisting cultural forms have a net balance of functional consequences either for the society considered as a unit or for subgroups sufficiently powerful to retain these forms intact" (1949, p. 86). The third postulate—the postulate of indispensability—relates to the idea that all cultural elements serve some purpose in maintaining the social system.

Merton argued that science had already established the legitimacy of functionalist approaches and that although the popularity of functionalism was not in itself proof of its relevancy, nonetheless "it does suggest that cumulative experience has forced this orientation upon disciplined observers of man as biological organism, psychological actor, member of society and bearer of culture" (1949, p. 102).

Inherent throughout Merton's discussion of functional analysis is the presumption that societies operate in a fashion akin to organisms in that system maintenance and survival are imperative. This presumption is consistent with the basic principles of society Tönnies, Durkheim, and Parsons adopt in their organic/functional representations of social life. From a functionalist perspective, even crime and poverty may be seen to serve some overarching purpose that in some way contributes positively to the overall society. Many of the students I interviewed revealed views rooted in a functionalist framework. But at the same time, they struggled with some of the logical conclusions functionalism suggests. For example, a student talked about an economics course he had taken in which the professor pointed out that a class of poor people or an "under class" is needed in order to provide a source of labor for lower paying jobs. "If there are not any poor, then who would assume some of the service sector positions offering marginal pay?" Such a perspective led this student to question whether helping the poor is a good idea or not. "If as a society we need to have a class of poor people, then why should we help them? I'm asking the question not because I have an answer but because the whole argument confuses me." Here we can see how the theoretical perspective one adopts suggests the possibility for action or inaction. I can imagine some students who might consider community service first saying to themselves, "If society needs to have poor people, then perhaps I should not help the poor to have a better life." Or, "Maybe I should not work to alter social and economic conditions that threaten poverty."

Functionalism goes hand in hand with social Darwinism and can lead to apathy among a citizenry. If social forms simply *evolve* because they are better suited to the society, why should citizens act as agents for social change? Functionalism fosters a sense that "things are the way they are for a reason, and therefore we shouldn't tamper with them." The student in the preceding paragraph highlights this stance.

When one argues that poverty serves a function to society, one must also ask: Which members of society benefit? Functionalists seem guilty of viewing society as a monolithic entity in which everyone benefits in equal fashion. Yet, if some live "high on the hog" and others suffer economic deprivation, how can we see their experiences in the same light and as part of some holistic portrait of the same society? Robert Serow speaks to this issue when he argued that in certain instances various individuals or subgroups within a society "may be asked to sacrifice for the greater good" (1983, p. 13). But who benefits from poverty, and is being homeless or hungry a reasonable sacrifice to ask an individual or group to make? One can almost envision an economics or sociology professor explaining to the poor that they are served by their own starvation or homelessness.

Merton provides an important connection to conflict theorists when he suggests that society at large is not always the beneficiary of certain social arrangements and that in some instances specific subgroups "sufficiently powerful" may be able to retain social forms for their own benefit. For Marx and Lukács, the subgroups of importance revolve around the distribution of property and the conflict between the bourgeoisie (property owners) and the proletariate (the working class).

Conflict Perspectives

From a functionalist perspective, conflict is seen as a disruptive force threatening the harmony and solidarity of the social system. Other theorists, however, have conceptualized conflict in a different manner. For Karl Marx, conflict was essential to the emergence of revolutionary action necessary for the achievement of a social utopia. Central to his discussion of conflict is the inevitable inequality of individual property ownership. The establishment of private property produces a sense of alienation resulting from our desire to "have" or to possess. Marx asserted that private property was at the source of inequities in that capitalism required people to associate value with ownership: Something can be of value only if it is possessed by someone. The quest for materialism served to pervert other aspects of human imagination. As Marx explained, "Thus all the physical and intellectual senses have been replaced by the simple alienation of all the senses, the sense of having" (1844, p. 151). His solution to the conflict or disharmony resulting from alienation lies in the overthrow of the bourgeoisie and ultimately the creation of a communist state—a social system in which private property is abolished. Marx posited, "Communism is the positive abolition of private property, of human self-alienation, and thus the real appropriation of human nature through and for man" (p. 149). "It is therefore," he added, "the return of man himself as a social, i.e. really human, being, a complete and conscious return which assimilates all the wealth of previous development" (p. 149).

Georg Lukács (1968), in building on the work of Marx, further elaborated the Marxian notion of "class consciousness"—the idea that a common sense of identity must emerge among the working class if the social revolution described by Marx is to occur. Lukács criticized bourgeois historians for "their belief that the concrete can be located in the empirical individual of history . . . and in his empirically given consciousness" (p. 50). As Marx had previously noted, social relations must be examined, not between one individual and another but through the relations of worker and capitalist, tenant and landlord. One's position within the system of materialist production is ultimately where identity resides—an identity grounded in one's class, a class consciousness so to speak. Lukács elaborated,

Class consciousness consists in the fact of the appropriate and rational reactions imputed [*zugerechnet*] to a particular typical position in the process of production. This consciousness is, therefore, neither the sum nor the average of what is thought or felt by the single individuals who make up the class. And yet historically significant actions of the class as a whole are determined in the last resort by this consciousness and not by the thought of the individual—and these actions can be understood only by reference to this consciousness. (p. 51)

Lukács further claimed that "the proletariate has been entrusted by history with the task of transforming society consciously" (p. 71). This, however, can occur only when the proletariate achieves a certain degree of maturity: "When the final economic crisis of capitalism develops, the fate of the revolution (and with it the fate of mankind) will depend on the ideological maturity of the proletariate, i.e., on its class consciousness" (p. 70). Maturity will be achieved only when the proletariate has recognized both immediate and long-term interests, as well as the difference between specific concrete concerns and those reflective of the totality of society. "Only when the immediate interests are integrated into a total view and related to the final goal of the process do they become revolutionary, pointing concretely and consciously beyond the confines of capitalist society" (p. 71).

For Marx and Lukács, the group supersedes the individual in that only through group action and commitment can social change occur. In this regard, the individual social actor is seen as relatively insignificant as the ultimate concern is with social transformation, which necessitates the development of a group consciousness.

Students working to serve the poor through community service projects cannot help but be confronted by the economic inequities inherent in our society. Although perhaps only a few considered social and economic structures from a Marxian perspective, nearly all of them faced personal conflicts related to seeing others with so much less than themselves. The economic differences between the "haves" and the "have nots" brought many to question their career objectives and what they truly valued in life. A student explained the crisis that working with homeless people stirred in her own life: "Seeing so many people with so little makes me feel very guilty. It makes me wonder about my own priorities and how important having money and security have become in my life. I want to have a successful career, a nice car, and even a nice house someday. But is it fair that I will probably have those things while someone else will be living in a cardboard box or sleeping under a plastic tarp tied to sewage grates? It makes me wonder if I ought to change my thinking and goals in life. But, honestly, I don't think I can. Maybe it's enough for me to give of my time to helping others."

Students such as the preceding one made connections between the internal conflicts they experienced and the larger issue of how a society distributes its resources. This only added to a state of incongruence resulting from their belief in individualism and a commitment to caring for others. Students attempted to reconcile this incongruence in a variety of ways. Some were able to push the issues aside and simply ritualize their service work and thus successfully avoid the paradoxical questions raised by simultaneous commitments to individualism and service. For others, resolving incongruence was not so easy. Some students talked about alternatives to pursuing their own career and personal interests. One student discussed her desire to work in social services and to serve low-income families, and yet she desperately wanted to have her own family some day. As the kind of individual who puts all her passion and energy into a commitment, she saw balancing the two as practically impossible. Many students considered changing their majors to service-oriented fields as part of letting go of their dreams of materialism and individualism. The struggles of these students bring to mind a passage from Margaret Sanger's autobiography in which she describes watching her house burn and all her material possessions go up in smoke:

> It was as though a chapter of my life had been brought to a close, and I was neither disappointed nor regretful. On the contrary, I was conscious of a certain relief, of a burden lifted. In that instant I learned the lesson of the futility of material substances. Of what great importance were they spiritually if they could go so quickly? Pains, thirsts, heartaches could be put into the creation of something external which in one sweep could be taken from you. With the destruction of the window, my scale of suburban values was consumed. I could never again pin my faith on concrete things; I must build on myself alone. (1971, p. 64)

One hears echoes of Margaret Sanger in the following student's voice as she contemplates some of the new meanings community service has brought to her life: "Meeting some of the homeless people I've met throughout the week has taught me a great deal about myself and my life. The things I have been taught to value are insignificant compared to helping someone in need. It has been so fulfilling for me that there is no way this can't have an impact on my life."

Again, the way we think about the social world shapes the way we experience it and vice versa. Culture shapes our social experience as we shape culture. As Clifford Geertz (1973) reminds us, we are trapped within the very webs that we ourselves construct. And yet, there is always the opportunity to resist and contest the way things are. This is what Marx and Lukács call to our attention, and this is what we hear from students as they contest more mainstream functionalist images of the world and struggle with the conflict surrounding them, made most visible through their community service work with the poor. How one interprets and makes meaning of life's experiences clearly shapes the choices to be made and the actions to be taken. Nowhere is this point made more vivid than in the works of symbolic theorists Mead, Blumer, and Burke.

Symbolic Perspectives

George Herbert Mead wrote, "Human society as we know it could not exist without minds and selves, since all its most characteristic features presuppose the possession of minds and selves by its individual members" (1934, p. 227). However, the self is contingent on the social: "Co-operative activity antedates the self" (p. 240). As I discussed in Chapter 1, the self emerges through a social process that involves taking the role of the other—the other being people with whom an individual interacts.

The act of taking the role of the other is a symbolic process in which we perceive ourselves as objects of our own previous or prospective actions. Taking the role of the other serves as a form of self-criticism and acts to exert social control over individuals. "Self-criticism is essentially social criticism, and behavior controlled socially" (Mead, 1934, p. 255). Mead argued that such a process, instead of crushing individuality, actually constitutes individuality as "the individual is what he is, as a conscious and individual personality, just as far as he is a member of society, involved in the social process of experience and activity, and thereby socially controlled in his conduct" (p. 255). Mead did not envision social control in the same oppressive light as Michel Foucault (1977, 1978) and other more recent postmodernists, who tend to see the power of the norm (and social control) as a source of confinement. Instead, for Mead, individuality or discord is possible only through the symbolic activities associated with social control and organization.

Blumer (1969) offered an interpretation similar to Mead's when, arguing from a symbolic interactionist perspective, he stated, "Human society is the framework inside of which social action takes place and is not the determinant of that action. Such organization and changes in it are the product of the activity of acting units and not of 'forces' which leave such acting units out of account" (p. 87). Throughout his work, Blumer deemphasized the role of culture and social structure. "Social organization enters into action only to the extent to which it shapes situations in which people act, and to the extent to which it supplies fixed sets of symbols which people use in interpreting their situations" (p. 88).

Blumer, like Mead, conferred a great deal of power on individuals in making indications to themselves and developing subsequent lines of action free from the influences of culture and social structure. Society, for Blumer, is merely the fitting together of individual lines of action to form joint action. From Blumer's perspective, society has a great capacity to tolerate discord because individuals can exist in conflict, possess different values, and, in general, be quite diverse but still be able to fit lines of action together to form a sense of social connection.

> It is held that conflict between values or the disintegration of values creates disunity, disorder, and instability. This conception of society becomes subject to great modification if we think of society as consisting of the fitting together of acts to form joint action. Such alignment may take place for any number of reasons, depending on the situations calling for joint action, and need not involve, or spring from, the sharing of common values. The participants may fit their acts to one another in orderly joint actions on the basis of compromise, out of duress, because it is the sensible thing to do, or out of sheer necessity. This is particularly likely to be true in our modern complex societies with their great diversity in composition, in lines of interest, and in their respective worlds of concern. (p. 76)

Inherent in the preceding passage is the notion that social bodies can exist in which differences are prevalent. Discord is not merely something to be resolved, but instead may abide as long as people are able to align their actions. Furthermore, in drawing from Mead, Blumer claimed that it is faulty thinking to presume that society necessarily requires a sharing of common values; the possibility for joint action remains despite diverse value orientations.

Kenneth Burke also painted a symbolic portrait of social life. For Burke, the most important step in comprehending society is understanding that people are symbol-using animals. "What is our 'reality' for today (beyond the paper-thin line of our own particular lives) but all this clutter of symbols about the past combined with whatever things we know mainly through maps, magazines, newspapers, and the like about the present. . . . And however important to us is the tiny sliver of reality each of us has experienced firsthand, the whole overall 'picture' is but a construct of our symbol systems" (1989, p. 58).

Burke's emphasis on the importance of symbols and symbolic communication points to the significance of the social construction of reality and how human experience is largely shaped through that which can be symbolized and, hence, communicated. Clearly, Burke envisioned culture as a central force in shaping human existence. For Burke, individuals exist as actors whose scripts are derived from the language and symbolic representations of their culture. Erving Goffman (1959) adopts a similar perspective in his theory of dramaturgy, in which actors exist to a large degree as by-products of their culture and society.

Recall George Watkins, whom I introduced in chapter 1. He talked about how he thinks people make sense of their world. I reintroduce some of his comments as he talked about one of his community service experiences: "I realized how much people learn by interpreting signals from others. It's so obvious in a situation like this—where you're working with people you hardly know. People learn so much without decisively learning it. Most of what I learned about people is obscure and circuitous. . . . People hide things from people, but they see through the masks. They see things you don't want them to see." The "signals" and the "masks" that George Watkins talks about may be understood as those aspects of culture that enable us to communicate in a shorthand kind of fashion. The masks that we believe hide something of ourselves perhaps reveal more than we realize. And the signals that are so quickly expressed shed so much information about one's self, one's identity. Information that is often too painful to express through precise words is revealed through subtleties. And yet, the signals and the masks also protect us, for perhaps we can offer disclaimers: "I never really said that you hurt my feelings. I'm sorry I left you with that impression. So you needn't apologize," says the individual whose feelings have been damaged but is unable to admit verbally to the hurt.

Symbolic theorists such as Mead, Blumer, and Burke remind us that so much is to be interpreted and many times misinterpreted. Social life provides the context for our interaction and is what makes us most human.

It is far too simplistic to argue that functionalists are correct and conflict theorists are wrong, or that conflict theorists miss the point and symbolic perspectives are on the mark. Social reality is too complex to be so neatly packaged theoretically. Instead, I contend that there are different aspects of these three schools of thought that can benefit contemporary understandings of community. For example, functionalists help us to understand the importance a sense of belonging has for human beings and the need to feel a part of a larger social fabric (not necessarily at the societal level, though). Conflict theorists help us to see how social transformation might come about and how conflict is important in the struggle to create a more just society. Symbolic theorists help us to understand how the individual and society interrelate through communication and language and how group action might be possible despite diverse realities. How might we use these views of social life to better understand today's social world? If we are truly amidst "the postmodern condition," then how is the social world to be understood? How do we create meaning in our lives? And how does such meaning help us to understand the self, and the other, in the context of community service and higher learning? To answer these questions, I first explore what postmodern views of society entail and how they might also influence our thinking about community.

POSTMODERN CONCEPTIONS OF COMMUNITY

Postmodern theorists often describe social life by discussing the centrality of difference. The emphasis on difference resists functionalist conceptions of community grounded in an essentialist view of identity. Such views also reject views of social life promoting similarity and assimilationist tactics. Instead, postmodernists see change and cultural diversity as fundamental aspects of the social body. "Multiculturalism" is a phrase that is often used to emphasize the idea that cultural difference is something to be considered not only across communities and societies but within them as well. "Multiculturalism does not lead us very far if it remains a question of difference only between one culture and another. Differences should also be understood within the same culture, just as multiculturalism as an explicit condition of our times exists within every self" (Minh-ha, 1991, p. 107).

The work of Michel Foucault is central to understanding postmodern conceptions of social life. Foucault's critique of modernity revolves around his views on power and its role in shaping human behavior. For example, in an interview entitled the "The Eye of Power" Foucault described power as "a machine in which everyone is caught, those who exercise power just as much as those over whom it is exercised" (1980, p. 156). Throughout much of Foucault's work he elaborated a conception of power that has a life of its own; this is contrary to traditional conceptions of power, in which it is seen as something that people possess or enact. "Power is everywhere; not because it embraces everything, but because it comes from everywhere" (1978, p. 93).

The central point of Foucault's theory is his view that power is more than a prohibiting, negative force; power also serves a productive role in shaping behavior. The productive capacity of power is most evident in *Discipline and Punish* and is captured in Foucault's discussion of the Panopticon, which represents an image of society in which power is omnipresent. A system of constraints and privations becomes the essence of a form of social control contingent not on fear of physical punishment, but instead founded on a political economy of the body in which the ultimate target becomes the human soul. The soul is acted on through disciplinary mechanisms evident throughout society. The major effect of the Panopticon is to regulate the entire operation of society through surveillance. Social control is accomplished by inducing in citizens a state of conscious and permanent awareness of expectations and potential punishments in the case of violations. This is the power of normalization and explains why Foucault saw power as originating from innumerable points.

While Foucault provided insights into how modernity has developed social mechanisms to control behavior, he also described a certain degree of resistance available to diverse groups and identities. Because power is everywhere in Foucault's conception of society, diverse individuals and groups have the opportunity to legitimize their own cultures, identities, and perspectives by taking hold of various levers to power's innumerable locations. His treatment of knowledge as socially constructed and of power as originating from multiple points raised the possibility that truth, which is no longer universal, can be turned upside down by those willing and able to offer resistance. The same can be said of identities as the accessibility of power opens the door to individual and group struggle and the possibility of using power's productive capacity to create new visions of identity. As power advances from a tool of repression to a productive tool available to the many, identity becomes multifarious and decentered as difference reigns.

As Foucault's work highlights, identity in the postmodern context is characterized by a decentering of the individual. For Turkle, postmodern identity is a mixture of complex "roles that can be mixed and matched, whose diverse demands need to be negotiated" (1995, p. 180). It is, as Kenneth Gergen noted, "a plurality of voices vying to be part of the good and the right" (1991, p. 7). For Gergen, the postmodern condition is synonymous with "social saturation"—"a multiplicity of incoherent and unrelated languages of the self" (p. 6). Gergen went on to explain: "For everything we 'know to be true' about ourselves, other voices within respond with doubt and even derision. This fragmentation of self-conceptions corresponds to a multiplicity of incoherent and disconnected relationships. These relationships pull us in myriad directions, inviting us to play such a variety of roles that the very concept of an 'authentic self' with knowable characteristics recedes from view. The fully saturated self becomes no self at all" (pp. 6–7).

Other cultural theorists also write about a decentered sense of self, often described in terms of "multiplicity." For example, Trinh Minh-ha addressed Gergen's concern about being pulled in "myriad directions" and suggested an alternative way of envisioning the social complexity accompanying multiplicity: "Perhaps life appears less agonizing when decentralization (and decentering) are no longer understood as chaos or absence—the opposite of presence—but as marvelous expansion, a multiplicity of independent centers" (1991, p. 142). Similarly, Edward Sampson offered a "nonequilibrium theory" of identity that rejects the traditional ideal of a coherent and ordered culture: "[A nonequilibrium understanding] introduces us to a new kind of entity: personhood as process, open-ended and dwelling always at the edge, far from equilibrium. We encounter a decentralized, multifaceted ensemble whose coherence as a being is sustained only by virtue of its continuous becoming" (1985, p. 1206).

How do we move toward a vision of social life characterized by difference and multiplicity and at the same time construct a view that offers hope for joint action and the development of community? From a traditionalist's perspective, the following question might be asked: How do we overcome our differences to create a common bond? However, because postmodernists do not envision difference as something that needs to be overcome (difference is not situated as a problem), they might instead ask: How do we build upon our differences to create joint action?

William Tierney (1993) wrote about the idea of "communities of difference" and suggested a way of conceptualizing academic communities so that difference is seen not as a barrier (as in most traditional conceptions of difference), but instead as a source of communication. He argued that communities ought to be framed around the notion of *agape*—the ideal of selfless love. Tierney elaborated,

> Postmodernism and critical theory ensure that we do not interpret agape as a consensual community based on similarity. Although some students of higher education might misinterpret agape as a synonym for what we have called a "collegial model," the collegial model is precisely what postmodernism has critiqued. The collegial is an idea of like-minded faculty battling over abstract ideas with the assumption that "truth ultimately succeeds." The assumption is that consensus will be reached and that the nature of community is real, concrete, and shared. The problem, of course, is that abstract notions of truth that obscure how we arrived at those definitions inevitably reward centric norms instead of bringing those norms into question. To engage in agape does not imply either that consensus will be, or ought to be, reached. We do not begin by assuming that one reality exists, but rather that there are multiple realities about issues and concerns that draw us into dialogue. (p. 24)

Agape, as the ideal of selfless love, is similar to the ideal of caring expressed throughout this book with one big exception: Instead of love being expressed as a selfless act, I see love and caring more as an essential aspect of the self. The self is not lost as a result of service to the other; instead, the self is intimately connected to the other. Acts of love and compassion, from my perspective, are not selfless acts but are acts deeply rooted in a caring self. In other words, we do not sacrifice for others at the expense of the self, but we give to others because love and compassion are essential to the self.

I suggest throughout this book that education ought to play a central role in fostering a caring sense of self. Caring selves encourage connections among diverse peoples and cultures and make "dialogue across differences" a possibility (Burbules & Rice, 1991). Caring is the cure for the common ailment of contemporary community—the lack of a sense of connection. Howard Radest spoke to this issue in his discussion of community service: "Community service is a praxis that both presumes and creates community in the act. It alerts us, however, to the evanescence and, paradoxically, the persistence of community and asks us to reflect on whether or not community can be had again and if so how and where" (1993, p. 33).

As I highlighted earlier in this chapter, functionalist conceptions of society, which arguably have been the most prominent lenses for examining social life, revolve around instrumentalism (the idea that everything serves a function) and social control. This is akin to what Sharon Welch (1990) described as an "ethic of control" and is Foucault's central criticism of modernity. For Welch, memories of American conquests such as the settling of the West, emergence as a technological and economic power, and the development of a military complex second to none leave many who are concerned with issues of social justice "paralyzed when we see that our work against the dangerous costs of this legacy of conquest does not have as much success as did campaigns for military and economic control. Given this disparity, the lack of control and precision in work for justice seems almost irresponsible. If control is the norm, then responsible action for justice is a contradiction in terms" (pp. 103–4). As Welch pointed out, work for social justice can be sloppy work as it lacks the precision of other instrumental accomplishments. The same can be said of community service work: "Compassion's value may not depend entirely on its being effective" (Wuthnow, 1991, p. 282). Listen to the frustrations inherent in the following comments from student volunteers:

> Sometimes I ask myself: 'What's the point?' We change a little piece of society here and there, but the larger structure endures. We feed someone today and someone else is born into starvation tomorrow.

> I really wanted to work hard! It's frustrating to not be able to finish every project. That seems odd to me. Part of me HAS to get the job done.

> My hope was that we would accomplish a lot more than we did. . . . I was disappointed in the work that we accomplished as a group. The project was more disorganized than I'm used to having things.

> I started getting really frustrated at one of the houses we painted. It looks so good but I know that it really wasn't fixed. The roof and the walls still leak. I guess every little bit helps but at the same time I felt frustrated that we couldn't do more.

> You don't know how many times I've had these debates with myself about why I do volunteer work and whether I should keep doing this stuff. There are times when I just don't think it does any good. A homeless person gets on his feet and someone else loses their home. A kid makes it out of the ghetto and gets shot the first day at his new job. Where's it all end and what the heck am I doing in the middle of Washington, D.C., when nothing ever changes?

Many students occasionally considered giving up because it seemed to them, and to me as well, that ultimately what we were battling against was beyond our control—that all we were doing was putting Band-Aids on slashed arteries and not really affecting deeply seeded social problems.

Concerns about the larger social issues and helping to end widespread poverty were paramount in the minds of many of the students. For example, a student who worked on a service project on one of the Sea Islands of Charleston, South Carolina, observed: "You can drive down the street and see a mansion and the rest of the people live in poverty." Another student from the same project added, "When we went on our walk we saw one side of the island where all the people have lots of money and yachts, nice houses. On the other side were a lot of people who need a lot of help." A third student who participated in a Habitat for Humanity project in rural Maryland expressed similar concerns: "I don't know if helping to build houses solves any serious social problems or not. Obviously, it helps a family out. But I'm not sure what we're doing has any impact on the broader problems that may cause people to be homeless or poor in the first place."

If we are to apply critical views of social life to community service and its educational influence, we must challenge students to think beyond the short-term approach to social change. However, the fact remains that bandages will be needed until the larger flow of blood and poverty can be slowed and social transformation brought about. We cannot stop caring for individuals because the problems are so deeply embedded in our society and our culture. We must care for individuals and families while seeking social transformation at the same time. I return to these issues in chapters 7 and 8 as I discuss the role of action and reflection in developing a critical consciousness and a commitment to social transformation through what I term "critical community service."

Feminism, as well as critical postmodernism, resists the ethic of control that Welch (1990) criticized in her support of liberation theology. Control, as a goal, is replaced by action and process. Frustration is to be expected at times. But to engage in social justice work, to struggle to transform inequities, is an end in itself. The battle may never be won, but we must join the struggle just the same. Welch described a commitment to social justice work, despite its frustrations, as "an ethic of risk": "Within an ethic of risk, actions begin with the recognition that far too much has been lost and there are no clear means of restitution. The fundamental risk constitutive of this ethic is the decision to care and to act although there are no guarantees of success. Such action requires immense daring and enables deep joy. It is an ethos in sharp contrast to the ethos of cynicism that often accompanies a recognition of the depth and persistence of evil" (p. 68).

Because postmodernism rejects instrumentalism and control, it fosters an ethic of risk and makes the possibility of caring more likely. Caring may be understood not only as an endeavor that builds connections with diverse others who inhabit the postmodern world, but caring may also be a more likely outcome of postmodernity because the controlling tendencies of modernity are slowly replaced by the unpredictability of multiplicity. As we grow more accustomed to multiplicity, and less accustomed to control, the postmodern condition opens up the potential for the "sloppy" noninstrumental work of social justice.

From Tönnies's discussion of *gemeinschaft*, communities characterized by social distance and impersonality and brought about by industrialization, to David Riesman, Nathan Glazer, and Reuel Denney's (1950) *The Lonely Crowd*, the sociological literature captures the rise and fall of modernity and a tidal wave of social alienation. The technological explosion of the late twentieth century has added to our sense of estrangement as diversity and difference have become defining characteristics of contemporary postmodern societies. But unlike modernist treatments of alienation and diffused selves, which tend to see commonality and synthesis as solutions, postmodernism envisions difference as a strength on which to build. The activity of building, however, involves the coming together of diverse individuals and identities as we seek to join our actions and attempt to develop communities around our differences. I argue that in order to build community within the context of modernist remnants and postmodern complications, caring as a guide to thought and action must be positioned at center stage. Furthermore, I argue that community service not only is a by-product of caring, but the activity itself fosters caring attitudes.

COMMUNITY SERVICE AS A CLASSROOM FOR UNDERSTANDING SELF, OTHERS, AND COMMUNITY

Is there a need for caring in today's schools? In the introduction to her book *The Challenge to Care in Schools*, Nel Noddings argued that there is. "At the present time, it is obvious that our main purpose is not the moral one of producing caring people, but, instead, a relentless—and, as it turns out, hapless—drive for academic adequacy. I am certainly not going to argue for academic inadequacy, but I will try to persuade readers that a reordering of priorities is essential" (1992, xii). She added, "I will suggest that education might best be organized around centers of care: care for self, for intimate others, for associates and acquaintances, for distant others, for nonhuman animals, for plants and the physical environment, for the human-made world of objects and instruments, and for ideas" (p. xiii). That which Noddings envisions as an imperative for schools (K–12) is true for colleges and universities as well. Human development is a lifelong process, and the possible selves we enact relate as much to adulthood as to child, youth, and adolescent growth (Ryff, 1991).

Educators and education ought to be involved as much in the development of caring attitudes toward others as they are in helping students grasp various fields of knowledge as part of their preparation for careers and advanced study. Traditionally, we have separated the nurturing role from the educational role. For example, Margo Culley, Arlyn Diamond, Lee Edwards, Sara Lennox, and Catherine Portuges elaborated on the distinction between nurturance and intellectual activity: "In our culture, the role of the nurturer and intellectual have been separated not just by gender, but by function; to try to recombine them [in the role of the feminist teacher] is to create confusion" (1985, p. 13). And Jennifer Gore commented, "The implication is that the teacher/professor (male, but sometimes female), as intellectual, has not traditionally functioned in a nurturing capacity. Moreover, the suggestion is that teaching is a patriarchal enterprise and that the position of the feminist teacher is particularly difficult because she (a few writers would add 'and occasionally he') must work within that system while trying to alter it" (1993, p. 69).

The distinction between nurturing and intellectual roles is captured in Kathryn Pauly Morgan's (1987) discussion of the paradox of the "bearded mother," which is the paradox of women educators. Morgan argued that women are expected to be "bearded" (malelike) in that they must embody traits such as rationality and objectivity, traits that are often seen to be the monopoly of men. At the same time, they must fill the traditional role of mother and be expected to provide nurturance, caring, and support. My contention is that male educators are needed who can also embrace the nurturing role. If we desire to foster an ethic of care among our students, we must embrace it as well. In elevating the nurturing role, we make it possible for women educators to begin to remove their beards, as the nurturing role becomes at least as important as, if not more important than, traditional male-centered roles organized around abstraction and intellectualism. Noddings offered her own passionate account of the nurturing role of the teacher: "When I became a mother, I entered a very special relation—possibly the prototypical caring relation. When I became a teacher, I also entered a very special—and more specialized—caring relation. No enterprise or special function I am called upon to serve can relieve me of my responsibilities as one-caring. Indeed, if an enterprise precludes my meeting the other in a caring relation, I must refuse to participate in the enterprise" (1984, p. 175). Noddings highlighted the central challenge that critical and feminist educators face: working within the system while at the same time trying to change it. If we heed the advice from Noddings, one way of transforming education might be to refuse to participate in activities that fail to foster caring relations.

Community service and service projects must be conceived as opportunities to both take the role of the other and walk with the other and thus provide an opportunity that is likely to foster thoughts and reflections related to issues of caring and community. Steven Schultz talked about the relationship between feminist notions of "connected knowing" (Belenky et al., 1986) and community service as an educational enterprise.

> The implications of this new understanding of "connected knowing" for civic education seem clear. The values of the heart—concern for the common good, a sense of compassion, courage to seek justice, devotion to one's community—all require a sense of connection to others which a completely abstract education cannot provide. I would suggest that these values and this kind of knowing are best nurtured and developed in an educational environment which provides the opportunity for engagement with others through service or in other kinds of action in the community. (1990, p. 214)

Like Schultz, I believe that community service as an educational endeavor generates a more caring sense of self through a realization of the role that a concern for others might play in one's life. Six years of participation in community service projects with college students provides empirical support for this conclusion, as does the research of people such as Robert Wuthnow who describes volunteering as "a special place in which to gain a more mature understanding of kindness" (1995, p. 226).

To ground Schultz's point in an example, I offer some comments from a Michigan State University student who talked about learning to be more empathetic and understanding of how others experience life: "People make decisions based on their own experiences, on what they think they know. For example, a boy I tutored last year had Tourette's Syndrome. People make jokes about Tourette's because it is so distant from how they experience the world. That really bothers me. He was a wonderful kid. People need to try to experience life through someone else. . . . I think the boy I tutored gave me a gift that has helped me to walk in other people's shoes. In a way it was given to me through the gift of a plant by that same boy. It's still alive in my dorm room. I haven't killed it yet. . . . It means a lot to me that I was able to help him."

A second student, this one from Pennsylvania State University, talked about the homeless people she met during a community service project in Washington, D.C.: "I used to think that homeless people were mostly bums who didn't want to work. I don't mean this to sound cruel because I still believe even if this were the case, that we are called to feed them nonetheless. But now that I've actually met so many of them I realize that many of my preconceptions, which amounted to stereotypes, were actually incorrect." This student went on to talk about the personal contacts she made and the value of community service as an educational experience: "I have made some friends among the homeless and they are not very different from myself. This has been perhaps the most valuable kind of learning experience I could have had during college. This is something you may read about in classes but it never really hits home until you experience it. I think it takes some kind of powerful experience to erase the stereotypes and generalizations we adopt about people."

Community service projects extend the idea of the classroom to the external world to the college or university campus and provide students the setting in which to think about and apply the abstract learning typical of the classroom. This is the classic idea of experiential learning represented most pointedly in John Dewey's discussion of a progressive philosophy of education: "I take it that the fundamental unity of the newer philosophy [of education] is found in the idea that there is an intimate and necessary relation between the processes of actual experience and education" (1938, p. 20). Building linkages between traditional classroom learning and lived experience has been a central project of many educators following in the Deweyian tradition (Kolb, 1984). Bridging knowledge and experience through understandings of the self is also a recent concern of student affairs professionals as addressed by Patricia King and Marcia Baxter Magolda when they argued, "How individuals construct knowledge and use their knowledge is closely tied to their sense of self" (1996, p. 166).

At the same time, instead of the educational activity being a self-serving activity from which only the student benefits, community service also provides an opportunity for others to benefit from a student's time and energy. As one student explained, "I've been a volunteer for the Nature Conservancy quite a bit. I have to find a purpose that's good for the community. I was a volunteer at the Special Olympics, and I participated in Adopt-a-Block in the early fall. I feel like I have to do something for the community, the state, or the nation. . . . I helped with the beach clean up. I want to help."

For George Watkins, community service is something he does, not because he wants anything in return, but because it seems like the right thing to do—to give to his community. From George we see education not only as a vehicle for learning, but as part of the struggle to improve society. Such a perspective connects the experiential quality of community service to the transformative ideals expressed in the work of Dewey, Freire, Tierney, Henry Giroux, bell hooks, Peter McLaren, and others. David Kolb highlighted how experiential learning might be linked to social change "by instilling in the population what Freire calls 'critical consciousness,' the active exploration of the personal, experiential meaning of abstract concepts through dialogue among equals" (1984, p. 16). Kolb saw this philosophy as an extension of the liberal humanist perspective characterized by "Deweyite progressive educators." "These views serve to highlight the central role of the dialectic between abstract concepts and subjective personal experience in educational/political conflicts between the right, which places priority on maintenance of the social order, and the left, which values more highly individual freedom and expression" (p. 16). Although individual thinking and commitment to transformation are clearly a concern of progressive educators, these ideals are united with the desire to advance the larger social body based on principles of democracy. This is clearly expressed in Dewey's discussion of the role of education in the development of a democratic society, in which he argues that democracy is inherently dependent on an educated citizenry and its ability to weigh matters and make decisions based on concerns for others.

Progressive and critical educators seek what at face value may seem like contradictory goals. They desire individual thinkers who are capable of critically examining social life and democracy. Simultaneously, they desire students who embrace a commitment to improving the social whole. The challenge is to grasp the dynamic complexities of knowledge through critical thought and self-reflection and to combine such understandings with a commitment to external action for the good of others. However, because knowledge is socially constructed, there is a strong social quality to one's self-reflections and critical thinking, as well as a self-interest in the well-being of others (as evidenced by the positive feelings students report through their community service work).

Experiential learning such as that engendered by community service, when combined with a feminist and critical emphasis on the importance of caring, has the potential to foster the kind of critical consciousness needed for community and societal transformation and for supporting the kind of democratic society envisioned by Dewey. If I am exposed to the inequalities suffered by others, and if I care about others, then I am more likely to engage in political and cultural struggle that leads to social transformation. Seen in this light, involvement in community service is an extension of the classroom in which theoretical and practical learning come together in a dialectical fashion as a means to challenge students to think critically, as in Freire's idea of critical consciousness. Feminist and critical pedagogies serve as guideposts to how service ought to be structured and how students might be engaged. These issues will be addressed in greater detail in chapters 7 and 8.

Educational experiences such as community service ought to be seen as crucial aspects of teaching and learning committed to nurturing students. Community service projects involve learning in the traditional sense—acquiring knowledge through interactions with others—and at the same time compel students to rethink their lives in terms of connections and relationships with others—experiences we typically associate with nurturing. Undertaking community service as an educational activity demands that we view intellectualism and nurturance as connected concerns and not as fragmented aspects of developing and clarifying identity.

SUMMARY

Based on the work of the diverse feminist, critical, and sociological theorists discussed in the first three chapters, I offer ten propositions that undergird the overall theoretical argument of this work.

Proposition 1: The self is formed relationally through social interactions. This is why the concepts of the "social self" and feminist notions of the "relational self" are helpful theoretical constructs.

Proposition 2: Culture provides the parameters for social interaction and at the same time is modified through social interaction. I describe this as a "dynamic and dialectical" view of culture.

Proposition 3: Identities are constituted within the parameters of culture and are highly related to the concept of the self. In many ways, identity is a narrative told about the self as object of our own past, present, and future.

Proposition 4: Power lies at the center of how culture contributes to notions of identity and the self, often serving to legitimize or delegitimize various cultural identities and possible selves.

Proposition 5: Postmodernism has resulted in significant cultural changes affecting the nature of communities and the nature of social interaction. Consequently, the parameters set by culture and the formation of identities and selves are different now than they were under modernist regimes.

Proposition 6: Postmodern identities are more fragmented and decentered, and the challenge to establish a clear sense of self is more vexing than ever before.

Proposition 7: College students are at a time in their lives when a multitude of forces influence their sense of self; thus they often are in the midst of a period of heightened self-discovery and identity confusion.

Proposition 8: Education plays a critical role in fostering student learning and development and thus provides a context for student self-exploration and identity development.

Proposition 9: Participation in community service provides a means to foster a sense of connectedness and offers an opportunity for students to understand themselves and to develop caring selves.

Proposition 10: Caring selves are critical to the process of democracy and the struggle to build a more just and equitable society. Without a strong concern for others as a vital aspect of the self, it is unlikely that democracy can be sustained in postmodern times.

These propositions, taken together, summarize the theoretical framework that guides my discussion of students' involvement in community service. No single proposition should be seen as more important than any other, but as a whole they form a web of ideas that must be considered as we examine the experiences of students engaged in community service learning. At various points throughout the remaining chapters, I will insert one of the propositions as a means of tying the findings and discussion of literature more clearly to the theoretical framework.

In the following four chapters (4–7) I shift the narrative somewhat as I focus more on the findings from my interviews and observations of students' involvement in various service projects. In each chapter I describe in some detail one of the intensive weeklong projects I participated in with students. Although I offer these more in-depth descriptions as a means to capture some of the flavor of the students' experiences, I want to stress that the findings discussed in the related chapters come from a variety of student experiences and not simply the week long intensive projects. In instances where it seems relevant, I will specify the kind of community service involvement the student had. Finally, I bring my research together and the book to a close in chapter 8 and the concluding chapter as I discuss what I term "critical community service" and some of the key implications for higher education.

Chapter 4

Otherness

*If you can't locate the other, how are you to
locate your-self?*

—*Trinh Minh-ha,*
When the Moon Waxes Red

*It was the summer of 1970. I remember it well because this was the sum-
mer my mother saved up enough money for me to take a bus from Grove City to
Pittsburgh to be part of Allied News Night at the newly opened Three Rivers
Stadium. The Allied News was the local newspaper and about sixty residents of
Grove City had traveled together to support their Pirates, who were in the
middle of the Eastern Division pennant race.*

*This was the only game I had seen since my first one back in 1967 when
my stepfather had taken the entire family. Back then, the Pirates played at old
Forbes Field in the Oakland section of Pittsburgh. Clemente had three hits on
that occasion and clinched the batting crown with a .357 average. He did not
fare so well however on this August evening in 1970 as the Pirates got trounced
by Lou Brock and the St. Louis Cardinals.*

*Whatever could be recalled of the game was soon forgotten by the ordeal
that followed. After the Pirates fell hopelessly behind, all of the fans who had
traveled on the bus together from Grove City headed to the exits early. All but
one fan I should say. Leaving a Pirates game before the final out was unfath-
omable to me. In fact, I was so intent on watching the game that I didn't even
notice the seats around me had been vacated.*

*When the game finally ended, I hurriedly made my way to where the bus
was parked. Having realized by now that the Grove City contingent had already
left the stadium, I expected that the early departers would be anxiously waiting
for the last stragglers to get there so they could begin the fifty-mile trek north.
My anxiety began to increase as I reached the spot where I thought the bus had*

been parked only to find a vacant parking spot. With sweat beginning to pour through my skin and tears swelling up in my eyes, I started running around the stadium, from one lot to the next, in search of the "Grove City Van Lines" marquee emblazed on the side of our bus.

I learned later that the driver had moved the bus and was about to leave when someone noticed that the little boy who sat in the front by himself was not present. When they finally noticed my absence, the bus was already on the other side of the stadium near one of the main exits. The police were no help; they were too busy directing traffic to help a lost, runny-nosed kid. Eventually, after about seven trips around the stadium and one near fall into the Ohio River, I spotted a bus in the distance that turned out to be my ticket home. The bus driver was pacing outside the bus obviously distraught over the missing kid. He and the rest of the Grove City contingent were quite relieved when I finally showed up. But no one was as relieved as I was.

I don't think I ever told my mother this story for fear she would not let me venture off on my own again. I also don't think I ever told her how special I felt by the fact that she had saved the money for me to see my Pirates and Roberto Clemente play in their new stadium.

It was a summer of few privileges and the trip to Pittsburgh helped to off-set a depressingly low point in my life. During the summer we had made one of those moves to save money as my mother found a house down the road for something like thirty dollars a month. The house had been condemned or was about to be condemned (I can't remember the exact details) but she convinced the landlord that we could make some of the repairs so it would be liveable. The previous tenants had dumped garbage in the well house, so trash had to be fished out of the well water, which then needed to be tested to see if it was drinkable. My mom and my Aunt Shirley did this and they also purchased paint through the landlord so we could fix up each room. There were at least ten rooms for it was a rather large old house. The inside of the house wasn't so bad. I mean we had grown use to multilayered linoleum floors so that was no big deal. But the outside! It looked like one would expect a condemned house to look. The roof resembled a lopsided ice cream cone about to slide off to one side or the other. The whole house leaned to the right, while the porch, with its broken steps, served as a counterbalance and tilted to the left. The brown tar paper siding was ripped in too many places to repair and several of the windows were broken and covered with cardboard and tape. The whole place left the impression that a stiff breeze would put it out of its misery.

Worse than the appearance was the house's reputation: It was one of the houses where the white trash in our hometown tended to live. There were a few other houses as well, but this one was the worst. We knew this and so did everybody else. Now we were the ones living there and all the cutting remarks we once tossed among ourselves about the Bryants or the Turcotts were sticking

in our own backs. "We" had become "them" by taking over their former resi-
dence, while they moved up in the world.

I spent much of the summer hiding from the friends I had made in my old
neighborhood, which was only about two miles down the road. I appeared
from time to time to play football and hang out at Becker's Store, but I never let
anyone get a fix on where we had actually moved. "Somewhere down the
road," I would say. Or, "Over by so and so's." When my sister Kim and I
played outside the house, we made sure to run inside when we heard a car
coming down the road for fear it might be the parents of one of our friends and
thus our new location would be revealed and the secret let out—that we had
become white trash.

As I look back on the summer of 1970, I am more embarrassed by my behavior than I am by the house in which we lived. My mother did the best she could and I should have embraced whatever she provided for us with a sense of pride in who we were as a family. I guess that's one of the down sides of human nature that I often struggle with—too much complaining about my circumstances and not enough gratitude for what I have. My involvement in community service has helped me to be vigilant about my attitudes toward what I have or don't have, but nonetheless, I often find myself to be something less than the idealized self I aspire to be.

The struggles I experience about "having" or "not having" were brought to mind by a recent article I read in the local paper—*The Lansing State Journal*. The article focused on a Michigan youth who was set to inherit roughly $500 million. Two things jumped out at me. First was the astronomical amount of money that he would come into on his eighteenth birthday, which was only a month away. It seemed unjustifiable to me that one individual in a society with so many poor people could be given so much, and not have done anything to earn it except to be born. I thought of all the homeless people I had met over the years, some too proud to accept welfare, and all the struggles they had been through trying to make it in this world. My feelings ranged from despair to anger. One of those pat sayings came to mind: "No one ever said life was fair."

The other thing that stood out for me was what seemed to be a complete lack of social consciousness evident in some of the comments the young man made. I know it's hard to fault a seventeen-year-old boy for not understanding or acknowledging the tremendous suffering in the world, and that a newspaper article only provides a quick snapshot of who he is as a person, but there is so much that *could* be done that, based on what I read, *would not* be done. He did mention that he would donate some money to a scholarship for underprivileged youths to attend a suburban prep school in Detroit, but for the most part, he seemed so indignant and "deserving" of his inheritance. As the newspaper reporter, Brian Akre, explained, he says he wants to invest the money and bristles when asked what he's going to do with his new fortune. "I hate that question, you know? The way I look at it is, it's my money and I'll do what I want with it."

Could an educational system oriented toward an ethic of care have altered the way this youth envisions the world? Can we influence another's sense of caring and commitment to the social good, be it the local community or more national concerns? And what of ourselves? How would we respond to new-found wealth? Would we donate a portion to the well-being of others? Should we do more with the financial resources we currently have? How would I respond? Can I do more now? Akre's article left me with these kinds of questions and induced reflections on my commitment to others and how responsive I see myself being to the world around me.

Where do others fit within our lives and our sense of self? This question serves to frame this chapter as I focus on the meaning and significance of the "other" or what might be termed "otherness." I call on some remarks from *The Call of Service* by Robert Coles (1993) as a means to situate an exploration of otherness. He described a memory of his mother and her remarks to him etched in a copy of Tolstoy's *Anna Karenina*. Coles's mother challenged her son to treasure his time with Tolstoy's characters: "Let them have a life in you, too, and let them teach you how to live your life. Let them teach you to avoid some of their mistakes, Tolstoy's mistakes. We all make them, blunder our way along. But we can step out of ourselves, now and then; we can take the hands of others and walk with them. That is what Tolstoy gives us in his characters; through them he approaches us and tries to be of help to us. We can return the favor with others" (p. 287). For Coles, and the many volunteer workers he grew to admire, understanding oneself through involvement in service is the vital foundation to a caring sense of self. Service "is a function not only of what we do but of who we are, which, of course, gives shape to what we do" (p. xxvi). Coles highlights the life of the great Catholic worker Dorothy Day and how the "call of service for her was a call toward others—heart, mind, and soul—but also a call inward, a call to oneself" (p. 284). He recalled her words from a Catholic Worker meeting held back in 1955: "There is a call to us, a call of service—that we join with others to try to make things better in this world" (p. xxiii).

The others with whom student volunteers will join throughout this chapter are homeless citizens of Washington, D.C. In particular, I discuss the experiences of Pennsylvania State University students and their community service work in soup kitchens in the D.C. area. I focus on what these students learned about the other and about themselves in the context of working with homeless people.

THE D.C. PROJECT

"It's my money and I'll do what I want with it." The wealth that the youth in the Lansing newspaper story was set to inherit is quite a contrast to the poverty and suffering described in the lives of Tolstoy's characters and in the lives of the homeless I met on a community service project in Washington, D.C. The youth's apparent lack of concern about human suffering and the potential to contribute to someone else's life in a positive way contrasts with the efforts I witnessed from college students who were frustrated by their inability to do more. I recall some remarks one student offered about his work with homeless people: "I feel like we are just sticking our finger in the dam. And that when we leave or when the other full-time volunteers move on, the dam will break. Unless of course someone else comes along and puts his finger in the hole. Sooner or later something tragic is going to happen. Someone is going to freeze to death on some park bench, and the work that we're doing will seem so meaningless. And the next day, someone else will get hit by a car because they are invisible to most people." This student was frustrated by his inability to significantly improve the lives of homeless people. He believed that a dramatic social and economic change was needed within our society, but he was at a loss to explain how such a transformation might occur. "I try to minimize the resources I use in my own life. I struggle to avoid becoming too materialistic, but I don't see how that really helps the poor. I'm still caught in the same system as they are."

For this student, the widespread problem of poverty in the United States is the result of two related phenomena: greed and a lack of caring for others. He thought greed in particular was widely embraced, especially by the most successful individuals in our society. "I guess, you can't really expect people who have gotten rich from the system to all of a sudden throw money at social programs. I don't see that happening. But is it too much to ask corporations and the wealthy to pay a greater share of taxes and give back in other ways to a system that has enabled them to achieve so much? The attitude is that they earned their money through hard work and that they should be able to keep it. But do they deserve it? Most people who are that successful started out in a lot better position than most of the homeless people we've met so far this week."

Students raised some interesting points about the various barriers individuals face throughout their lifetimes. They talked about how mental illness and drug problems often contribute to homelessness. Students mentioned the role of broken homes and how some families are just not able to make ends meet. They discussed factories closing and people losing their jobs. They pointed out the lack of educational opportunities some inner-city youths face. The youth who was set to inherit $500 million certainly had few financial barriers to overcome, especially in comparison to the homeless people of Washington, D.C.

In his book *Tell Them Who I Am*, Elliot Liebow wrote about the lives of twenty women who, by most accounts, can be classified as "homeless." Like the students working on the D.C. project, Liebow also sought to make sense of homelessness: "We live in a society that is very competitive. After adding individual differences to handicaps/advantages of race, class, and sex, it turns out that some people run faster than others. Those who run very fast are highly rewarded. Those who run at an average pace do pretty well most of the time. For a variety of reasons, seldom if ever any fault of their own, some poor people and some homeless people . . . can't run fast at all" (1993, p. 234). Liebow introduced a homeless woman named Shirley as an example: "I'm 53 years old. I failed at two marriages and I failed at every job I ever had. Is that any reason I have to live on the street?" Liebow responded, "A society that answers 'yes,' that is prepared to treat a large number of its citizens as surplus people, is . . . in steep decline" (p. 234).

Frank Gardner is a homeless man living in D.C. who was born sometime around the beginning of World War II. He could not recall his precise birth date, but he was sure it was right around the start of the war because, as he stated, "I can remember soldiers coming back from the war and I think I must have been around four or five then." So Frank is somewhere in his early fifties and has been living in the streets for about three years. He has stayed in shelters from time to time, but he doesn't like all the rules they impose or the way he has been treated by the people who run them: "Most of them were homeless at one time or another but they act like they are somehow better than you."

Frank has experienced many ups and downs during his lifetime. At one time he had a decent job and a family. But after a divorce, the loss of his job, and declining health (Frank was recently diagnosed with diabetes), he fell on hard times. "It's not easy living like this—not having a home and eating in soup kitchens. I still hope for something better but getting things back together is harder than you might think. How do you get a job when you look like this [he points to himself and his clothes]?" His dirty and tattered clothes certainly would be seen as inappropriate in the context of a job interview.

The first time I met Frank was at a soup kitchen in D.C. known as Mariam's Kitchen. I bumped into him several times more at other soup kitchens around the city, including Zacchaeus' Community Kitchen, as well as at a mobile soup kitchen delivering food to homeless people at a D.C. park. I talked to Frank in between his card games while I was helping to serve meals at Zacchaeus' Kitchen. With his broad smile and deeply creased wrinkles across his forehead, Frank fit the warm and affable grandfatherly image, looking closer to seventy than to his fifty-some years. Students took a special liking to Frank and often engaged in good-natured teasing with him. Frank was among a group of homeless citizens who provided students with a more personalized understanding of some of the struggles they had to endure. Not only did his openness provide a great deal of insight into his life, but his personality made the community service experience that much more rewarding for many of the students and myself as well. Frank was one of the reasons the experience has become a lasting memory for many of us. As one student commented, "I thought about all the statistics I have heard about the homeless—and the lady they found frozen to death in the park. It's frightening yet they were never real people to me. They were somewhere out there in an abstract kind of way. The last day I worked at SOME (So Others May Eat) and it really hit me. I thought about Frank, William, Alvin, and Ritchie. They aren't statistics any more. They are friends now."

It was early January 1991, and about thirty-five students and a few staff from Pennsylvania State University had volunteered to work in soup kitchens over their winter break. This was the first D.C. project, and it would be followed by two more during subsequent winter breaks. The vast majority of students participating in these projects were White students (approximately 90 percent), and there were more women than men (about a 60 to 40 ratio). During each trip we stayed in the basement of a church on the corner of 4th and Independence (in the southeast quadrant of D.C.), just a few blocks from the Capitol building. Students and staff worked in teams to prepare our own meals and carry out various cleaning chores around the church. A typical day involved getting up at 5 or 6 a.m., eating breakfast, and then taking public transportation or a university van to one of several soup kitchens within the city. Most groups returned to the church by 5 in the afternoon, at which time a team prepared and then served dinner. After dinner there was a series of small-group activities, often involving extensive reflection and discussion of issues related to community service and homelessness. Social service and volunteer workers from the D.C. area were invited to stop by and give perspective to some of the problems associated with homelessness and urban poverty. One entire day was spent visiting legislators at the Capitol and meeting with activists involved in political, economic, and social issues connected with homelessness.

Each morning, students traveled to one of four soup kitchens, all of which serve a hot meal to anyone in need of food: Zacchaeus' Kitchen, So Others Might Eat, Mariam's Kitchen, and the Church of the Brethren (on North Carolina Avenue, SE). The last site, which was within walking distance from where we stayed, served only lunch so students assigned there did not have to arrive until about 9:30 a.m. The other three sites required volunteers to arrive by about 6 or 7 a.m.

I will never forget my first experience at Zacchaeus' Kitchen and the swarm of roaches that scurried out from under the rag I picked up to wipe off counters. My eyes, which hardly had been open, soon took on an all-alert, on-roach-patrol look. I still get chills just thinking about all those antennae scurrying in all directions, including up the sleeve of my shirt.

Each soup kitchen has its own personality. Things are very regimented at SOME and the Church of the Brethren. At SOME, people are pretty much hurried in and hurried out. As they say during basic training in the Army: "Swallow your food now and chew it later." SOME has hundreds of people to feed and their cafeteria is small in comparison to the one at Zacchaeus' Kitchen. The "eat and get out" attitude seems a bit heavy handed at first, but when one considers that SOME serves about 1,200 meals a day, it is easier to understand (not to mention the fact that the line of homeless citizens waiting to sit down and eat often extends down the street and January in D.C. is rarely very comfortable). Many of the volunteers are ex-homeless citizens themselves and are the most vociferous in prodding the clientele to their seats and then out the door. At one point during our work at SOME, the yelling between one of the volunteers and a client was so loud that some of us thought a fight might soon break out. However, we quickly judged by the minimal reaction from the regular voluntccrs that thcre was no reason for concern. It appeared to me that both the volunteer and the homeless man were more or less engaged in a struggle to save face in front of the rest of the homeless population and that both seemed unwilling to give up the last word edgewise.

Mariam's Kitchen provides a personal touch to its meals, and the regular volunteer staff interacts with the homeless citizens often on a first-name basis. The same is true to a somewhat lesser degree at the Church of the Brethren. Perhaps the most interesting site from a purely sociological perspective is Zacchaeus' Kitchen. Unlike most of the other soup kitchens, which have limited space and for the most part do not allow the clients to linger in the dining hall for too long, Zacchaeus' Kitchen encourages people to hang out and socialize, at least until cleanup begins at around 2 p.m. In part, this is because the cafeteria at Zacchaeus' is much larger than the eating areas in other soup kitchens. Homeless citizens or anyone else needing a free meal (not everyone who eats at a soup kitchen is homeless) can spend about a three-hour block of time there. For some, this time is key to maintaining a sense of community with other homeless citizens. People are free to play cards, sleep, read newspapers, or just visit. I remember one group of women entertaining themselves by imitating the "church lady" made famous by Dana Carvey from Saturday Night Live. I joined them for a few minutes and offered my own impersonation, which judging by their laughter they got a kick out of. I also visited with several men who were debating the demise of the Washington Redskins. Other groups that caught my eye were the various pockets of card players. Playing Spades and Hearts had become a passion for me and some of the students on the D.C. trip, and we took every opportunity to learn what we could from the homeless people we met, who had their own derivations of the same games we played. One interesting aspect of Spades was the various styles of "making one's play," depending on the quality or strength of the card to be thrown. In tossing out a meaningless card, there was the "lean-back-in-your-chair-and-just-fling-it-and-if-the-winner-has-to-pick-it-up-so-what" style. The opposite was the "slam-dunk-from-three-feet-above-the-head-with-enough-force-to-send-the-other-cards-flying" style, which was reserved for key points in the game. Some of the students and I learned to incorporate these moves into our own card playing, much to the annoyance of our opponents.

Most of the students preferred working at Zacchaeus' Kitchen (despite the roaches) because there they had a chance to interact more with homeless citizens. This was the highlight of the D.C. experience for many of them. A first-year student majoring in elementary education commented on her work at Zacchaeus' and the D.C. project in general: "Talking to the homeless people and with the volunteers in the various soup kitchens was something else. Being out in the crowd of people as they were eating and sharing eye contact and small conversation and lending a listening ear was a learning experience that challenged my attitudes. I learned that there are many homeless people in our world and that everything I and someone else does as far as service is concerned is important no matter how large or small. I learned that eye contact is one of the best gifts I can give to people on the street."

A few students were somewhat intimidated by the idea of mingling in the eating area. Many of these students preferred to keep their distance and work behind the serving counters, but even they began to venture out into the cafeteria once they became more accustomed to their new social context.

For those students who took the time to visit with homeless citizens, to play cards, to participate in the good-natured teasing that was so prevalent at Zacchaeus' (there were outbreaks of arguing from time to time as well), the experience was beyond any expectation they had carried with them to D.C. A student commented, "I expected that I would be working side-by-side with people who were quite different from myself. . . . I learned that my coming here *did* have a significant impact not only on myself, but also on the lives that our group touched during the week. What I learned from others will leave a permanent mark on me and hopefully on those I interacted with." This student called attention to how the "other" often informs one's understandings of the self. For him, the homeless people he interacted with left a lasting impression on him, and he hoped he had influenced their lives as well. In the following pages, I discuss theoretical issues related to exploring otherness and highlight some of the reactions and thoughts students shared during and after their work in Washington, D.C.

EXPLORING UNDERSTANDINGS OF THE OTHER

Frank Gardner is hardly representative of all homeless people. No one is for that matter. However, in introducing Frank I run the risk of creating a certain vision or representation of homeless people. Although I believe it is important to talk about real lives and real people, at the same time any description of someone's life must be recognized as only a brief, piercing glance. We must approach such a representation carefully, being mindful of the multiplicity of human experience and identity.

Understanding the multiplicity of identity and of the self is central to the work of Trinh Minh-ha. In examining ethnographic and documentary representations of the other, Minh-ha offers a challenge to recent practices that suppose the deep inner self can somehow be represented by the filmmaker or author. Things are not always as they appear, and people frequently give misleading impressions of who they really are and often are driven by opposing inclinations and intentions in their lives. Hence, the ethnographer's search for the deep and inner self of the other has come to replace overly simplistic accounts that tended to portray entire social groups or cultures as homogeneous. But the search for the inner self is problematic as well. Minh-ha commented: "The move from obnoxious exteriority to obtrusive interiority, the race for the so-called *hidden* values of a person or a culture, has given rise to a form of legitimized (but acknowledged as such) voyeurism and subtle arrogance—namely, the pretense to see into or to *own* the others' *minds*, whose *knowledge* these others cannot, supposedly, have themselves; and the need to define, hence confine, providing them thereby with a standard of self-evaluation on which they necessarily depend" (1991, p. 66).

In seeking to represent the other's identity, we misrepresent. In depicting reality, we lose sight of the fact that multiple realities coexist. To counterbalance the problems of representation, we often resort to the "giving of voice"—the act of allowing the other to speak, either in our films or in our stories. Susan Krieger discussed her attempt in *The Mirror Dance* to introduce a structure in which her research subjects created their own portrait of social life in an all-women's community. Krieger explained: "My desire was to have the voices and language of the women I had interviewed provide their own systematic self-reflection, to have them suggest, in their own terms, the form of a pattern that might explain the problems of individuality the community posed for its members" (1983, p. 191).

Although Krieger's effort to allow others to write their own narrative may be commendable, it nonetheless represents a certain naïveté. In suggesting that the women's voices and language might offer, on their own, a thematic pattern revealing some of the strains between individuality and community, she loses sight of the fact that she, as author, links the women's narratives together and thus creates the structure (or the pattern) herself. In presupposing that a pattern would emerge from the women's narratives, Krieger, through the structure of her book, guarantees that a pattern emerges. Without a pattern, how do we tell a story? So where life offers no such pattern or structure, we create one as a means of explaining the social world in which the other and the self coexist. Even if our text reflects the voices of only those we interviewed, as revealed through their own words, we are still the producer of the text, the arranger of the narrative. The author is the one who makes connections to create some kind of meaning, whether loosely structured or tightly woven. I cannot escape the fact that any narrative I create, any representation I offer, reflects a large part of who I am. The challenge is not to ignore our own voices, or our own lives, but to embrace our sense of self and how it shapes what we see, what we question, and ultimately, what we write.

The problem that Krieger fails to highlight, and that other ethnographies and documentary films often fail to come to terms with, is that in "giving voice" the author still maintains a position of power. Once again, Minh-ha is instructive: "Power creates its very constraints, for the Powerful is also necessarily defined by the Powerless. Power therefore has to be shared so that its effect may continue to circulate; but it will be shared only partly, with much caution to circulate, and on the condition that the share is given, not taken" (1991, p. 67). The solution suggested by Minh-ha involves a degree of "interdependency" and is akin to what I discuss in chapter 5 as the idea of "mutuality." Mutuality applied to an understanding of representation of otherness involves creating a mutual space and opportunity for the creation of diverse identities. It means the ethnographer/author goes beyond the "giving of voice" and becomes dependent to a large degree on the other for the images and imagination necessary to create representations. As Minh-ha states, "Interdependency cannot be reduced to a mere question of mutual enslavement. It also consists in creating a ground that belongs to no one, not even to the 'creator.' Otherness becomes empowering critical difference when it is not given, but re-created. Defined with the Other's newly formed criteria" (p. 71). Minh-ha's work reminds us that issues of power, culture, and identity are interwoven. (Recall from chapter 3—*Proposition 4: Power lies at the center of how culture contributes to notions of identity and the self often serving to legitimize or delegitimize various cultural identities and possible selves.*)

To put this in more practical terms, ethnographers must find ways of involving the creativity and imagination of their subjects as research participants in the construction of their own identities. Such a process necessarily requires that critical reflections take place between the observer (the ethnographer) and the observed (research participants) in a way that subjects become observers. In a sense, this is akin to what Yvonna Lincoln and Egon Guba (1986) discuss as "member checks"—the practice of involving research participants in the creation and analysis of qualitative data. In terms of the research studies that inform this book, students (the primary subjects of my observations) were involved in a variety of ways. For example, as part of the community service projects, reflection groups were used not only as a means to process community service involvement but also as a tool to challenge students to critically examine their assumptions about self and others. In addition, students were asked, as part of the interviewing process, to reflect on their sense of self as a community service volunteer. Questions such as the following were stressed:

What does community service mean to you?
How do you see yourself fitting into this community service project?
How have you thought about yourself through the community service experience?
What have you learned about yourself through your participation in community service in general?
What have you learned about others through your participation?

Responses to these kinds of questions were helpful in gaining insights into how students situate themselves in relation to others, especially within the context of community service encounters. Data derived from students' reflections about the self and the other provide a context for a narrative that may more fully capture the complexity and multiplicity of their lives.

At the same time, however, the reader must recognize that contents of this narrative are my impressions, realities, and experiences in struggling to capture the complexities and multiplicities of social experience related to community service and students' contact with poverty. This is why it is important to understand and keep in mind my own positionality, as I discussed in chapter 1. What I see as important, what I embrace as my reality, and how I create the other are clearly different from what another writer might present. With that said, I offer some of the data collected during the past six years (including, but not limited to, the D.C. projects) related to students' involvement in community service work with homeless citizens.

STUDENTS' EXPERIENCES
WITH HOMELESS CITIZENS

One of the striking things that my research on community service highlights is the limited knowledge students have about those whose lives are different from their own. It appears that community service is often, as Howard Radest (1993) claimed, an "encounter with strangers." Radest argued that this may be especially true as society becomes increasingly diverse: "Being embedded in a plurality of life-worlds is now 'normal.' So, the community service project always involves crossing some cultural line and entails a meeting of strangers" (p. 120). Radest also alludes to the interaction that goes on internally as a result of interacting with diverse peoples and in diverse settings: "Diversity appears not only between myself and others but in a confusing way within the 'self' by itself. In the meeting of strangers I also meet myself as a stranger" (p. 120).

For the students who participated in the Washington, D.C. project, homeless citizens were indeed strangers to their world. This is revealed by the fact that nearly every student commented on how his or her view of homeless people and homelessness had dramatically changed after working in the soup kitchens and actually meeting homeless citizens. For many students, the most significant learning experience was personalizing homelessness—being able to put faces and names with the alarming statistics and endless policy debates. One student reflected on her experience and the importance of personalizing social issues such as homelessness: "Service is not glamorous. People are hungry and we need to feed many. Beyond that primary concern, I learned by talking to many homeless people that they are very human—not faceless, second-class citizens. I learned a lot about love at SOME from the people we helped and from the incredible volunteers I worked with. After feeling insignificant early in the week, I learned that my little effort was important. Homeless people are real. They laugh and cry and have a lot to offer." Other students also discussed the personal side of the community service work they did in D.C.:

> Every homeless person has a name, a story.

> They just want to be recognized and treated as human beings. There are names behind the statistics.

> Working with the people of the streets has transformed "those people" into real faces, real lives, and real friends. I can no longer confront the issue without seeing the faces of my new friends. This has an incredible effect on my impetus to help.

> Hearing the homeless talk about their lives was enlightening. I had these preconceived ideas about what their lives were like. They are more educated than I expected.

> Expressing what it has meant to me to actually have the chance to engage in conversations with people who used to be total strangers is next to impossible. It has been eye opening. My understanding of homeless people was based on what I'd see on the news, in magazines, or on TV shows. They were not real people and I could easily turn my back on them and the problem in general.

In terms of their interactions with homeless citizens, students involved in the D.C. project made several points. Some discussed becoming more empathetic with the plight of homeless citizens. One student elaborated, "I learned that the homeless in general do not earn their predicament. Instead, their problems are brought on by a series of events that are largely beyond their control. Such events could make myself or anyone wind up homeless." A junior majoring in psychology talked about how people often distance themselves from the homeless by making reference to "those people" as if they are somehow better than homeless people. This student also commented on how her work had left her with a different feeling about the homeless: "I feel entirely different about homeless people than I did previously. I understand better some of the circumstances that contribute to people losing their jobs, or their homes. But I also understand that many of the people I've met through this work are not helpless victims. They are more than capable of working and maintaining a normal life if there were just more opportunities."

A common theme delineated by students was the fact that community service work with people of diverse cultural backgrounds forced students to confront generalizations they had of the other. For example, students talked about various stereotypes they held or had witnessed in the media with regard to homeless people and how such stereotypes were erased as a result of their service work. Several students noted how surprised they were to find so many intelligent and educated people without jobs or places to live. One student maintained that the only accurate stereotype relates to the amount of bad luck that most homeless people have experienced. A second added, "I learned that all people are innately afraid and that no one deserves to be without a voice and a safe place and that stereotypes can be more damaging than can be fathomed." A third student talked about how his preconceptions about homeless people had been shattered through his interactions with them. As he explained, "This experience gave my beliefs and convictions about the homeless a personal basis that I'll never forget."

Another example is a senior in wildlife management who commented, "My most significant learning experience was that the people I served did not want someone to feel sorry for them, but to just be recognized and treated as a human being with likes, dislikes, and a story. That they are names and not just statistics. This is impetus for me to do more. I can't just walk away from these problems when they are so close to me now." A senior majoring in nutrition added, "Homeless people have a lot to offer. Everyone has a part deep down inside that longs for respect and understanding. If we each try to find that part in ourselves and look for it in each other we can create bonds and break down barriers."

Often students entered community service interactions with unrealistic expectations of the influence they might be able to have. Optimism tended to flow from an inadequate understanding of the complexities of another's life. They discovered that there are many reasons why someone is homeless and that the solutions are often just as complex. A student reflected on a service experience she had had at an earlier point in her life: "It's harder to help people than I thought. I worked with a young boy as part of a student mentoring program, and I thought I could go and encourage him and help him with his homework and he'd get all A's. But there were so many things that influenced what was going on in his life, and I was not as big an influence as I had hoped to be." A student involved in the D.C. project shared some similar thoughts: "I always go into these kinds of things thinking that I'm going to change the world somehow. It's pretty silly when you think about it. As if I'm going to be able to leave a big dent in the huge problems the homeless face."

Not all the students who participated in the D.C. project grew from their experience of facing homelessness. Several seemed unable to cope with the poverty they witnessed and remained behind the food counters while they served meals. These students tended to keep the homeless at least a soup ladle away and refused to venture into the eating areas where they could interact with those they had come to serve. The lives of homeless people as diverse others seemed too foreign and depressing for these students to handle. A student commented on some of her fellow volunteers' inability to deal with diverse others and the struggles the homeless face: "A number of students in our group didn't understand the issues. When we walked into this one room where there was this very dirty family, some of the students had blank looks on their faces, as if to hide their disbelief that anyone could live this way. I don't think the students wanted to have anything to do with them. They were just 'too dirty' for them to deal with. I think it threatened their vision of America as the land of opportunity."

In addition to participating in the D.C. project, I also interviewed students from Michigan State University who had worked with homeless citizens in either New York City or Louisville, Kentucky, over their spring break in 1995. Although nearly every student I interviewed described the experience as very rewarding and as one that taught them a great deal about themselves and their commitment to others, at least one student was traumatized by it all. This student was overwhelmed by the pain and suffering she had witnessed among the homeless in New York. She shared her thoughts and feelings: "The work in New York was very intense. Very hard for me. I was so upset for about a month. One of the things I did was work in one of the soup kitchens in the city. It was so hard being with the people. One lady had two little children with her and I couldn't help but think that they should be in school. They looked so sad and hungry. I couldn't deal with it. On another occasion we saw a man with one leg and he was screaming for help and all we did was walk right past him. A group of four of us who went all the way to New York to help others just walked away. Everywhere I turned I saw homeless people. I love everybody. And they have nothing. It's just so upsetting." This student decided she never wanted to work with homeless people again. "I learned that I am very fortunate. It was right there in my face. I learned that I am extremely sensitive to it. It's not that I don't care. I just can't deal with it. I just can't deal with the first-hand experience. I need to help in some other kind of way." When asked about what other kind of way she might select, she was unable to articulate a vision of her role in confronting issues of poverty. She struggled to make sense of her turning away from concerns for the poor: "I'm a very independent person. Maybe kind of selfish. I tend to get upset and I go into myself. I'm not sure I'm able to learn about others when I do that."

My fear was that she had already disconnected herself from the poorest in our society and that her decision might be a permanent one. The New York City project was coordinated and supervised completely by students, and no reflective component was built into the week's activities. The lack of a reflective component left me to wonder whether this young woman might have handled the experience differently had there been an experienced volunteer with whom to share her fears and possibly work through some of them. I discuss the importance of reflection in greater detail in chapters 7 and 8.

Some encounters with homeless people were more frightening than students had expected. The following two incidents highlight some of the fears that were stirred among the students. "While we were working at the homeless shelter," explained one student, "I heard a mother beating her child in one of the apartments—you could just tell. It was scary to stand by and hear that. It was very frightening for me. But I needed to recognize that people are doing what they can to try to improve their lives and that it might not be what I would do." A second student added, "I wasn't as prepared as I thought I'd be. I was scared a lot of times. There was this man from the shelter. We had served dinner to him the night before, and I was walking down the street the next day and he started coming toward me. He was yelling at me and calling me a white bitch. It was really scary. I didn't know what to do, so I just walked away as fast as I could."

In addition to putting a personal face on homelessness, the experiences students had led some of them to question the broad implications and social justice issues related to the problems of poverty. Many wanted to know more about recent legislative actions concerning economic policies. Robert Wuthnow noted that a growing concern about social justice issues and social policy among volunteers and community service workers is a common trend: "Some volunteers in our society have been forced to turn toward broader questions of justice and exploitation. At first their efforts have been directed more to specific individuals in need. But as they become more involved with volunteer work, their vision expands. Like Margaret Sanger, they realize that individual suffering is rooted in larger social arrangements" (1991, p. 253). This was clearly the case with many of the students who worked in Washington, D.C., as well as with other student volunteers I have met over the years.

Along with gaining an increased concern for social justice issues and policy implications, students became more aware of the physical and psychological consequences of being homeless. They learned a little bit about how a person is affected by the physical strain of being cold for extended periods of time. They learned something about what it does to one's sense of self to have to depend on others for food and shelter. A sophomore in biology commented, "Homelessness can cause some serious mental illnesses associated with feelings of despair, hopelessness, loneliness, and lack of trust in society. I never knew that this problem of mental illness was that bad in society and deserving of everybody's attention." This student added, "I learned how different people cope with homelessness. There are some who are still cheerful in their situation, who still have hope and continue to struggle and try to succeed in life. I learned that there are others who are very bitter and are afraid of trusting in other people. I also learned that there are those who seek to escape the reality of their situation by turning to drugs and alcohol."

The same student also talked about some of the little things homeless people do to retain their sanity despite dealing with circumstances that have turned their worlds upside down. She talked about how important playing cards in the afternoon was to a group of older men she met. It was their chance to build and maintain friendships and community. Many also liked to read the newspaper and talk about sports, politics, and crime. At first, she was surprised and then realized how her stereotypes about "the homeless" were interfering with her ability to get to know them as individuals, as real people. Some were quite well educated and had graduated from college. She revised her thinking and went about learning more about their diverse lives. Some of the homeless people she met loved to watch and talk about weekly television sit-coms. "Where did they watch television?" she wondered. So she asked them. "In the shelters, in front of store windows, at bars, at a friend's place," someone informed her. The things she learned about their lives surprised and amazed her. Their trials and tribulations did not seem any less difficult, but their lives certainly became more vivid for her. She was beginning to be able to relate to many of the homeless people she met throughout her work in D.C. She still did not fully understand what it meant to live on the streets, but her thoughts about the homeless were now rooted in a shared conversation, some giving and some taking.

In this section I have offered brief comments from students who largely appear as anonymous voices with some of their own life stories attached to the narratives. I think it is helpful to ground the various community service projects described in this book and the related learning experiences with more personalized accounts of students. With this in mind, I want to introduce Carolyn Fisher and discuss her involvement in community service and social activism and how these experiences both reflect and contribute to her own sense of self. It was through her participation in one of the first D.C. trips that I met Carolyn.

A STUDENT PROFILE

In the spring of 1995 I was doing research on engineering education at the University of Washington. Although my work was scheduled to begin on Monday, I had flown into Seattle on a Saturday to take advantage of reduced airfare for weekend travelers. This left me with a full day to explore the Seattle area, so when Sunday morning arrived I headed downtown to take in the sites of the Emerald City.

It was a warm and sunny April day, and after exploring the site of the World's Fair, I found myself at the market section of the city. I bought some fresh fruit for lunch at one of the stands and then proceeded to a nearby park and a grassy knoll overlooking Puget Sound. Amid a crowd of alternative-looking youths and young adults, I selected a seat from which to observe a fundamentalist preacher who was creating quite a stir. The people in the park, whose ages probably ranged from sixteen to thirty, wore black leather jackets, boots, belts, and accessories. Flannel shirts, bandannas, and well-worn jeans were popular, too. The style was a mixture of grunge and leather, with a number of body piercings and tattoos evident as well.

The preacher's topic was clear: sex and immorality. The favorite target of his venomous wrath were "the homosexuals" and "the fornicators." "Sex has become the devil's primary tool. He has lulled us to sleep with sex. Look around you, it's everywhere. Homosexuals, teen pregnancy, abortion, AIDS. It's all evil."

From somewhere behind me and off to the right a woman responded, "You are the one who's evil." I turned around to see whether I could locate the antagonist and was astounded to spot a familiar face, but one that was so out of context that I just could not believe it was truly she.

The same woman answered another comment from the preacher: "You're the one who's preaching hate." Her comment increased my state of incongruence because even her voice matched my mind's storage file known as "Carolyn Fisher." I had to pinch myself to make sure that I was in Seattle and not in State College, Pennsylvania, where I had known Carolyn when I was a doctoral student and she was an undergraduate.

I got up and walked over to make certain of the identity of this familiar but out-of-place person who was wearing a vest, T-shirt, and ragged jeans. When I was about ten feet from her our eyes met, and at that instant I knew I was not seeing things because suddenly she took on a look of incredulity that probably matched my own.

As it turned out, Carolyn had taken a year off from college and had traveled to the West Coast to figure out some things about her life. She was about to enter her senior year at Penn State but had become disenchanted with her major. Instead of finishing her degree in a field that no longer inspired her, she decided to take some time to mull things over and see the West Coast. As she informed me a year later when I caught up with her again, "There are two kinds of learning. There's academic learning that you do in school. You know, with books and professors. And there's another kind of learning that comes from traveling, from experience, from living. I needed to do some living before I could be sure about the kind of academic stuff I wanted to study and the kind of career I wanted to have." Eventually, Carolyn had come to realize that she wanted to be in an academic program committed to social justice issues, one that might in turn serve as a stepping stone for law school. When I last spoke with her, she was in the process of transferring to the University of California at Berkeley to enter such a program.

For a variety of reasons, including that strange encounter in Seattle, Carolyn Fisher has left an indelible mark on my life. One reason I remember her so fondly is that she was committed to social justice issues and willing to engage in political battles to create social change. From the first time I met her in Washington, D.C., to our encounter in Seattle, to the last time we crossed paths when I formally interviewed her, Carolyn's identity as a caring activist came across loud and clear.

During the interview, Carolyn spoke of her frustrations and concerns about our country's policies and leaders. She sees too many short-term solutions being applied to complex social problems. From her perspective, political leaders and their advisors fail to deal with the deepest issues that lead to some of the more obvious social concerns. Carolyn used the abortion debate as an example of superficial treament of a much deeper social ill. Politicians debate pro-choice and pro-life but, "They don't see the lack of love and community that causes people to suffer." She also spoke about the country's national debt and efforts to balance the budget by cutting education and social programs. The irony for Carolyn is that these same programs may be understood as part of an effort by political leaders to act in a caring and compassionate manner and yet they are the first programs to be eliminated. Again, if building community and advancing a concern for others truly mattered, Carolyn believes that such programs would be strengthened.

Carolyn had recently returned from a trip to Mexico, Guatemala, Nicaragua, and Honduras, where she and about one hundred other volunteers had collected and then transported school and hospital supplies to communities in need. While in Central America, Carolyn heard numerous horror stories of atrocities perpetuated at the hands of United States-backed forces. "I learned a lot about how our country has its sticky fingers in everything. I mean I heard some real horror stories. . . . It's so hard to know what's true and what's not true. Some of it I don't even want to believe. . . . It makes me ashamed. But at the same time, it makes me even more committed. That's one reason I am considering law school. I want to be able to speak the language of politicians and lawyers so that I can fight for fair policies." Unlike many other people in our country who seem to have given up hope of creating change or were never able to embrace such a vision in the first place, Carolyn remains determined: "We hear people all the time say that 'I'm only one person. What can I do?' But one person can love another person and create change. We need to raise a society that cares more about people and less about greed."

In addition to Carolyn's commitment, I will always remember her talent as an artist. During the D.C. project, she brought great joy to several of the homeless people of whom she drew sketches, which she offered to them as gifts. She used a technique she later described as "blind drawing." "That's not the technical term," she noted, explaining that blind drawing involves focusing on an object, such as someone's face in this case, and drawing what one sees without looking down at the paper. As I watched her, I guessed that she had developed through practice (or perhaps it was a gift) a feel for where her hands were on the paper. Many of us tried to mimic this technique, but our sketches were more likely to resemble a two-year-old's art work than Carolyn's intricate lines that recreated the face of another. More interesting than watching her weave her art was witnessing the reactions of the homeless citizens she sketched and the warm hugs and glowing smiles they returned to Carolyn. One gift for another.

Carolyn has struggled to combine her commitment to social justice and her artistic talent. In fact, her year off from school was partially an effort to resolve a heartfelt tension between her desire to create and her desire to serve others. The two seemed mutually exclusive, and the struggle pulled her in multiple directions, leaving her sense of self somewhat in turmoil. Finally, it all came together when she created a portrait that touched several of her friends. "I have this one piece that I did of an elderly Black homeless man, and he looks so sad and beaten up by the world. I call the piece 'Racism.'" Through this effort, as much as anything else she had accomplished, Carolyn had come to realize that art could be used as a tool to reach people's hearts, to influence their attitudes. As she explained, "What is the biggest barrier that keeps people from caring? It's their attitudes and their vision of life. Art has the power to make people think about what they value, what they care about."

Obviously, someone's life is more than a portrait. But because of her talent, Carolyn was able to offer a passing glimpse into the life of one homeless man whose suffering could be read between the lines and wrinkles of his face. His pain and anguish called out and his life was no longer invisible.

THE IMPORTANCE OF STORIES

An experience homeless people often describe is that of "feeling invisible." This comes in part from the fact that many people intentionally avoid making eye contact with the homeless, perhaps out of fear or maybe out of a desire to avoid being asked for a handout. Regardless of the reason, people will go out of their way to avoid acknowledging the homeless. In part, the attitude conveyed seems to be, "If I avoid seeing 'them,' then I do not have to think about the awful circumstances and conditions others are forced to confront." It is kind of the "out of sight, out of mind" idea. The lengths people will go to avoid homeless people and the issue of homelessness is one reason why it is so important to make their lives and the related issues visible. Liebow speaks to this concern in his portrait of homeless women in D.C.: "None of the women ever said 'Tell them who I am' in just those words, but they demand to be seen—and have a right to be seen—as they are, with many warts and human frailties, but fully human nonetheless" (1993, p. 21).

Not everyone agrees that homeless citizens have a right to be seen. Numerous cities around the country have made or are making it illegal to live in their communities without a home. In essence, they are trying to outlaw homelessness. As one social activist said over e-mail: "They are trying to make it illegal to be nowhere!"

Palo Alto is one example. The city recently spent $20,000 for two months to increase police protection after a survey of businesses in the area indicated strong support for prohibiting panhandling. In the meantime, the city spends only $102,939 a year on services for the homeless out of some $80 million in general funds. Some of the suggestions offered by downtown business owners included: buy the homeless a one-way ticket out of town, reconfigure areas where they congregate to discourage their presence, have the police keep them moving and not allow them to set up any permanent stations, and ticket people who give money to panhandlers. One individual was quoted as saying, "We all seem to worry about infringing on their First Amendment rights. When do they begin to infringe on our rights?" I can't help but ask: Since when is surviving in the streets a violation of someone else's rights?

Where are the homeless left to go? A passage from the autobiography of Angela Davis comes to mind. In the passage she discusses a letter she received from James Baldwin. A sentence from that letter seems apropos: "If they take you in the morning, they will be coming for us that night" (1974, p. 306). If homeless citizens can be swept off the streets, presumably the last place they have left, then who is next?

When a homeless man or woman is found dead in the streets, few speak of the death as a tragedy. In fact, in 1992 a homeless man in Annapolis was attacked by two twenty-one-year-old men who used baseball bats to beat what they described as a "worthless bum" to death. When they got off with a lesser manslaughter charge, a clear message was sent that homeless citizens do not have the same rights as others in our society. And if cities like Palo Alto have their way, the homeless won't even have a sidewalk to rest on. Recent legislation and the general attitude conveyed by some members of our society suggest that many do not see homeless citizens as real people having normal human rights.

The community service work in D.C. enabled students to learn about the lives of homeless people and in this way helped students to see homeless citizens as real people with real problems and concerns. For example, a senior majoring in management and journalism commented on what he thought was most significant about his work: "I enjoyed talking with a homeless man who had served in the Navy. But since then he had suffered a stroke and had paralysis on his left side. When I asked if he was in contact with his family back in Ohio where he was born, he said he was 'too gay' for them. He couldn't even recall the last time he had spoken to them." A junior majoring in health education also discussed what she thought was important about her experience: "My most significant learning experiences came from talking with some homeless people and trying to learn about their struggles. It was a real awakening for me to hear about their lives in great detail."

A senior in nursing participated in the D.C. project because she wanted to be able to better relate to and understand the problem of homelessness. She was ignorant of many of the issues and concerns homeless people face and thought that interacting with some of them might serve to educate herself about the issues. She commented, "One-on-one discussions with different homeless people was the most significant aspect of the project. I realized that in part what they need is to be heard—to be able to share their experiences and feelings." A sophomore in sociology described an unforgettable moment she had experienced on a repeat community service trip to D.C.: "What sticks in my mind was meeting and remembering someone whom I had met in a soup kitchen last year and talking to him on a very deep and personal level. I think he remembered me too."

Liebow (1993) and many of the students involved in the D.C. project highlight that the telling of stories is one way to make visible the lives of homeless people. When we hear about their lives and the problems they face, they become more real to us. A connection forms between the self and the other. As Howard Radest maintained, this is especially true when cultural differences exist among individuals involved in community service: "Community service is also built on assumptions of relationship. So, we assume that it is both possible and appropriate for culturally diverse persons to move, although not without difficulty, into each others' worlds and to have a shared world as well" (1993, p. 114).

Radest talked about how community service is one way to help overcome the "lost connection"—the sense of community that seems to have eroded in today's technologically advanced, postmodern society. (Recall from chapter 3—*Proposition 5: Postmodernism has resulted in significant cultural changes affecting the nature of communities and the nature of social interaction. Consequently, the parameters set by culture and the formation of identities and selves are different now than they were under modernist regimes.*) Radest did not suggest a return to the "old connections," characterized by the conservative rhetoric of former President George Bush and his "Thousand Points of Light," which seems to call out to some overglorified America of the past grounded in a vision of rugged individualism, free markets, and close-knit communities that provide charity but only to those who are "deserving." As Radest explained, "It is striking that so much energy is expended to build a third sector in order to avoid direct action by the government. Yet, the market place is also suspect as an agency for meeting communal needs. Hidden by the ideological debate on the 'privatization of public services' are the echoes of the once-upon-a-time narrative of a world of clear distinctions and communal connections" (p. 41). Thus, for Radest, building lost connections is not about erasing cultural difference and returning to American traditions grounded in visions of harmony and similarity. Instead, overcoming our sense of alienation involves recognizing real differences, and, at the same time, understanding that we can build some common connections—that the stranger is not so different from myself and that we can engage one another in a common struggle or cause. (Recall from chapter 3—*Proposition 9: Participation in community service provides a means to foster a sense of connectedness and offers an opportunity for students to understand themselves and to develop caring selves.*) The story of the other is real and has much to offer the self and vise versa. The challenge is, as Peter McLaren explained in his discussion of narrative and identity, to use narrative as a means to decipher the identity of the self and the other while recognizing the dynamic and evolving nature of identity, the relevance of history, and the importance of "networks of social power" (1995, p. 97).

At times students had a hard time understanding the point Radest made about connecting with others who are different from ourselves and tended to ignore differences related to the other. Despite their efforts to understand the complexities of the lives of homeless citizens, students seemed at times to essentialize homeless lives. A variety of student comments offer insight into some of the simplistic generalizations applied to homeless people. The following are some examples:

> I learned how beautiful the homeless are.

> I don't see any difference between me and people who are homeless. They have the same needs and concerns as I have. Everybody wants to be loved and have a place they call home.

> All people are basically good, more similar to one another than different, and have love somewhere within themselves.

Homeless people are just like you and I. They are no different. They just do not have homes.

Everybody thinks of homeless people as criminals and as bums. But what I learned through this project is that they are just like everybody else.

Another student involved in a community service project designed to serve low-income rural families, most of whom were African American, offered some relevant comments: "What's great about working with the people I've met here is that racism kind of falls by the wayside when you get to know them." Clearly, racism is in part rooted in ignorance of the other. At the same time, however, racial and cultural differences exist, and the tendency of many White students involved in community service is to see difference as a barrier to understanding and thus adopt strategies in which cultural diversity is ignored. The phrase "We're all the same," usually uttered by middle-class White students in reference to low-income African Americans, is perhaps the most frequently mentioned comment heard throughout my work with students. The challenge is to learn from one another and seek common connections, while at the same time envisioning our differences as something to understand and respect. For too many White students involved in community service, difference was something that frightened them, so they took solace in blanketing that which was foreign to them.

Students I interviewed had developed certain images of the poor and of homeless citizens that, to a large degree, they had derived from the media. In expressing that homeless people are beautiful, one student implied that for one reason or another, she had previously perceived them as the opposite—as somehow not beautiful. Another student, in pointing out that "homeless people are just like you and I," suggested that at one time he believed there were inherent qualities that make homeless people different from people who have homes. A third student stated, "Everybody wants to be loved," as if to imply that even homeless people deserve to be loved. And other students revealed former images of homeless people as "bums" or as "lazy" and thereby deserving of their place in life, at least until these students learned more about them through their community service work. Although the experience of working with homeless citizens helped students move past simplistic and stereotypical views, one is still left to ponder not only how such views had evolved to begin with, but also the level of understanding students ultimately reached. Let us now explore these two issues: the origins of students' stereotypes and the complexities of their more experientially based understandings.

One student offered some insight into his own prejudice and misconceptions about the poor, the homeless, and African Americans: "Meeting homeless people and talking with them taught me that some of my stereotypes about the poor, about Blacks, have been rooted in my own life of White, middle-class privilege. I have never had to work that hard to get a college education, for example, yet I've bought into the idea that others who have less than me are somehow lazy because they are poor. Heck, they may have worked twice as hard as I have. I've never really had my views of the poor challenged until this experience working with homeless people."

Some of the generalizations and stereotypes to which students referred were seen as the by-product of the media. As one student, a senior in geography, pointed out, "I learned that my perceptions of poverty, crime, and homelessness are influenced and perhaps shaped by misconstrued images that I see on television." Another student also talked about how television had played a major role in how she had come to envision African Americans. She pointed out that in her rural Pennsylvania community "there wasn't a single African American family. I never even met an African American until I attended college."

A sophomore talked about the difference she felt between herself and the large number of homeless African Americans she encountered during her volunteer work: "I definitely feel a major barrier between Blacks and Whites in this country. There were times working in the soup kitchens where I felt very uncomfortable." A college junior studying mathematics commented on a similar feeling: "It was an experience for me simply to be placed in the awkward environment of walking around in predominantly African American, poor neighborhoods. I want to remember that feeling of insecurity. It reminds me of the vast differences between races in our society." A student who worked with low-income families on a rural community service project in South Carolina provides some personal insights: "There is something that I'm not proud of and I always considered myself open minded and not prejudiced, but when I worked at Sharon's house [Sharon is an African American woman who needed some repairs done to her home] it reminded me that some of my previous thinking about the poor had been based on stereotypes. I mean I've always kind of thought in the back of my mind that people become poor or destitute because they are not motivated or not as intelligent. But Sharon has a master's degree and is very articulate. I see now that there may be many causes or barriers that people face that can limit them. It was an eye opener and I see now that I was carrying this misconception about their being to blame for their plight."

A number of students expressed different perceptions of community service depending on the population to be served. Janie Dreshbach, who we will meet again in chapter 7, talked about her experience working with homeless people in Louisville, Kentucky: "I learned that I can handle something more real life. I had done volunteer work before but with teenagers from the middle class. I hadn't worked with low-income people or with minorities. This was a new experience for me." It is more than interesting that Janie hints at the fact that working with people from similar backgrounds to herself is not "real life" community service, but working with minority or low-income families is. There seems to be an underlying assumption here that "real" community service involves working with diverse others who are in some way needy. The implication is that community was not at the heart of working with people like oneself. Taken a step further, Janie seems to imply that Whites and the middle class are essentially the same and therefore community building is not really necessary among this group. Benjamin Barber spoke to the perception expressed by Janie: "Many draw a misleading and dangerous (to democracy) picture of service as the rich helping the poor (charity) or the poor paying a debt to their country (service in exchange for college scholarships) as if 'community' means only the disadvantaged and needy and does not include those performing service" (1992, pp. 248–49). Barber's point is that in a true democracy where active participation as a citizen is key, we should all be involved in community building and we all benefit from service that seeks to build community, even when the service is for and with members of our own race or among those of a similar economic standing. This is opposed to the idea of charity spoken of so frequently by political leaders such as George Bush and Bill Clinton, both of whom tend to envision involvement in helping others as a charitable act, and not as something from which the doer also benefits.

The comments from the preceding student and other White students as well who suggested that service work with members of their own race may not be "real" community service may be interpreted as a lack of consciousness of their own racial identity; there is a tendency for Whites to fail to see "whiteness" as a source of identity. Of consequence, whiteness becomes a universal, invisible, and uncontestable barometer for situating blackness and other racial identities as marginal. As McLaren argues, "White groups need to examine their own ethnic histories so that they are less likely to judge their own cultural norms as neutral or universal. The supposed neutrality of white culture enables it to commodify blackness to its own advantage and ends. It allows it to manipulate the 'other' but does not see this 'otherness' as a white tool of exploitation" (1995, p. 133).

Many of the students I observed throughout my project did not have experience with people of different racial and cultural backgrounds, and as a result had confused expectations of how open and caring they would be toward diverse others and how in turn those diverse others would treat them. They were surprised when they saw a bit of themselves in the other. But some of their comments also reveal the deep divisions in our country between Blacks and Whites, and between lower-class and middle-class people. The fact that students who have the time and resources to work for the benefit of others who are less well off financially report being *surprised* at times by their ability to love those same others is telling. Did students truly expect homeless citizens to be unworthy of their love in some way? A junior who participated in a rural service project to Yonges Island, South Carolina (the focus of chapter 6), offers some related thoughts: "I was able to truly love these people here on the island. I was a bit surprised by how comfortable I felt and how easy it was to share."

All in all, students' comments frequently revealed a certain naïveté about the other and about race and class. They desired either a color-blind world or one in which Blacks were somehow transformed into Whites—a world in which "we are all the same." As a senior in elementary education commented, "There is only one race—the human race." Students seemed unable to grasp the positive aspects of difference and were trapped within a modernist and functionalist discourse of homogeneity. Rarely did a White student comment that he or she enjoyed trying to understand the world from the perspective of an African American.

Perhaps I am being overly critical. The reality is that I would be one of the first in line to celebrate the willingness of college students to give of themselves to others. Another interpretation of the struggle middle-class White volunteers face in making sense of race and class issues may be more reflective of the inadequacy of our language to come to terms with otherness and to adequately address the connection between the self and the other in any way that moves beyond a Cartesian dualism. How do we talk about the self and the other without resorting to a subject/object dualism? How can the two be seen as intertwined and interdependent? If Robert Bellah (1985) and his coauthors are correct when they argue that we lack a language that effectively bridges individualism and community, then it is not too great a leap of faith to believe that our language may also lack a vocabulary for articulating a sense of self and other as interconnected. In part, this is a goal I have along with other critical postmodern writers such as McLaren and Henry Giroux (1992, 1993), who seek to create a border language capable of bridging what until now has been largely unexplainable.

The challenge in working with students involved in community service projects is to help them understand that as human beings we do have many things in common, yet as a result of how race and class have situated us within our society, we cannot ignore important identity differences. We also must recognize that, simply because someone is of the same racial or class background, this does not mean that we can somehow automatically understand how he or she has experienced her life. In other words, everyone is the other and in possession of a unique and complex self that we must work hard to understand and get to know. Making assumptions about people based on race and class may offer shortcuts to complex sense-making processes, but such shortcuts may short-circuit a sincere and caring understanding of the other.

SUMMARY

The data throughout this chapter suggest that a more personalized understanding of homeless people's lives helps students confront some of their stereotypes and generalizations about diverse others. Students talked about becoming more aware of the complexity of the problems homeless citizens face, and many began to question larger structural arrangements. Students were less prone to pass judgement on the lives of homeless people. These students seemed to arrive at an understanding suggested in Liebow's account of homelessness: that homelessness is a matter of poverty and economic inequalities and not necessarily the blame of alcohol, mental illness, or laziness. Liebow elaborated: "People are not homeless because they are physically disabled, mentally ill, abusers of alcohol or other drugs, or unemployed. However destructive and relevant these conditions may be, they do not explain homelessness; most physically disabled people, most mentally ill people, most alcoholics and drug addicts, and most unemployed persons do have places to live" (1993, pp. 223–24). In general, students were beginning to understand homelessness as a wider problem of race, class, and economic inequality.

McLaren argued that "students need to be able to cross over into different zones of cultural diversity and form . . . hybrid and hyphenated identities in order to rethink the relationship of self to society, of self to other, and to deepen the moral vision of the social order" (1995, p. 22). This chapter highlighted the fact that students' involvement in community service is often an experience of "border crossing," where borders represent the different zones of cultural diversity that McLaren delineates throughout his work. Border crossing hence may be understood as a process involving social interaction and engagement with others from diverse backgrounds. However, cultural borders must not be treated in a simplistic manner: "Culture is not viewed as monolithic or unchanging, but as a shifting sphere of multiple and heterogeneous borders where different histories, languages, experiences, and voices intermingle amid diverse relations of power and privilege" (Giroux, 1992, p. 32).

In attempting to cross cultural borders defined by the basic privilege of having a home or not and all the histories and languages that go along with that dichotimization, students began to learn a little about themselves and the other. In general, students enter into community service interactions with certain assumptions and expectations that often relate to generalizations, even stereotypes, they might have about the poor. Some students entered community service interactions believing that the poor may be deserving of their position in life. Others did not imagine homeless people to be as intelligent or as educated as themselves. Students continually were surprised to learn that the identities and backgrounds of the homeless were complex and diverse. The only generalization that seemed to fit was that the homeless are without homes.

Through their border crossing, students were challenged to think in terms of the multiplicity of homeless citizens' identities. At the same time, this caused a certain degree of discomfort among some who looked for easy and generalizable notions to describe and understand the other. Some students resorted to what amounted to essentializing homeless citizens through such notions as "they are the same as me," thereby rendering invisible uniqueness, complexity, and diversity.

Because many of the homeless citizens were African American and the vast majority of student volunteers were White, racial tension was also a significant aspect of the students' experience. Many of the students were not used to working with and around African Americans and were challenged to confront race and their own racist assumptions. Once again, students in many cases resorted to essentializing the identities of the African American homeless citizens they met and tended to regard racial differences as irrelevant. The general attitude students conveyed was that we are all the same, regardless of our racial identity.

A concern raised in this chapter relates to the need to develop community service projects that help students confront otherness while challenging them to see the complexity and diversity of the other, without resorting to simplistic explanations that conceal cultural differences. Within this criticism, however, is the recognition of the incredibly positive learning opportunities students had through their interactions with homeless citizens. For the most part, students found their interactions with the homeless to be some of the most enlightening experiences of their lives, and many left D.C. with fond and heartfelt memories.

Chapter 5

Mutuality

If you have come to help me, you are wasting
your time. But if you have come because your
liberation is bound up with mine then let us
work together.
  —Lila Watson, source unknown

It's funny how children's recollections are often so different from those of
their parents. When I reflect on my childhood, certain experiences get caught in
my fishing-net memory that holds some and allows others to slip away. I
remember getting hand-me-downs from my Uncle Bob and Aunt Phyllis—hand-
me-downs that had belonged to their son Wayne, who despite being a year
younger always was a few inches taller than I was. His blue jeans in particular
stood out for their quality and because I had to cuff them three to four inches
just to keep them from dragging on the ground. When I was in grade school, a
kid could get away with big cuffs. It sure is hard to imagine a third or fourth
grader dressing like that in today's world of fashion with expensive, profes-
sional sports team jackets and high-flying, high-priced tennis shoes.

I was happy and grateful to receive the clothes that were too small for my
cousin. Getting hand-me-downs from Wayne didn't pose a threat to my sense of
self or to my pride. That was not true, however, of other clothes that local
churches or charitable organizations gave to me. I always had the same fear—
wearing a distinctive shirt to school that had belonged to one of my class-
mates: "Hey, Bobby. That's the same shirt I got for Christmas last year. My
mother donated it to the Salvation Army and now you're wearing it. Isn't that
funny?" No, it isn't funny, and although I played that scenario out in my mind
a hundred times, fortunately for me it never happened.

During the years when my clothes were most limited, I had to take extra
time in the evenings to get them ready for the next day. I remember laying out

my school clothes each night before going to bed. I had to plan things right so that the other kids didn't realize that I wore the same shirt two or even three times in the same week. If I wore my favorite shirt on Monday, then I could wear it again on Wednesday, and possibly once again on Friday, which was the day I always wanted to look my best. Friday was the last day of school for the week, and that was always an event worth celebrating by looking my best. Part of the evening ritual included not only selecting a shirt for the next day but also ironing my pants. I figured if I had to wear the same one or two pairs of pants, the other kids would be less likely to notice them if they were finely creased and wrinkle free. It might have been a humorous sight for an outsider to visit our house and see a third-grade boy ironing his pants, underwear, socks, and shirt each night before going to bed.

———————

Having experienced economic difficulties at different times during my childhood left me with certain impressions of the world of poverty and of working to serve the poor. It seems to me that people need to be more understanding of the diverse experiences and beliefs poor people have of the world, instead of making assumptions or generalizations about their lives. As I mentioned in chapter 1, there are better ways to help low-income individuals and families than many of the strategies our society enacts.

I remember a conversation I had with Mary Edens, director of the Service Learning Center at Michigan State University. We were talking about the idea of "mutuality"—the belief that service ought to be a two-way relationship in which all parties give and receive and all parties participate equally in the planning of service activities. She shared an experience she had with a group of sorority women who wanted to raise money to purchase Christmas gifts for low-income hospitalized children. Their idea seemed like a nice gesture on the surface, but Mary raised questions about the project. Her primary concern related to the following: How would the parents feel about a group of college women providing things for their children that they could not provide? When Mary suggested that the students ought to meet with the parents to develop, as a group, some possible ideas for serving the children (an example of mutuality in practice), the students balked and decided on a different service project. They were uncomfortable with the idea of meeting with the parents and obtaining their insights.

The point Mary Edens made in sharing this example is something I experienced as a child on the receiving end of community service: Too often community service is structured as a one-way activity in which those who have resources make decisions about the needs of those who lack resources. It is one more example of the "haves" of our society shaping the lives of the "have nots."

Service that lacks mutuality is not community service. Instead, such action is charity because community building is not at its heart. A student provided some insights into the difference between community service and charity: "The little bit of time and effort that I can give has a ripple effect. My time and effort is probably many times more powerful and more significant than any change from my pocket." A second student also alluded to the difference between community service and charity: "I think the biggest reason I participate in community service is the opportunity to meet and interact with real people. So often we find ourselves going through the motions and never truly experiencing people who have lives that are a lot different from ours. I love to interact with people who face struggles that I've been fortunate enough to never have to deal with. They teach me about what it means to support one another. They teach me about what a real community is. If I didn't need these kinds of interactions, I guess I would probably just give money to some worthwhile cause and use my time in a way that benefits my own career or my own family."

Charity does not encourage the intimate connections and personal relationships that result from service built on mutuality. When mutuality is the guiding framework, a sense of connection becomes a possibility for students and for those in the community who may benefit from their service. A student drew an analogy from some work he had done on the house of a resident of Johns Island, South Carolina: "We started working on the front of the house, but by the end of the week we were on the back porch. I think that symbolizes how quickly they opened their lives and their homes up to us. The front porch is open for all visitors, but the back porch is for your closest friends." A second student who participated in the same project discussed the influence a member of the community had on him. "Whenever I get outside my own world, my community gets larger. . . . My sense of community is not defined by a certain race or population. I had a conversation with Uncle Leroy today. He started the conversation yesterday about the difference between a White man and a Black man. The way he talked was very interesting. He used lots of metaphors and told a lot of stories, and eventually he got to his point. He taught me that family values are important to everyone, yet they're defined differently. He believes that White people start with nothing, but make something from that. But Blacks have learned helplessness. His wife, he said, wouldn't give living in the country a try. He bought all new furniture for the house to encourage her to move, but his wife wouldn't leave the city. He'd promised his father at his deathbed that he'd go back to the family home on Johns Island, but his wife never came. 'In White America, you would just jump up and move away. There's not such a strong sense of family responsibility,' he said. He made me think about my grandfather."

The point here is not whether Uncle Leroy's interpretations of Whites and Blacks and their routes to success or how they value family ring true or not.

What is important is that the student and Uncle Leroy shared some intimate moments and learned from one another. While riding in the back of the van from the University of South Carolina to Johns Island, it had never crossed this student's mind that he would meet an elderly African American man who would remind him of how much he missed his grandfather.

The preceding student narrative informs us of a specific quality of interactions between service workers and community members: That quality is mutuality. The ideal of mutuality and how it gets played out through community service contexts is the focus of this chapter. I use an intensive community service project conducted on Johns Island, South Carolina, to introduce issues related to mutuality. A central concern of this chapter is the struggle students endured in coming to terms with the gifts they received through their service efforts.

THE JOHNS ISLAND PROJECT

Many of the experiences I had as a child with church and community service workers haunted me during the week I spent on Johns Island with a group of students from the University of South Carolina. We were there to help restore and renovate the homes of low-income families of the island. Some had been damaged by a recent hurricane. Others had been slowly worn by the Atlantic winds that sweep like giant brooms across the eastern coast from northern Florida to southern Virginia to the outer banks of Maryland's eastern shore. Time and endless dampness had been the enemy to others as the roofs, walls, and floors rotted at the hands of winter's rain and summer's humidity.

Throughout our weeklong project, we all seemed forced at one time or another to confront our own values and beliefs about material wealth and how we should situate our own lives within our society and our communities. Many of us talked about the complicity of our career hopes and personal interests and wondered what we could reasonably change. We talked a great deal about our wealth and privilege as each day challenged us that much more to reflect on our lives and those of others. "Lately, I've realized how lucky I've been," reflected one student. "I need to give back. Maybe it's a selfish reason. I don't know. But I need to give something, give something back to my community." A second added, "Because of this experience, I've learned that my problems aren't big. Not compared to some of the problems of the people who live on Johns Island." And a third student explained, "This was an opportunity to get back into service to others. I feel on one level that I can make a difference, but on another level I question why I was so lucky to be born into an upper-class family in the first place."

We were all challenged at different times to reflect on our own values and how they might differ from those of members of the Johns Island community, as well as from the values of other members of the group. I recall a conversation I had with several students and my friend Julie Neururer, a faculty member at the University of South Carolina and advisor to the students who had planned the trip. Litter was scattered everywhere throughout the island, and some students raised the possibility of doing another project at some other time to clean up trash along the highways. We debated whether we should make such an offer; some were supportive of the idea and others opposed it. "If it was a concern to the people who live here," exclaimed one student, "then they would do it themselves or ask for help in doing it." All of us found the trash to be an eyesore, but we were torn as to whether or not we should play a role in cleaning it up. A second student reflected on this and some related issues: "A lot of people drive around and complain about garbage in people's yards. It bothers them. But some people don't have materialistic priorities because they don't have those kind of values. I got sick before this trip and went to the doctor. I was seeing a nurse practitioner, and when she found out where I was going for spring break she started talking about the 'funny colors of the houses.' A lot of people know there's poor people, but they only see them as poor."

The conversation about the trash along the roadways underscores some of the issues associated with mutuality: How we serve others and what we do in action with and for others needs to reflect what they desire and what they see as important, as well as our own abilities to provide different kinds of service. Most important, for the activity to reflect mutuality, it must involve the input of those who will be most affected by the service. As Jane Kendall argued, "People must decide what their own needs are and how those needs will be met" (1990, p. 9). A concern for mutuality requires that the planning of community service involves, in a meaningful manner, those to be served. It should not be a matter of the "haves" doing for the "have nots."

Johns Island is one of the Charleston Sea Islands and part of the region along the Atlantic seaboard described as the "low-country." In her anthropological account of language use in the Piedmont region of the South, Shirley Brice Heath differentiates the "low-country" from the "up country": "Separating the central Piedmont of the Carolinas from the Coastal Plain is a strip of sand hills with no vegetation except jack pines and scrub oak. Along this strip is a geological fault called the 'fall line.' River rapids and shoals mark this point at which rushing waters of rivers falling from the Appalachians across the foothills enter into the Coastal Plain. Above this line is 'the up country,' and below it the 'low-country'" (1983, p. 19). Although limited vegetation may mark the point between the low- and high-country, the low-country itself is a region of exceptional beauty, with ancient oak and cypress trees separating the various small farms throughout the area and hosting front-yard swings, and often demarking neighborhood churches. There is a stretch of highway cutting across Johns Island and leading to its wealthy neighbors—Kiawah and

Seabrook Islands—that is lined on each side with giant oaks whose limbs reach across the road like outstretched arms intertwining some twenty-five to thirty feet above the roadway. The Spanish moss dangles down from their sleeves as the color guard of this southern island offers both a welcoming salutatory hello and a somewhat eerie farewell. The darkness of the tunnel one enters passing through the oaks hints at something to come on the other side. Heading east, the impending ocean is given away by its scent and vacant horizon. Heading west, one can almost sense the miles of landscape that lie ahead, rolling on like time itself.

Johns Island hardly seems like an island in the traditional sense of the word. The western edge of the island is a series of swamps and smaller inlets, most of them barely navigable. A highway passes through the western boundary and only the drawbridge one passes over hints at the fact that Johns Island is indeed an island. Although the western edge of the island might raise questions about its geological classification, the other side is adjacent to a series of deeper inlets and bays that are travelled by the largest of family yachts. The vast majority of these ocean passages serve the residents of Kiawah and Seabrook Islands.

On Johns Island is a facility known as the Rural Mission, which provides human services to low-income Sea Island and migrant farm workers' families. Services include home improvements and repairs, day care, community education, and special assistance in the form of food and clothing for those in need. The mission facilities are in need of significant repairs themselves and comprise a central building, which is about 100 feet by 50 feet, and several smaller buildings that are used as cabins, tool sheds, and bathrooms. The central building is connected to a wing in the back, thus forming a T-shaped structure. The back wing extends for about 70 feet to the edge of an ocean passageway connecting the Atlantic to Seabrook Island. This wing of the central building houses the sleeping quarters, comprising three bunk rooms. The entire wing is supported by a series of steel poles and is elevated about 5 to 10 feet above the edge of the shore and then above the bay itself. The fact that the sleeping quarters extend over a body of water was apparent every morning when we awoke in damp sleeping bags, which had collected the perspiration from our own bodies struggling to keep warm (the temperatures were in the 30s and 40s at night), as well as the moisture rising off the water. The three bunk rooms are connected by a screened walkway running the length of the wing and ending on a back deck overlooking the bay. The deck became the evening's final resting place for many a reflective meeting.

Visible off to the southeast of the Rural Mission deck are the yacht houses of Seabrook Island. The majestic masts rising in front of the residences appear like flagpoles of faraway castles, proclaiming and protecting the site for its owner. We stood on the deck of the rundown Rural Mission created to serve the poorest people of the area and were amazed by the beauty of the yachts and yacht houses in the distance. The swamps and swamp grass separating Johns Island from Seabrook Island served as a motelike reminder to us that Seabrook was a private resort community and inaccessible to the residents of Johns Island, unless, of course, they were hired to work in one of the restaurants or marinas. As we explored the vista throughout the week, the contrast between rich and poor had never seemed quite so clear and in the darker moments reminded us of how little we could really change.

It was from the Rural Mission deck that we witnessed two of the most beautiful natural sights I have ever seen. On one occasion, early in the morning, we saw two dolphins swimming in the bay. What struck me most about this event was the fact that one student had spotted the dolphins from the back deck and, rather than cherish the fleeting moment for himself, he ran down the walkway to get the rest of us to share the wonder. We all followed, running as fast as we could, and sure enough there they were: two bluish gray dolphins arching in and out of the water as if in slow motion. One descended into the depths of the deep green water as the other rose two to three feet and at its apex arched its back and returned home. For a few seconds, nothing. And then some twenty or thirty feet away from where they were last seen, they rose again, this time simultaneously. It was a breathtaking morning portrait.

On another evening we watched the most beautiful sunset I had ever seen. It was a chilly evening, and several of us were wrapped in blankets and enjoying the deep rainbow-colored tapestry slowly unveiling itself across the horizon to the right of the deck, just beyond the inlet and swamps off to the west. It was a light for our reflection, and the week unfolded before us as the fruits of labor bloomed right before our eyes. When I read Gloria Naylor's *Mama Day* about a year or so later, I knew that we were kindred spirits for having shared one of the same sea island canvases: "It seems like God reached way down into His box of paints, found the purest reds, the deepest purples, and a dash of midnight blue, then just kinda trailed His fingers along the curve of the horizon and let 'em all bleed down. And when the streaks of color hit the hush-a-by green of the marsh grass with the blue of The Sound behind 'em, you ain't never had to set foot in a church to know you looking at a living prayer" (1988, p. 78).

The week was one of contrasts, especially in terms of economic disparity. As the following comments from students indicate, many were taken aback and had not expected to see such poverty or such wealth:

> It's really kind of weird to see so many poor people and then contrast that to the wealth in the city of Charleston and the other wealthy islands around here.

I think the odd thing about the communities here is that there is no clear-cut wealthy neighborhood. It's like it's every other house. I'd like to think that if my neighbor's house was in bad shape I would do something to help them out. There is a definite polarization here—a rich house and then a poor house.

It's been somewhat shocking to me to see such a difference in lifestyles between the wealthy and the poor.

The quality of the homes that many of the poorest on this island live in is troubling. I'm concerned that I was unaware that people in this country live in such degrading conditions.

The community service project to Johns Island was planned by a group of students from the University of South Carolina as part of a national program known as Alternative Spring Break (ASB). Because of our common interests in community service, my friend and colleague Julie Neururer had graciously invited me to join the USC group. Julie and I tagged along with two goals in mind: to participate in the community service work out of our own desire to do something constructive over our break, and to record observations and conduct interviews with students during the weeklong experience.

Twenty-four students and three staff were housed in the Rural Mission building on Johns Island. The students and staff shared housekeeping duties for the week. Some packed peanut butter and jelly lunches the night before, others got up early to make breakfast, and still others returned from working all day only to begin the evening meal. Everyone was more than willing to do whatever they could to help with group chores. There was little free time each day, but what we had was spent reflecting about the day's and week's activities. Much of this was done in groups, whereas other reflections took place as part of the interviews that Julie and I conducted.

Several of the students who participated in the Johns Island project were repeat participants from the previous year. For others, it was their first visit to that area of South Carolina. As a result, students had a variety of mixed expectations and motivations for joining the project. The following comments capture some of the students' feelings and attitudes toward their participation in the spring break project. "My expectation was that this would involve intense work and intense feelings," explained one student. "I expected I'd be getting to know people, and help the community here. I expected to give something." A second student stated, "I like to learn and to help other people. I love to learn. And it's great to do things that benefit others." And a third student with a great deal of community service experience talked about helping other volunteers make the most of the trip: "I wanted to help the other students reflect on what's going on, especially if they hadn't seen conditions like those on Johns Island."

Other students talked about their dissatisfaction with the traditional college spring break and how they wanted to do something different. As one student explained, "I was looking for something to do over spring break. I didn't want to go home, and I didn't want to sit around doing nothing. I felt I had to do something. And I had to do something I could pay for myself. My parents said they would pay for me to come home, but anything else I'd have to pay for myself. They said since I was doing this, they'd pay for it. And my friend said it would be fun." Jokingly she added, "And since I was a kid, I liked to hammer with my dad."

For several students, their participation in the project reflected their emerging commitment to community service. "My choices this year for spring break were Florida or the Alternative Spring Break trip to Johns Island," commented one student. "This is where my heart is." A second student explained why she participated in the project: "Usually during spring break everyone spends their time laying in the sun and drinking. I wanted to relax but at the same time do something for someone else." She laughed and added, "I'm certainly not in it for the carpentry experience." A third student talked about her evolving values as well as her changing sense of self: "The reason I decided to do this is for years I'd been saying 'volunteer!' But I always made excuses like 'no time,' 'too tired,' 'I have to study.' I saw the ads for Alternative Spring Break in the college paper. After putting it off for a long time, I decided to go through with this. In previous years, I've spent lots of money on spring break. I'd always go somewhere. But this time, I decided to do this. I wanted to give back to the community."

Another student contrasted her experience on the community service project to Johns Island with charity work she had done for her sorority. "At USC, I do philanthropy through my sorority. We did a Halloween carnival, and work at the Nurturing Center. But I get more out of this. The sorority efforts take only a couple of hours. When you're done you don't feel like you've done anything. . . . I ask my friends, 'Why don't you want to do this?' I tell them, 'I'm going to work on someone's house.' I don't think they understand what it means to do real community service."

A few of the students were unsure about what the Johns Island project might entail. As one student explained, "I didn't know what to expect." A second added, "I hardly knew anything about Johns Island. That's why I had so many questions for Anderson [the supervisor at the Rural Mission who guided our work]. I'd heard of Gullah, but I didn't really know much about the people here." A third student also commented on his limited knowledge of the area: "I had a vague idea of the people who live here. When I was in junior high, I remember hearing some of the spiritual songs and stories from this area. . . . And I've read Pat Conroy's *The Water Is Wide* [Conroy's novel, like *Mama Day* by Naylor, takes place in the same region]. So I had a vague impression of the community."

The preceding students offer insights into some of the expectations and motivations students had, as well as revealing some of their experiences with community service. I want to add to this discussion by introducing a personal account of a student and some of the struggles, expectations, and experiences she had in conjunction with the Johns Island project. The student is Kaitlyn Johnson, who at the time was a junior majoring in education.

A STUDENT PORTRAIT

For Kaitlyn Johnson, the trip to Johns Island was an opportunity to learn more about herself while at the same time doing something to serve others over her spring break. "I'm kind of searching right now, and this trip is part of that search. I just don't know yet what kind of person I want to become. I'm still struggling to figure it all out. These kinds of things help. I'm most genuine in these settings." (Recall from chapter 3—_Proposition 7: College students are at a time in their lives when a multitude of forces influence their sense of self; thus they often are in the midst of a period of heightened self-discovery and identity confusion._) The trip represented a chance to explore her life and the kinds of things Kaitlyn was coming to value: friends, community, understanding, and caring. "I have given more thought and effort in recent years to making and keeping friends. Maybe it's something that comes with age, but I'm beginning to value much more all the connections I have with people."

Kaitlyn had gone on the trip the previous year and was somewhat apprehensive of this year's group. She didn't know many of the other student volunteers and found a few students to be intimidating because of their strong personalities. She often was insecure among groups of students and had little self-confidence in her own personality and talents. As a junior whose goal was to become a teacher, she knew that she had to resolve some of these issues, and the Johns Island project was an opportunity to work on her self-confidence and her ability to relate to others. By the end of the week, she had discovered something about her peers as well as herself. "There are people in our group who have really strong personalities. I tend to see people like that as one-sided: They are always funny. Never say anything stupid. And they always look good. I always felt they have something more than me, that I'm not as special as they are. But this week helped me to see that even they say and do stupid things sometimes." (Recall from chapter 3—_Proposition 1: The self is formed relationally through social interactions._)

The trip had a spiritual quality for Kaitlyn that she found to be quite compelling. "I'm a Christian, and I think it's hypocritical just to take and take and never give back to others or to one's community. For my own spiritual growth, I think actions say a lot more than words. God's love is about giving and not just talking and discipling." She also noted the spiritual emphasis among the people of Johns Island. "There's something that threads through the people here. There's something that connects us all. For me it's a spiritual connection. God's love is about giving."

Kaitlyn talked about the important aspects of community service and focused on the interactional component to the experience. She explained how she perceived her own role throughout the project: "The chance to visit with Uncle Leroy may have meant more than the work we did for him. It was great to be able to visit with him. I really felt like that was my role. Building friendships with the people was rewarding enough." She thought that the most important aspect of community service was creating an opportunity for interaction among people, which for her meant establishing a caring setting in which community service might take place. "It's OK that we all have different interpretations of things that happen in our lives. The people around here see us coming as an act of Jesus. And some of us see it another way. But all that matters is that we're here and they're here and we're making connections."

The trip to Johns Island was part of a long history of Kaitlyn's involvement in community service. She had worked for low-income families in parts of Appalachia and had done more than forty hours of community service as part of her high school's graduation requirements. Community service was something she expected of herself and needed to do as part of feeling good about her life. Other students on the Johns Island project came for similar reasons. "I expected to see some people living in conditions that would make me feel like I was making a real contribution. That I could make a difference for someone. And, to get something back—positive feelings about myself. And I did." The comment from this student, as well as some of the remarks offered by Kaitlyn, remind us that community service is not only about giving; it also involves receiving.

MUTUALITY AND COMMUNITY SERVICE

Any discussion of community service must in some way deal with a central quality of the experience—the nature of the interaction between, in Howard Radest's terms, the "doer" and the "done-to." Radest (1993) argued that, in an idealized sense, an act of community service ought to involve not only the act of giving but the act of receiving as well. In giving to others, one receives in return. Radest pointed out that the idea of mutuality calls attention to the fact that the relationship between "doer" and "done-to" ought to be reciprocal: "Community service is a particular way of learning my human 'being' precisely because it is an encounter of strangers with whom I am nevertheless connected by the possibility of a reciprocal interchange of positions. I can be doer; I can be done-to" (p. 179). Radest's conception of community service challenges relationships that separate the "haves" and the "have-nots" of power and position. "To be a doer in the presence of the done-to is to mirror the other in myself; to be the done-to in the presence of the doer is to respond to the other in myself. Both of us are active; neither is passive" (p. 180).

Radest in no way implied that mutuality should result in the elimination of cultural differences between the service worker and the community member in need. He resisted the tendency of community service participants to essentialize the other and hence conclude that we are all the same—a common conclusion that students throughout my research tended to draw. Radest explained, "Mutuality should not be confused with similarity. It is precisely because the other remains the other and I remain myself that community service works out. The persistence of otherness provides community service with a permanent tension that generates its interest and our energy" (p. 180).

An idea similar to what Radest described as mutuality appears throughout much of the literature on community service and service learning, although the idea is often expressed in a different language or terminology. For example, Jane Kendall discussed "reciprocity"—"the exchange of both giving and receiving between the 'server' and the person or group 'being served'" (1990, pp. 21–22). Kendall claimed that one of the fundamental errors of the student community service movement of the 1960s and 1970s was its failure to build on the ideals of reciprocity: "We were learning that without an emphasis on the relationship between the server and 'those served' as a reciprocal exchange between equals, that relationship can easily break down. . . . Paternalism, unequal relationships between the parties involved, and a tendency to focus only on charity—'doing for' or 'helping' others—rather than on supporting others to meet their own needs all became gaping pitfalls" (pp. 9–10). For Kendall, avoiding paternalism is vital to the success of service.

> All parties in service-learning are learners and help determine what is to be learned. Both the server and those served teach, and both learn. Such a service-learning exchange avoids the traditionally paternalistic, one-way approach to service in which one person or group has resources which they share "charitably" or "voluntarily" with a person or group that lacks resources. In service-learning, those being served control the service provided; the needs of the community determine what the service tasks will be. It is this sense of reciprocity that creates a sense of mutual responsibility and respect between individuals in the service-learning exchange. (p. 22)

Although Kendall's primary concern was defining "service-learning" in such a way that it benefited both students and communities, much of her argument applies to community service work as well, especially those activities that are designed to foster students' learning (such as the Johns Island project). I say this to point out that not all community service projects have an intentional learning component built into their design. Those that do, however, seem to fit Kendall's definition of "service-learning" and I believe have a much deeper influence on students' lives.

The notion captured in the terms "mutuality" or "reciprocity" is also suggested in discussions of caring as set forth in the work of Nel Noddings: "Caring involves, for the one caring, a 'feeling with' the other. . . . The notion of 'feeling with' . . . does not involve projection but reception" (1984, p. 30). Noddings made a careful distinction between "feeling with" as an act of caring and the typical conception that might involve trying to walk in someone else's shoes or an effort to see life through someone else's eyes. The traditional view that Noddings rejected is perhaps similar to the symbolic interactionist idea of taking the role of the other. As I pointed out in chapter 2, Noddings's idea of caring seeks not to understand the world from someone else's perspective, but instead attempts to make connections to another's world. Instead of asking how one would feel if they were in a certain situation or faced the same dilemma that another faces, Noddings suggested that an individual ought to receive the other as part of his or her own self.

Noddings offered a more affective and perhaps more advanced understanding of the interactionist idea of taking the role of the other. Instead of the act being some sort of rational response in an effort to experience the world through the other, one actually becomes, in an emotional sense, connected to the other. It may be more than coincidence that most interactionists are men and tend to explain social life and acts of caring as more of a rational process, whereas feminists such as Noddings provide a vision of caring as an affectional and emotional act. The difference between the two perspectives highlights gendered ways of knowing. This, however, is not to say that all men or all women tend to be only rational or affectional knowers.

For example, Robert Coles (1993) discusses a working-class man he met through his many experiences with community service. The man had become distraught when he and his wife had a child born with Down's syndrome. The couple already had five girls, and he was working two jobs to make ends meet. When the boy was born, the man and his wife had to decide whether to care for him themselves or trust his care to an institution. They decided to keep the boy, but the husband was unable to connect emotionally with the child and sank into a deep depression. Eventually, the wife suggested that her husband see a doctor, who in turn recommended he get involved with older retarded children by volunteering at a local hospital. The doctor hoped that in time the father would have a better understanding of children with special educational needs and thus might be better equipped to interact with his own son as he matured. In time, he grew fond of three or four of the boys at the hospital. "Pretty soon he and his boys were quite a team—in sports and games and cleanup activities, in doing routines and assisting the staff with other children. Pretty soon he began to figure out ways to connect with his own son, to show the boy and his mother and sisters that there was a lot this busy mechanic could do to fix the way a home was running" (Coles, 1993, p. 84).

As the years passed, the father became more involved in his son's life and even organized a Little League team for his son and other children in the area. He recalls a response he had to a friend who called his team "special": "I didn't like the way he used the word. I felt myself getting weak. I was a little teary for a second, and my knees felt as though if someone touched me, I'd fall over. But in another second I was up for anything. I said, 'You bet we're special.' I meant it. Me and the kids, we were doing great, and we'd show him, we'd be thrilled to show him! It was then I knew I'd crossed some big street, and I was walking on the other side and my head was up, not down, and it was working with those kids that did it. They're the ones who got me across to the other side—do you see?" (p. 84). Coles added his own commentary concerning this man's struggle: "In the end . . . his pain responded to the visible, concrete opportunities a few children offered him. The gifts he bought on their birthdays and at Christmas signaled not only what these children had come to mean to him, but what they had enabled him to find and affirm in himself" (p. 85).

Through the other, we come to experience the self. Mutuality is about how we both give and receive because we connect to the other through a concern, which, in the name of caring, bridges whatever differences we have. Clearly, finding oneself through acts of caring and building connections with others is not limited to women's experience. Again, although it may be true that women are more likely to define themselves in relation to others, men also have the chance to ground their sense of self in the lives of others as opposed to more autonomous pursuits. The example Coles offers highlights how important the receiving aspect of community service experience can be for those who engage in service for and with others. To better understand the role receiving plays in community service encounters and how such experiences might inform an advanced understanding of mutuality, I introduce additional findings derived from the Johns Island project.

STUDENTS' EXPERIENCES OF RECEIVING

"I get fulfillment from doing good. I wanted to do this for myself and for other people; there's a lot of satisfaction in giving," stated a graduate student, who added emphatically, "I like to help." A second student also acknowledged the return he gets from service. "I participated in this project for selfish reasons, because of the positive feelings I get from helping others. I don't think my reasons are bad, though. I believe it is in my community's best interest to tackle social problems through volunteering and working with others." And a third student commented, "I think if I ever have a family, I'll use volunteering as a family thing because of what you get out of it."

Students talked about the feelings they experienced related to the warmth and giving of the people of Johns Island. "I realize that I have a hard time accepting gratitude in any fashion. I'm not accustomed to receiving it. I'm not used to so much sincerity," reflected one student. A second echoed those remarks, "I think now I understand why I've heard so many people talk about the low-country. This place is a really beautiful area, and the people are genuinely nice people and care about almost anyone who passes by their house." Other students were surprised and confused as to how to respond to the sincerity and acts of kindness they received. "Sometimes I feel like we get way more out of these things than we should. Do people have the right to use someone else's life for their experience? Sometimes we do things because we don't want to feel bad about ourselves by not doing anything."

The highlight of the Johns Island project for many of the students was the intimate interactions they were able to have with members of the community. Two members of the community who had a particularly profound influence on the students were Uncle Leroy, whom we have already met, and his neighbor, Miss Virginia. Both were in their sixties or seventies and had known each other since they were small children. In fact, according to Uncle Leroy, he and the rest of the neighborhood boys had a crush on Miss Virginia when they were growing up. Students spoke fondly of the two longtime island residents, and their responses call attention to the fact that mutuality was at the heart of their community service encounter. As one student explained, "Miss Virginia's house wasn't very big and we were working on a pretty big portion of it, and she was so trusting of us. And she'd never even met us. She was doing just as much for us as we were for her." Another student added, "I will never forget Miss Virginia and how she trusted us enough to welcome us into her home. I learned some things about her life. She has grandchildren and great-grandchildren. Uncle Leroy used to pick cherries for her when they were younger. He lives only about 100 yards away, and they have known each other their entire lives." A third student offered the following thoughts: "I learned about the lives of the people who live here. They opened their hearts and their homes to us. Miss Virginia gave us everything she had—frying up sausages and giving us sodas. I may never meet the woman again, but she'll always be in the back of my mind." "I like the idea of interacting with the people here on the islands," explained a fourth student, who added, "Serving people and getting to know them at the same time is so rewarding. Like Uncle Leroy. He said he was born at the beginning of the Depression, and so he's about seventy. He has an elementary school education. His father died when he was real young and had wanted Leroy to go to college and become a doctor, but he only went as far as the third grade. He worked for an electrical company and then got laid off in Charleston."

One student commented on the general outcomes associated with having personal interactions in service settings: "The whole experience helps you to see that others are real people and have real problems and yet can come together to help one another. . . . When you work with the people on their houses or in their backyard it adds to the experience. You get a chance to know the people. You have a face or a personality to go with the work." A second student contributed, "When you have so little but give so much . . . I realized how deep their faith is, and even though they only have a little they give thanks a lot."

Other members of the community also left an effect on the student volunteers. Students painted the house of a middle-aged woman with two little children. "When I was painting the house I asked myself—why are we helping these people? We are painting a house and there's dirt around it everywhere. It will probably be covered with dirt in no time. But it made me feel good to see her smile and express so much gratitude. When I met some of the people, like the kids, it put a more personal side on community service. Having the two little kids work with us was fun." A second student added, "I've learned a lot by talking with the people in the houses we're working on. There's a neat family with two little girls where we're painting the house. My impression is they're a very close-knit family."

Students' work at another site involved tearing down Mrs. Chisolm's burned-out house. The house was a five-room building with two rooms in the front, two in the middle, and a kitchen in the back. The front and middle rooms were very small; each was probably no more than eight feet square. The fire had destroyed most of the house, but because of new building codes we had to leave part of the house standing; the house was too close to another residence, and if it were to be completely torn down and rebuilt from scratch the new zoning codes would apply and thus require that it be relocated. The "strategic" plan was to tear down everything but the kitchen and then build onto the remaining structure. Eventually, the kitchen would be torn down and in effect a new house would be built, but in stages. Clearly, it was a case of circumventing the building codes.

Although many of the work sites were fun and involved a great deal of energetic interaction and sharing with the residents, this was not the case with this site, where Mrs. Chisolm had lost most of her personal possessions. I recall arriving at the house on Monday morning. One of our first steps was to examine the inside of the house and figure out what could be saved. The fire apparently had started in the corner of one of the front rooms, where a small propane heater was still standing amid its own destruction. The house was obviously a fire trap. There were two other portable electric heaters, and judging by their location, they both had been plugged into the same overburdened electrical outlet. There was no furnace, and even though it was South Carolina it could still get quite cold around the sea islands as the nights we spent at the Rural Mission confirmed. The fire had swished across the wall from the heater and broken like a wave down the opposite side of the room, melting several family portraits into oblivion. The fire had stopped about two feet from the floor and then apparently moved to the other areas of the house by way of the ceiling and then the roof. A few charred two-by-fours were all that remained of what once kept Mrs. Chisolm safe from the southern rain.

Our job was to remove all the personal items and then tear down about 80 percent of the structure. We had no idea of how to go about our work, but learned as we went. We carried various items to Mrs. Chisolm, who sat in an old charred chair positioned about fifteen feet from the front steps to the house, which remained invitingly intact. She was too elderly and delicate to be of help with the physical challenge that lay ahead but offered her assistance in making decisions about what to keep and what to throw away. For this task, she was more than sturdy enough, for she seemed to handle the pain of seeing most of her material past disappear with the grace of an angel. Many of us were not nearly so graceful and struggled to create the right attitude within ourselves and among the group at what for us was a hallowed work site. As the week and the project progressed, we gradually replaced the sentimentality of tearing down a house with the more cheerful and joyous notion of building a new home for Mrs. Chisolm.

As I removed the shredded and charred furnishings by throwing them out a large hole burned in the side of the house, I came upon a stack of pictures. One was of a young man in an Army uniform. Another appeared to be Mrs. Chisolm standing in front of an old dark blue Buick, perhaps a '58 or '59. I handed her the pictures, and she identified the soldier as her son and herself standing in front of "dat ol' Buick." I asked her how long she had lived in the house. "Ever since 1950 when I moved from the plantation." I had a strong desire to learn more about her life on the plantation, but at the same time I felt like an intruder. I went back to the task at hand, all the while daydreaming about the interactions and lives that had once intersected this sea island home. I wondered if much had changed for Mrs. Chisolm over the past forty years. Judging by the few appliances and the burnt furniture that looked like stuff my grandmother once owned, little seemed to have transpired. But then again, I was guessing about her life by her possessions. Does the material trail we leave behind reveal to others who we are?

A number of students had to deal with feelings of guilt as a result of receiving so much kindness from the Johns Island residents. Some questioned the rightness of it all. The following comments offer insight into some of the thoughts and feelings the students had throughout the project:

I've always liked to do volunteer work because it makes me feel wonderful. I feel guilty to get so much out of it.

These people have given me so much. What I've given is superficial compared to what they gave to me.

I think you get more out of these kinds of experiences than you put in. The people on this island gave us an appreciation and kindness that is so genuine. You can't fake that.

I'm reluctant to acknowledge what we are doing as anything that deserves recognition or a reward of any kind. I think just getting a chance to talk to Uncle Leroy is a big enough reward.

These students call attention to a point Robert Wuthnow made when he wrote, "We can really be of no use to anyone else unless we take care of ourselves" (1991, p. 286). A message that might be conveyed to new volunteers is the following: It is all right to feel good about yourself for giving time and energy toward serving another.

Apparent throughout this section is the degree of satisfaction and indeed joy the students experienced as part of their efforts to serve the residents of Johns Island. The attitude of the students in general was captured by two students who wrote the following passages in a group journal:

I really didn't know what to expect when I signed up for ASB, but I didn't expect it to be as wonderful as it was. I haven't worked this hard in years, but I'm not even sore because it has felt so good. This has been a wonderful week for making friends and helping others. I think we've all learned a little about ourselves and much about how our lives differ from others'. The words family and community mean much more to me now. I think I'll call my mom and dad when I get home.

I have absolutely no regrets being a part of ASB. I've always felt that I had a civic duty to serve society, but now I realize that I can actually have fun doing it! My main "job" was to help destroy and rebuild a porch for Miss Virginia. I felt a great deal of accomplishment after standing back in her yard and looking at this new structure that I helped build. But I felt an even greater sense of accomplishment after seeing Miss Virginia's face light up as she stood on her new porch. Her smile and her warm hugs captured the essence and the spirit of why we came to John's Island in the first place—to serve those less fortunate than ourselves.

Although I disagree with any language that categorizes those with less wealth than ourselves as "less fortunate" (and I am guilty of this myself sometimes—in part because we lack an effective language for deciphering the relationship between the self and the other), the preceding comments nonetheless capture how giving often has nothing to do with the financial measure of a person. We seem to have a hard time escaping the trap of basing definitions of the "fortunate" and "unfortunate" solely on the grounds of materialism and income. Yet the students involved in this project learned a great deal about the wealth of the people of the Johns Island community and their spirit of giving.

A prime example of the giving spirit of the community was a seafood jamboree that residents of the island planned and then hosted at the Rural Mission for the volunteers. During the jamboree, elderly women from a local church choir sat around the perimeter of the dining area and sang hymns to the student volunteers, who were seated at the center tables. The women also helped in serving the meal to the volunteers and then took their turn eating as well. Students were unsure of how to handle all the attention and service bestowed on them. After all, they were the ones who had come to serve. Or so they thought. "Some of us were uncomfortable with them sitting around the edge of the room and us as the center of attention. Them doing all the giving. It's as if we don't feel we are worthy of receiving. If you are willing to give, then I guess you must be willing to receive. That's what makes a community—a degree of sharing."

Feelings of guilt were prevalent among students who saw themselves as having so much more in terms of financial security and resources than the people of Johns Island. Coles points out that this is sometimes cause for despair among community service workers and volunteers: "This distinction between one's own prospects and the prospects of those with whom one is working may well account for despair in many volunteers. They feel considerable discomfort at the disparity and an increased consciousness of their own good luck; in contrast, the misfortunes of others seem engraved fatefully in stone" (1993, p. 133). The combination of being situated as the privileged (in terms of materialism) and then having to be on the receiving end of the generosity of the Johns Island residents was more than a challenge for some of the students.

Not only did students feel guilty about receiving, some felt bad about not being able to do more. The following comments from one student are insightful: "Some of us had a conversation about judging Sharon [a Johns Island resident whose home needed repairs]. In two days we only spent thirteen hours at her house. That's not long enough to judge someone. We don't know the circumstances that caused her to let her house go. I thought of the cleaning and the painting as a job to do, but today, I thought of her as someone who needs and deserves my help. And not 40, 50, or 60 percent of my help. All of my help. It meant a lot to give to her. . . . There's no material satisfaction from doing this, but inside I know there's more important things than financial or material rewards. And I felt bad because we weren't able to get enough done on her house."

Throughout the Johns Island project, students experienced the challenges and benefits of a mutually structured service experience. They learned that in giving you must be willing to receive. Otherwise, the service encounter becomes nothing more than charity, with the volunteer situated in a position of privilege, which is likely to be disempowering for community members with a need. One student who participated in the Johns Island project had some important thoughts on working with low-income families, both during this project and during a project from the previous year. His name is Jack Burkeholder.

A STUDENT PROFILE

Jack Burkeholder was a graduate student at the University of South Carolina studying student affairs administration when I first met him in the spring of 1994. This was the second time he had participated in a spring break project to Johns Island, but this time he was one of the student leaders who had helped to plan the project. I interviewed Jack twice during the weeklong project and again nearly a year later, after he had graduated and taken a position working in student activities at another southern university.

During the first interview, he talked about his involvement from the previous year. Jack thought that the experience he had gained during the first project to Johns Island gave him some insights that helped him assume more of a leadership role the second time around. He was able to explain to students some of the unique social and cultural aspects of Johns Island and thought that the students were better prepared the second year. He talked briefly about his experience from the first year: "At the end of the week I realized how much I had learned from the group and from the community. Last year I met Mrs. Guilford, and it put a face with the service I did. It was a good feeling for me to do something for somebody else. I think all of us fed off the appreciation we received from the residents of Johns Island. There is this energy that is contagious."

Jack went on to talk about his expectations for this year's trip. He was eager to learn more about the members of the group and was excited about meeting additional people from the community. "I expect to have more interaction with members of the community. I think there is a lot of fear when you meet someone who is different than you, but after a while you begin to feel more comfortable. I think it helps you to get to know yourself better, too. You learn about some of your fears and have a chance to grow from what you learn. And people who have had different life experiences are able to show you things that you've never seen before—sometimes even things about yourself." (Recall from chapter 3—*Proposition 9: Participation in community service provides a means to foster a sense of connectedness and offers an opportunity for students to understand themselves and to develop caring selves.*)

At the end of the week, I asked Jack to reflect on the week's experiences and describe the things that were most important to him. He talked about his interactions with Miss Virginia and with the other students who participated in the trip. What was most important to him were the friends he had made. As Jack pointed out, there is a natural bonding that goes on among people who are involved in community service work. "That's one of the reasons I enjoy community service so much. It's not just the joy I have about giving to someone else, but it's also the fun and excitement you experience when you're really wrapped up in a project with a group of people who also want to give to others. It reminds me that the kid in me still exists."

Nearly a year later, when I caught up with Jack again, I asked him to think about community service issues in general and what he thought was most important to consider in structuring activities such as the Johns Island project. He mentioned some of the important aspects of planning and carrying out community service projects, but I pushed him to delve deeper into the relational qualities of service. "How should students relate to those they work to serve?" He responded, "I think you have to see things in terms of broader issues. You need to understand that there is a great deal of unfairness and inequality and that you can play a part in creating change. You can't blame the poor for being poor, at least not in most cases. You have to understand that people have different barriers to overcome. I have found that meeting people and interacting with them helps me to see that the barriers they face are real and if I care about living in a better society, then I need to contribute in some way, even if it's only helping to fix someone's roof, or their porch. You have to be willing to treat all people with dignity. Everyone deserves that." (Recall from chapter 3— *Proposition 10: Caring selves are critical to the process of democracy and the struggle to build a more just and equitable society. Without a strong concern for others as a vital aspect of the self, it is unlikely that democracy can be sustained within postmodern times.*)

During Jack's first year at his new job he was left with too little time to participate as often as he desired in community service. He had worked with some student groups to plan and conduct a harvest festival for some of the economically disadvantaged youth of the area and he enjoyed that a great deal. He longed for more of those kinds of experiences and seemed a bit down about not being able to touch the part of himself that the work on Johns Island had brought out so vividly.

COLLABORATION AND EQUITY

Radest maintained, "Mutuality announces the actual meeting of strangers in a particular way, the reciprocal encounters of doer and done-to, the capacity to be active, to accept, to move between, and to sustain self respect in the exchange" (1993, p. 190). When Jack Burkeholder talked about ways that he believed community service workers ought to relate to community members, he alluded to his concern about "living in a better society" and went on to mention the importance of "treating all people with dignity." Interestingly enough, Jack relied on what might be considered a classic male-centered approach to making sense of mutuality by embracing a language of equality and social justice. Compare his comments to those offered by Kaitlyn earlier in this chapter. Recall how she described mutuality between community service workers and community members. For example, she stated that she saw as her primary role making connections with members of the community and talked about visiting with Uncle Leroy: "The chance to visit with Uncle Leroy may have meant more than the work we did for him. It was great to be able to visit with him. I really felt like that was my role. Building friendships with the people was rewarding enough." Kaitlyn explained that to her the most important aspect of community service was to create a "caring atmosphere" in which differences between doer and done-to may be embraced and not silenced. As she explained, "It's OK that we all have different interpretations of things that happen in our lives. The people around here see us coming as an act of Jesus. And some of us see it another way. But all that matters is that we're here and they're here and we're making connections."

Jack also discussed his involvement in service from what seems like a more relational orientation when he talks about the excitement he gets from interacting with community members and the friendships that develop with fellow volunteers. The community service experience reminds him that the kid in him still exists. Like Jack, Kaitlyn also reveals both patterns of reasoning. Although relational ways of knowing seemed to be most prevalent in her discussion of the Johns Island project—"building friendships" with the residents of the island was first and foremost in Kaitlyn's mind—she also alluded to aspects of service and the project, which reflected a moral and rational tone. An example was when she spoke of her religious commitments and motivation for serving others: "I'm a Christian and I think it's hypocritical just to take and take and never give back to others or to one's community."

Jack and Kaitlyn highlight the notion that although generalized patterns of knowing often are tied to gender through male and female socialization, there are multiple ways people come to know their worlds and that some students are able to incorporate diverse patterns of understanding. Both Jack and Kaitlyn have learned to "take the role of the other" as well as to "walk with the other."

In general, I did not observe any significant differences in how the men and women involved in this study made sense of acts of caring or the meaning of community service. Some demonstrated relational styles, whereas others offered moralistic and rational explanations, but gender was not an obvious factor. And some students such as Jack and Kaitlyn revealed complex ways of knowing in that they seemed to incorporate both relational and moralistic understandings into their discussions of caring and service. The one difference between men and women that I did note was discussed in chapter 1, when I pointed out that women were more likely to raise questions about various social structures and policies. I maintain that women's tendency to question the social system possibly is rooted in their nonprivileged positions as women in a patriarchal society.

From Jack and Kaitlyn, as well as others such as Samuel Frias and Carolyn Fisher, we can see that community service is an educational activity that fosters a good deal of thought about the meaning and importance of caring. Too often, educational activities are centered on competition and individualism, in which students rarely get a chance to build diverse ways of understanding their social worlds.

Throughout my observations and interviews with students, I was somewhat surprised to find that many of the men adopt relational styles of knowing. The explanation I offer is that the men who volunteer to do service work may be more inclined to care for others than perhaps the general male population. Another explanation is that the community service context forces men to think about relationships and connectedness, and these thoughts often come out during interviews and small-group reflections. I think both explanations make sense, but the latter offers support for encouraging other, less relationally inclined men to become involved in community service.

One of the primary points of this book is that educational contexts tend to favor male-oriented perspectives, and greater opportunities and structures are needed that foster what typically have been thought of as women's ways of knowing. I contend that both men and women stand to benefit from greater emphasis on relational forms of knowing; women will feel more confident about the ways they have come to understand the world, and men will learn more about the other and the importance of relationships. In addition, when we foster relational ways of knowing and enhance an ethic of care, society benefits as the possibility for building community becomes greater. I discuss the issue of community building in more detail in the next chapter.

Community service, therefore, is one aspect of higher learning that may be used to highlight and encourage diverse ways of understanding the self and the other and thus tends to foster a more caring sense of self. As Brian Morris pointed out, feminists such as Gilligan do not necessarily reject moral reasoning based on rights and equality but instead tend to argue "for an enlarged and revised conception of morality that takes into account the ideals of compassion and caring for others that are articulated by women" (1994, p. 177). What is needed is a higher education grounded in an expanded view of morality that emphasizes diverse ways of knowing. (Recall from chapter 3—*Proposition 8: Education plays a critical role in fostering student learning and development and thus provides a context for student self-exploration and identity development.*) Therefore, efforts to advance connected ways of knowing, such as encouraging student involvement in community service, must be brought forward to center stage.

The examples of Jack Burkeholder and Kaitlyn Johnson highlight the idea that community service workers also receive benefits from the service encounter. Mutuality implies a degree of collaboration and equality between parties involved in service and rejects the patronizing perspectives often suggested in the idea of charity. "Rather than helping, some people view volunteering as a way to put people in their place, or as trying to save them," one student explained. "I believe everyone should help—including those in need—and everyone has a responsibility to help people out. My father is a dentist, so I know I've been privileged. It's luck. . . . We all have limitations, so it's important to help people out and stop complaining about other people." For this student, "everyone" includes not only those who are well off financially but anyone who has a neighbor in need.

Students repeatedly expressed the positive results of being able to work with residents of Johns Island. Although not all work sites involved collaborative efforts between the student volunteers and community members, those that did provided a different kind of learning context for the students. In particular, students who helped at the house of one woman who tried to work between watching her two children enjoyed the camaraderie that evolved over the two-day project. Again, there was a sense among the students at this site that they were working together—to borrow Radest's language—the doers and the done-tos striving together to improve conditions.

SUMMARY

Students were quick to acknowledge the fact that they had received a great deal in return for their efforts. It is somewhat surprising that students occasionally were taken aback by this aspect of service. In fact, many seemed ill prepared to receive, and they exhibited a certain degree of awkwardness and reluctance. Recall how one student described feeling somewhat out of place during the seafood jamboree because the volunteers had been made the center of attention and the community residents—supposedly the people to be served—were doing the serving.

At other times, students were caught off guard by acts of caring and giving offered by the residents of the island. Miss Virginia provided sausages and sodas to the students who built her porch, and some of them felt guilty for accepting the offer. In part, students saw the limited resources of some residents of the community and did not want to subtract from those resources by accepting food and drinks that obviously cost money. They accepted the offers obligingly, but later in the evening reflected on their ambiguous feelings and attitudes toward receiving.

Students were more receptive to the knowledge that was shared with them by the residents with whom they interacted. Uncle Leroy told stories about his experiences growing up on the island and picking cherries for Miss Virginia when they were kids. He also talked about his father, who had wanted him to become a doctor, but unfortunately he had to quit school in the third grade to get a job. Students found the sharing of experiences to be an easier gift to accept and cherish than the food and beverages that often were handed to them by the humblest of hands.

Although students recognized the rewards of working alongside the community members of Johns Island, for the most part they did not comprehend or at least did not discuss the significance of community members themselves participating in the service activity. Students tended to see the benefits they received from mutuality, but they failed to see how involvement on the part of community members served some of the residents' intrinsic needs. Whereas the extrinsic benefits derived by the community members was obvious to students, by the excitement and smiles of Johns Island residents, intrinsic rewards rarely came up in students' conversations. However, in discussions with the residents, it was seen that working alongside or interacting with the students was a joyous opportunity that led at least two of the women of the island to claim a couple of the students as their adopted children.

This chapter highlighted the idea that community service ideally ought to involve a degree of mutuality in which reciprocity exists between the community service workers and the community members. Mutuality needs to be understood in two ways. First, acts of community service ought to involve both parties in the development and structuring of the service project or activity. Community members must be engaged in identifying the needs to be met by the service activity as well as in determining how best to go about meeting such needs. Too often, service is undertaken as a patronizing endeavor in which community members—those designated to receive—rarely are consulted about what their real needs are. Such service is not community service, at least not in the truest sense of what "community" means.

The second aspect of mutuality involves more of a recognition than a conscious plan. The idea is that both those in the community with a designated need and those participating in the service act receive benefits from the encounter. This was clearly revealed by the students who participated in the Johns Island project. They reported receiving in a variety of ways. For many, this was an unexpected outcome. Some of the students had a hard time recognizing that it was acceptable to embrace the good feelings that often come with working with others to improve their lives. And clearly, the members of the community were excited about the improvements to their homes that the students helped to accomplish. They were also warmed by their interactions with the students and thus benefited from the sense of community advanced between the two groups. The mutual benefits that community service workers and community members receive need to be addressed more openly so that both parties recognize that each is doing for and with the other. Mutuality reminds us that the encounter needs to be seen for what it ought to be—a joint action involving equal decision making and offering benefits to all parties.

Chapter 6

Community Building

*A shared sense of community replaces the void
of individual estrangement. Only by acting for
the other does one come to know one's self, not
in isolation from the ties that bind each to all
but in affirmation of them.*
　　　　—Tom Regan, The Thee Generation

In 1965 we moved from a farmhouse in Hickory, Pennsylvania to an apartment in the Farrell projects. What was most interesting about our move was the fact that we left a predominantly White, rural neighborhood for a more urban, Black neighborhood where we were one of only two White families. Our apartment building was in the middle of a U-shaped section of three buildings situated on a hill overlooking a large factory called the Sharon Steel. The steel mill was the largest employer in this region known as the Shenango Valley and produced a distinctively foul odor that came to be a part of our experience in Farrell.

Life as one of only two White families was a little intimidating at first. After a while though I grew to like the Farrell projects because I enjoyed having so many kids around to play basketball, baseball, and football with. Every evening a group of us would gather on the steps of one of the nearby apartments and engage in the daily conversations about who was better at basketball, or baseball, or who was the fastest runner. The bragging eventually shifted to personal challenges as the conversations turned to foot races around the block. As a kid in a low-income neighborhood, being athletically inclined made making friends a piece of cake.

The same was not true for my older brother Gary, who tended to be drawn toward interests other than sports. For example, Gary was a mechanical wizard and could take just about anything apart and put it back together again—at least most of the time. While I found the atmosphere of the projects inviting, Gary made few friends and in fact was at war with many of our neighbors. He and the neighbors traded insults on almost a daily basis and it was hard to say who resented the other more.

Although my sister Kim seemed to get along all right (she was only five years old), and Jamie was still a baby (she was two years old), as a family we were not very accepted in our new surroundings. I remember the tension we experienced as we walked from the street to our apartment at the end of the sidewalk. Our neighbors, who sat on their steps laughing and joking, were suddenly hush, until we walked by and then snickers could be heard, and then an uproar, and then a return to the previous joviality.

To put things in perspective, it is important to note that it was 1965 and the Watts riots in California were still fresh in everybody's mind. The Civil Rights movement was in full swing and the increased consciousness of Blacks to White privilege was paramount. From the perspective of the Blacks in the Farrell projects, we were just one more example of White privilege and if they weren't careful, pretty soon the entire projects would be overrun with Whites. The fact that we also were a low-income family made little difference; the projects were Black space and we were infringing.

The daily tensions that included name calling, an occasional rock thrown haphazardly in someone's general direction, or simply dirty looks, came to a head one late summer day. I can't remember all the details, but I do remember a group of about fifteen to twenty Black teenagers and young adults banging on our front door and screaming at us to "get the hell out of our neighborhood!" I also can remember my brother going upstairs to the bathroom and tossing water on the people down below. Gary, ever the antagonist, was never one to back down from a confrontation, even when it seemed like the prudent thing to do.

As it turned out, Gary had had a run-in with several of the youth and the name calling had escalated into a confrontation at our front door. My mother did not know what to do (we did not have a phone), but she came to realize on this day that we had to move out of the Farrell projects. As for the ruckus at our door, as best as I can recollect, the cops were called and calm was eventually restored. A few days later we moved to the projects in Reynolds, Pennsylvania, a predominantly White neighborhood. My mother found a job at Blazon (a factory in Reynolds that made children's toys) and economically things improved for awhile.

———

Race, and the meaning we construct around race in our society, played the central role in my family's negative experience in the Farrell projects. We played a role and the Blacks living near us played a role. We feared them because they were Black. They resented us because we were White. From time to time, one of us, a member of my family or one of our neighbors, saw more than simply a White or a Black person and became friends or at least friendly. In the end, however, the fear and the resentment were too strong to overcome and we never became part of the community existing within the Farrell projects.

In this chapter, I highlight some key issues related to building community and the role caring and community service play in such activities. I use a community service project conducted on Yonges Island, South Carolina to make several points. One point in particular deals with the contemporary challenge to build community within a culturally diverse and at times fragmented society. Unlike many traditional views of community, which tend to situate cultural differences as a barrier, I treat diversity as a source of community building. Central to the process of community building is an ethic of care, which I argue may be fostered among students by community service participation. I use my childhood experience in the Farrell projects as a backdrop, which I return to from time to time to reinforce various points related to community. Before proceeding to discuss the Yonges Island project and its implications, I believe a brief review may be helpful.

A BRIEF REVIEW

Community service often involves encountering diverse others in a variety of dynamic cultural and interactional contexts. (Recall from chapter 3— *Proposition 2: Culture provides the parameters for social interaction and at the same time is modified through social interaction.*) As a result, community service offers many students the opportunity to develop a more advanced understanding of diverse cultural identities. Despite a more advanced understanding of the diverse other, there is nonetheless a tendency to essentialize identity as a means of dealing with the challenges of diversity. Thus, for many of the students who participated in this study, the other was situated either as the same as oneself or as completely different from oneself. Only a few students were able to grasp the dynamic and complex nature of difference and similarity. These students seemed to recognize (in their own vocabulary) that people have multiple selves that connect to and disconnect from others in a variety of complex ways. (Recall from chapter 3—*Proposition 6: Postmodern identities are more fragmented and decentered, and the challenge to establish a clear sense of self is more vexing than ever before.*)

In addition, mutuality plays a fundamental role in community service work with others and has two aspects. One aspect relates to the notion that both the community service worker and the community member benefit from the service activity. A second aspect of mutuality involves an idealized vision of community service, which stresses equal participation in identifying needs and planning how such needs might be met. Mutuality thus emphasizes collaboration and equality between community service workers and those in need of service. It is when the ideal of mutuality is met that volunteerism becomes something more than charity and hence contributes to community building and in the truest sense becomes *community* service.

Community building often requires that those involved in community service cross cultural borders defined by race and/or social class. Throughout this research project, students stressed how activities such as community service are helpful in bridging cultural differences and in making connections with diverse others. (Recall from chapter 3—*Proposition 9: Participation in community service provides a means to foster a sense of connectedness and offers an opportunity for students to understand themselves and to develop caring selves.*) "Everyone has a part deep down inside that longs for respect and understanding," stated one student. He went on, "If we each try to find that part in ourselves and look for it in each other we can create bonds and break down barriers." The challenge we face in today's culturally diverse society is to cross cultural borders through community building activities such as community service. However, we must avoid the modernist tendency to view social life as a unified whole, in which cultural difference is seen as a threat to the social good and a common identity is demanded of everyone. Such a view promotes an uncaring attitude toward difference and tends to silence cultural diversity.

Two examples from students' experiences highlight the potential for community building to be central to the service encounter. An undergraduate who participated in a Habitat for Humanity project on Maryland's eastern shore commented on a family who worked with us to build what was to become their home. There were a mother and two little boys, roughly eight and ten years old. "It's great to be able to work with the family and help them to build their own house. The kids take such pride in being able to pound in some nails or give someone a hand." Habitat for Humanity has long had a policy encouraging future home owners to help with the construction. As a result, community service workers and community members in need work alongside one another, thus not only creating a dwelling but fostering community as well. Students involved in the D.C. project also enjoyed opportunities to interact with homeless volunteers who worked in the soup kitchens. Many of these volunteers would not accept free meals unless they were allowed to help. The students thus had numerous opportunities to work alongside homeless citizens and could share with one another as they literally rubbed elbows washing dishes or stirring a giant vat of soup. One student commented on her experience: "For me, getting a chance to actually work in a soup kitchen with the people we came to serve was the most rewarding part of the experience. There's more of a feeling of being in something together, even if it's only preparing a meal." Community service involves something more than building homes and preparing meals. There is the additional possibility for a meaningful connection between the doer and the done-to. In fact, in the ideal sense of community service, it may be difficult to determine who is the doer and who is the done-to.

In chapter 5, I described the community of Johns Island and an area of South Carolina known as the low-country. I noted that Johns Island is one of four islands constituting the Charleston Sea Islands. The others are Edisto, Wadmalaw, and Yonges Islands. The last island—Yonges—is the setting for this chapter as I focus on the ideal of community and how it relates to students and their involvement in service. Two students offer some insights and help to highlight the community-building quality of effective community service. "I never expected to have such a deep and meaningful experience. I just thought I'd paint a few walls, put up some playground equipment, and catch some rays. I admit that getting a chance to go to South Carolina for less than a hundred bucks had a great deal to do with why I went. But what sticks out for me is the incredible contact I had with members of the community. I learned so much about their lives. You know, they are not very poor at all if you look beyond their financial situation and consider other things that matter in life." And a second student added, "I cannot explain what the whole project meant to me. To have the chance to get to know the people on a first-name basis meant everything."

Although much of the ensuing discussion about community building revolves around our work on Yonges Island, additional data from a wide range of students' experiences with community service are also included. More often than not, I specify the source of the students' service experience and whether their involvement was part of the Yonges Island project or some other service project. Again, the data from this book were not derived solely from week-long intensive experiences such as Alternative Spring Breaks. I simply use some of these weeklong excursions to highlight key issues that perhaps get magnified under such intense circumstances (such as the importance of "border crossing"). I believe the magnification of the intense experiences does not distort the students' learning outcomes and self-exploration, but instead serves to make more vivid the significance of different aspects of service. The data I collected from students involved in other service contexts tend to support such a conclusion because similar learning outcomes were revealed.

THE YONGES ISLAND PROJECT

The low-country region of South Carolina and Georgia has attracted considerable attention from both cultural anthropologists and novelists. For example, both Gloria Naylor's (1988) *Mama Day* and Pat Conroy's (1972) *The Water Is Wide* are set in the low-country region bordering these two southern states. Conroy's description of the fictional Yamacraw Island could apply to several of the sea islands within the area stretching from Savannah to Charleston as they might have existed two decades ago.

> Yamacraw is an island off the South Carolina mainland not far from Savannah, Georgia. The island is fringed with green undulating marshes of the southern coast; shrimp boats ply the waters around her and fishermen cast their lines along her bountiful shores. Deer cut through her forests in small silent herds. The great southern oaks stand broodingly on her banks. The island and the water around her teem with life. There is something eternal and indestructible about the tide-eroded shores and the dark threatening silences of the swamps in the heart of the island. Yamacraw is beautiful because man has not yet had time to destroy this beauty. (p. 3)

Conroy went on to write that the twentieth century had basically passed by this area of the South. Since his novel was published, however, much has changed about the region as development on the islands has expanded rapidly. Hilton Head, Kiawah, and Seabrook Islands are examples of the rapid growth in the development of tourism centered on improved beachfronts, marinas, vacation homes, and restaurants. Many of the longtime residents have been caught in the middle of the rapid economic expansion that has left their rich cultural traditions dangling in the balance of time. Students were struck by the contrast between modernization and development and the rich island traditions. A student reflected on a church service she attended on the island and on how it seemed to contradict so much else that she saw there. "It was quite strange for me to go to the Pentecostal service. It reminded me of being back in the 1950s. Everything about the church was so old fashioned. I liked it. I enjoyed the friendliness of it all. The love that they conveyed for us was truly sincere. But what stands out for me is it's such a striking contrast to all the other things going on around here. You can travel down the road and pass an old-fashioned country church and then you'll see a marina with yachts and yacht houses. It's just so strange to me." A second student also highlighted the stark contrasts: "Have you ever watched the Twilight Zone? Yonges Island kind of makes me think of that show. Things are kind of bizarre. It's very advanced in parts and then it's like time stopped. Like all the clocks stopped ticking and nothing changed. And people just went on living and were happy that progress seemed to pass them by. Kind of makes you think about what progress is, doesn't it?"

Many of the African American residents who live in the sea island area, such as Johns and Yonges Islands, are descendants of slaves and practice some of the traditions passed down through years since well before the Emancipation Proclamation. Tradition is important to many of the low-country residents, as Conroy points out in his discussion of Yamacraw: "It is not a large island, nor an important one, but it represents an era and a segment of history that is rapidly dying in America. The people of the island have changed very little since the Emancipation Proclamation. . . . They love their island with genuine affection but have watched the young people move to the city, to the lands far away and removed from Yamacraw. The island is dying, and the people know it" (p. 4).

The islands are dying because of the changing economy of the area and of the country. Small-time farming and fishing no longer can compete with the larger agricultural and fishing conglomerates, and the residents of the sea islands have been forced to seek employment within a service industry catering to tourism. Gaining employment has required relocation for some and traveling long distances to work for others. For the young, it has meant leaving the area upon graduation from high school or college or suffering the same economic woes of their parents. This has added to the intergenerational tension between the youths and their elders. Both the problems of the development and its effect on the relationships between the young and the old are highlighted by one of the central characters in Naylor's book: "Hadn't we seen it happen back in the '80s on St. Helena, Daufuskie, and St. John's? And before that on Hilton Head? Got them folks' land, built fences around it first thing, and then brought in all the builders and high-paid managers from mainside—ain't nobody on them islands benefited. And the only dark faces you see now in them 'vacation paradises' is the ones cleaning the toilets and cutting the grass. On their own land, mind you, their own land" (p. 6).

The increased accessibility of islands such as Yonges parallels a rapidly evolving culture that threatens the deeply held traditions of the community's elders. Naylor's work, whose setting is a fictional sea island close to Charleston called Willow Springs, captures some of the unique cultural traditions of the low-country region, which have evolved out of a combination of African and Caribbean customs (including Haitian voodoo or "hoodoo" to the residents of Willow Springs) mixed in with Western beliefs such as Christianity. Mama Day, the matriarch of Willow Springs, combines Christian spirituality with many of the cures, spells, and traditions of voodoo and knowledge of the woods, winds, and whispers. In the following passage, Naylor offers some insight into the magical powers of Mama Day as she evaluates an upcoming storm: "They can storm warn all they want, hurricane-watch till they're silly— she didn't have to stand by for no further bulletins. The only news that mattered started coming in a week ago; the final warnings she needed was in them snake trails she had to cross. . . . Them diamondbacks and copperheads was always the last to smarten up. No, next to the last; after the snakes came all them meters and graphs down at the Hurricane Center" (p. 243). Mama Day represents a fading figure within island communities such as the fictional Willow Springs and the real-life Yonges Island. She stands as a symbol of the past—the mother of the life whom residents of the sea islands once knew.

Another fading element of the culture of the sea island area is the language of Gullah, which is a combination of English and African languages. Although most of the residents speak English, a few of the elders still speak Gullah. During a community dinner, some of us were able to listen in on a conversation among five elderly women who conversed using what sounded to us like it might be Gullah. Occasionally, we were able to comprehend a word or two as we recognized some English that they used, but with strange accents and crescendos. Eventually, I tried my luck interacting with this group of women. I wanted to learn more about a wild weed or herb that supposedly grew in the woods around Yonges Island and that had been described to us by one of the community's elders as "life everlasting." The elder had described a variety of "medicinal" uses for the weed: "You can use it for anything from a cold or flu to stiff joints to the chills. It even cures just being sad. You can cut it up and mix it with your tea, or you can roll it up and put it in your pipe like tobacco." Life everlasting sounded strangely similar to another weed I had once heard of. I was interested in locating some of this wondrous weed—for its medicinal value, of course!

All five of the women laughed and smiled when I mentioned life everlasting, but they nearly rolled over and split a gut when I asked them where I could get some. Were these people pulling my leg? Or did they merely appreciate my eagerness to participate in an aspect of their culture?

When the laughter finally subsided, they began to respond to my request. I could comprehend only a few words, but what I understood them to say was that the local sheriff wasn't too fond of their using life everlasting and that it was best to keep it a secret. Whoops!

The community of Yonges Island, like other low-country communities, found itself caught in the crossroads between the past, with its predictable and knowable patterns of communication, and an ever-changing outside world that was hanging over their heads like a southern storm. The traditions, superstitions, and beliefs that had lasted for hundreds of years were vanishing as more and more youths either escaped the island or rejected their parents' ways. The rising skepticism of the youths of the area paralleled their growing interest in and dependence on popular culture. While the elders of the island, such as Mrs. Multree, one of the matriarchs of the community, held to the strength of their spiritual convictions, the young more and more frequently turned toward materialism and the fast-paced world depicted on television. For many of the younger people, the pace of life on the island was just too snail-like; they desired a more modernized setting in which there were more job opportunities and chances to pursue some of their material interests. The elders faced the reality that the community as they once had known it was eroding; the young were slowly leaving, and there were fewer and fewer of them to carry on the past.

The rich traditions of the low-country region were not lost on the students who participated in the Yonges Island project. "I can only imagine how interesting it must be to have such a rich sense of one's past," commented one student, who went on to say, "Heck, I'm not even sure of what my nationality is. I'm an American, but other than that I'm not sure where my ancestors are from." And yet, despite the rich sense of tradition, Yonges Island has not been immune to the music videos of MTV, the jackets of the Oakland Raiders, the Nike hats and T-shirts of Michael Jordan, or teenage and young-adult violence that has progressively crept to the forefront of the youth culture in our society. (Before the service work on Yonges Island, a youth had been killed in a drive-by shooting while playing at a local playground.) It was the tide of popular culture, including youth violence, that many of the elders found themselves battling. We were part of their plan, in that they hoped we could somehow contribute to their effort to engage the youths of the island in more productive activities, such as school and community involvement. Specifically, they had asked a local church in Charleston to provide some financial support as well as some able bodies to renovate their community center and help them get a community education program up and running. A campus ministry at Pennsylvania State University had found out about the request through colleagues in Charleston and had, in turn, organized a group of about twenty students to participate in the project over their spring break. Another trip was conducted the following year, with a similar number of students. The data concerning the Yonges Island project thus were derived from both trips.

In addition to representing some of the rich traditions of African Americans of the area—such as the Gullah language—Yonges Island also reflected many of the oppressive aspects of the broader culture and social structure of the United States. For example, a large percentage of the people of Yonges Island were unemployed and existed well below the poverty level. Many of those who were employed had to be bused daily to the tourist areas such as Hilton Head Island, which held the only real job opportunities for the residents. The bused workers often returned late in the evenings, and those with children were forced to leave them with friends or relatives or to their own devices. One of the challenges we faced, in cooperation with the community, was trying to start an after-school program and recruiting volunteers from the community to provide structured activities for these school-age children.

Yonges Island evidenced the changing economics of the area and indeed of the broader society in that, whereas local workers formerly were transported to the fields to pick cotton, tobacco, or soybeans, now they were transported to the tourist areas as part of the growing service sector of the economy. The irony, of course, is that living conditions had hardly changed for the longtime

African American residents of the area, despite the tremendous influx of wealth. A senior majoring in mechanical engineering was struck by the social structure and economics of the island: "The effects of racism and economic injustice run extremely deep here. These people are proud people. They are proud of their heritage. They neither want nor need our culture . . . just our acknowledgment as fellow human beings."

Although few Whites live on Yonges Island, most of them seemed friendly and at ease with the African American majority. However, at least one police officer was mistrustful of the "coloreds" in the area and warned us that we should "watch our backs because the island ain't safe for Whites." Although his comments did frighten more than a few students (nearly all of the students who participated both years were White), others of us attributed his remarks to the pervasiveness of racism that many of us had grown up with and recognized in our own parents, families, and communities.

During both community service projects to Yonges Island, the students from Penn State were housed in the same community center they were asked to renovate. Most of the major renovations were accomplished the first year, and the initial phases of a community education program, namely an after-school program, were also put into place. During the second trip to Yonges Island, the students focused on playground improvements and provided additional assistance for the after-school program.

The community center was a one-room facility measuring about sixty feet by forty feet, with separate toilet facilities for men and women and a tiny kitchen area complete with a small stove and refrigerator. There were outside showers that had become overgrown with weeds but had all the free-flowing, colder-than-cold water one desired. This was where we bathed during the time we spent on Yonges Island.

Our task, upon arrival the first year, was to clean the inside of the building so that we could use it for sleeping and eating. This was an overwhelming challenge, considering that we had traveled all the way from State College, Pennsylvania, and had had only a few hours of sleep the night before at a church in Charleston. None of us had any idea of what to expect. We knew we were supposed to help renovate a building that had once been used for community meetings, but what we faced when we walked into Jefferson Community Center was enough to make most of us want to head a few hundred miles further south to Daytona or Fort Lauderdale or some other place where fun might be had. And although most of us wanted to give of ourselves over spring break, we also wanted to have a little bit of pleasure. What awaited us on Yonges Island certainly was not going to involve anything remotely related to fun—or so we thought.

Two challenges were presented to us by a group of elders of the island, who included among their group Mrs. Multree. The first challenge required physical labor: The building needed to be cleaned, junk had to be removed, playground equipment around the community center needed to be installed, and other equipment needed repairs. Fortunately, the building was structurally sound and did not need any major work. We did not have the tools or expertise for such an undertaking anyway. Tools? We had no tools or cleaning supplies, so one of the first tasks was to make a hardware store run all the way to Johns Island, some fifteen to twenty miles away. We got organized and divided into various teams, with each group making a list of cleaning supplies and tools they needed to perform their work. We purchased what we needed through a $1,000 account established for our group by the Presbyterian church in Charleston that had helped to organize the overall project.

By the end of the week, the community center hardly resembled the building we had first faced some six days earlier; and around the yard were a new basketball hoop and backboard and three giant swing sets constructed of heavy-duty wooden railroad beams. Little of what we accomplished could have been done without the help of Mr. and Mrs. Multree. They lived next door to the community center and loaned us a variety of equipment throughout the week. There were too many to recall the number of times we interrupted Mr. Multree's spring plowing to request a hammer or a shovel. The other key community member on whom we depended was Coach Brown, who launched an air ball on our ceremonial opening of the new basketball hoop, which quickly was attacked by a group of about fifteen sharklike kids seeking new meat to embarrass on the court. Later in the day, some of us took time to join them and made some new friends in the process.

Coach Brown was a large African American man, probably in his late forties or early fifties, who had worked at the local high school for nearly twenty years. He stood about 6' 2" and must have weighed about 240 pounds. His devotion to and concern for his community were evidenced by the number of extra hours he put in during the week to help us with the work at the community center. Coach Brown gave up most of his free time (lunches and evenings) throughout the week to give us direction on some of the technical tasks that required greater expertise than we had—such as erecting the large swing sets. It was his concern and kindness that led to our first warm shower of the week when he garnered access to some outdoor showers across from the high school. The joy of standing in a hot (actually, slightly warm) drizzle for the first time in four or five days reminded several of us of the everyday things we took for granted.

The other challenge we faced at Yonges Island was to start a children's after-school program that we hoped would be led by local volunteers once we left at the end of the week. As "outsiders," we faced a major problem: How do we foster enough community excitement to get residents involved throughout the week and then identify a few who have the time, energy, and desire to provide leadership to the program? This was a naive and unrealistic goal on our part. The primary factor that ultimately led to community support and assistance was the stimulus from Mrs. Multree and her influence over her fellow residents. Her involvement was crucial to the evening meetings that were held throughout the week, which served to generate support for the program.

The goal of the after-school program was to create a supervised tutorial and recreational program that would provide structure for the children. The idea was to mix some organized play with time for study and creative expression, such as finger painting and sidewalk chalking. We also hoped to leave behind enough supplies for many of the activities to be continued.

For the first few days, we had two different groups of workers; one team focused on the physical chores that needed to be accomplished and the other planned and conducted the after-school program. Word of our presence spread throughout the community as fast as "the storm of the century" that eventually chased our two vans up the Atlantic coast. On the first school day after our arrival (the third day of our trip) and much to our dismay, about fifty school-age children showed up. Even though we were barely prepared for any children, we got prepared rather quickly. What the Penn State students were about to experience during their week in the community was, for many of them, one of the most tender experiences of their lives: A southern rural African American community completely embraced a group composed predominantly of White college students from up north.

STUDENTS' EXPERIENCES OF COMMUNITY

As I indicated in chapter 5, charity and community service are two different ideas. Charity involves giving to another person who is in need in some way. Like charity, community service is about giving. However, community service also involves giving and receiving through a relationship based on mutuality. Service encounters of this variety are designed not only to enhance the living conditions of another person, but also to build a connection between the parties involved and thus contribute to a common sense of community. For example, a student who participated in the Yonges Island project offered the following comments: "The fact that we were able to interact a great deal with the people of the island added so much to the overall experience. I've done volunteer work in the past where I never really got the chance to meet with the people who I was actually trying to help. It left me wondering who they are. But this project was different. I got a good feel for the residents of the island and they truly are wonderful people." This student highlights how community service may be seen as community building.

As part of a commitment to community building, community service is concerned not only with temporary solutions, but because individuals care for those they serve and those with whom they serve, a desire also exists to alter conditions permanently for those in need. Thus, the idea of "community building" involves both serving others and working with them to permanently change social conditions. Jane Kendall addressed this quality of community service and what she described as "service-learning":

> A service-learning program might encourage participants working in a local soup kitchen, for example, to ask why people are hungry, what policies in our country do or do not contribute to this problem, and what economic, cultural and logistical factors result in hunger in a world that already knows how to grow enough food to feed everyone. Participants in a program that focuses primarily on charity, on the other hand, might serve food in the same soup kitchen, but they would not be encouraged and supported to ask these types of questions. (1990, p. 21)

In chapter 4, I talked about the Washington, D.C., project and how one day out of each of the three trips was spent meeting with legislative representatives and full-time volunteers to discuss issues of homelessness and economic policy. As Kendall noted, our goal was not merely to involve students in charity but also to challenge them to think about the larger social issues and how they might be able to contribute to change as members of a connected society. Indeed, community and social responsibility ought to be at the heart of community service and the kind of service learning that Kendall highlights. She went on to explain that the idea of community in the definition of service-learning programs may include the local neighborhood, or it may have a broader meaning implying the state, national, or international community. For Kendall, service learning has as part of its goal "developing the skills and awareness needed for responsible global citizenship" (p. 21).

Kendall calls attention to some clarification that perhaps is called for. I need to distinguish between the concepts of "community service" and "service learning" (which I briefly discussed in the introduction to this book). These two terms inevitably are interwoven and often are misconstrued. For the purposes of my writing, community service refers to any kind of service activity that has an interactional component that in some way fosters community. This view of community service suggests that service activity is not only designed to meet some need but also seeks to build a sense of connectedness. In relation to college students, community service endeavors may be tied to a course or may be part of the extracurriculum and not formally connected to academic work (as when a group of students from a residence hall volunteers to paint houses). Service learning, on the other hand, may involve community service types of activities but is most typically tied in some formal way to a course or to academic credit. Both are important. However, the primary focus of this book is community service. I may occasionally speak of or refer to service learning because, clearly, community service involving college students often is linked to the academic educational experience and thus may be classified as both community service and service learning. To complicate matters even further, some of my colleagues, such as Jeffrey Howard, editor of the *Michigan Journal of Community Service Learning*, use a third phrase—"community service learning." The intention of this phrase is to capture a broader meaning of service learning and ground it in the goals of community development. I occasionally use this term in the remainder of this book as a means to address the learning outcomes related to community service, which become more central to chapters 7 and 8.

To repeat a point I made earlier in chapter 3, I prefer to think of the extracurriculum and the curriculum as integrated, and from my perspective all forms of community service ought to be considered as part of a student's overall "formal" educational experience and therefore can be thought of as "community service learning." Thus, from my perspective, community service and service learning ought to be more closely identified with one another, hence, Howard's term makes a great deal of sense.

With the preceding points in mind, my goal in the upcoming section is to discuss some of the students' experiences that contributed to their sense of community and what they learned through their engagement in community building. In what follows, I organize students' thoughts on community and community building around two themes: (1) students' perceptions of community and the communities they served, and (2) students' thoughts on the community of volunteers with whom they worked. Although the data for this section were derived primarily from students' experiences on Yonges Island, additional comments come from students who participated in other service projects, including intensive kinds of experiences such as the Washington, D.C. and Johns Island projects and ongoing service work in their home and university communities.

Perceptions of Community

Most of the students who participated in the Yonges Island project, as well as other service projects, had not given too much thought to community and what it means to work to build community. The community service project to Yonges Island, however, forced many of these students to reflect on community-related matters. A number of students thought that they had learned a great deal about community from the residents of the island. Although many of the students had lived in rural communities in Pennsylvania, few had witnessed the closeness evidenced by members of their adopted community. "Our world has gotten to be too individualistic," commented one student. "The whole trip reminded me that community is the answer." Another student talked about how he felt welcomed by the Yonges Island residents: "I felt like we were adopted by the community. Everyone was so warm and friendly, and they accepted us as part of the community. I didn't feel like an outsider in any way."

Several mentioned how important community is for having a sense of connectedness to others and as a source of support and love. One student talked about the importance of community and his involvement in service in general: "Throughout my involvement in service I have learned that all of us really want and deserve love and community." Another student echoed such sentiments when she talked about the role community plays as a support system: "One thing that I learned is that people sometimes need someone to fall back on. I think a lot of families fall through the cracks, and the system isn't helping them. That's what I think community is all about—not letting people fall through the cracks. Helping people when they have fallen on hard times." And a third added, "I learned the true meaning of patience and what it's like to work together as part of a community. I learned that the children are the light of the world. They are perfect examples of a love that knows no boundaries of color. I believe good shines in each of us in different but uniquely special ways. No one is perfect, and we must love one another as we are. We function together as a community, and when one part breaks down we all do."

A Michigan State student who was actively involved in community service in the Lansing area offered the following thoughts on community and service: "Community service is more than doing work for people who could use extra help. You also learn about why doing work with others is so important. It's not about planting a tree that needs to be planted. It's not a one shot-thing, either. It's something natural that appeals to people. Everyone in our country can't live on their own—we're all connected in some way. In order to be a good citizen, you need to be able to give your time and resources to others. Community service is a way of sharing resources across society."

Students who worked on the Johns Island project also had a great deal to say about community. One student commented, "The people of Johns Island may not have an elm-lined street but it's a real community because they care for each other. They have that and maybe that's something we can take with us— talking with our neighbors and giving to them." Another explained, "It's been one of the best weeks of my life. . . . I wish more people could experience stuff like this. One of the residents told me she would remember me for the rest of her life. That's an incredible feeling. The sense of community here is different from where I grew up. I may not even know my neighbors. But not here. That's the wonderful part of it all. Everyone here is so neighborly."

Another student talked about how one's definition of community and how and where one draws the lines between communities influence how they define themselves in relation to others: "What you define as *your* community is important to each individual, because each person sees their community in a different way and therefore it is important to know when you are overstepping your bounds—

when you might be imposing your value system on someone else. It's hard to determine. Whose community is it? Are we a part of their community? How you define the limits of your community affects what you feel comfortable doing."

This student's thoughts bring to mind my family's experiences in the Farrell projects and the difficulty we had in becoming part of that community. Race was a significant barrier at the time as the historical circumstances of the 1960s and the Civil Rights movement clearly acted as a backdrop for all that happened during our attempted integration into the projects. Tension between Blacks and Whites was perhaps at an all-time high and the movement of a White family into a predominantly Black neighborhood, as poor as it was, seemed to be interpreted as one more intrusion into the lives of Blacks in America.

Tensions between Whites and Blacks certainly existed in the spring of 1993 and 1994, but the racial climate on Yonges Island was quite a bit different from that of the Farrell projects in 1965. Also, the circumstances were dramatically altered: In one case a family was seen to be intruding on another's space, whereas in the other case, a group of individuals were invited to share space for awhile. The residents of Yonges Island were happy to expand their community for a few weeks to a group of northern students. There was a high degree of mutuality between the residents and the Penn State delegation. Mutuality, however, did not exist during the period my family lived in the Farrell projects. The definition my family had of community back in 1965 was unlikely to have included our African American neighbors in the projects, and their definition certainly did not seem to include us.

The Volunteer Community

Paul Loeb talked about the importance of community in the lives of student activists and volunteers: "In the face of inevitable frustrations, students sustain involvement through community, through sharing beliefs and concerns, hopes and disappointments, with others of kindred spirit" (1994, p. 208). Loeb's comments speak directly to the experiences of many of the students in my study. For example, students talked about the importance of community in terms of working as a member of a group of volunteers with similar commitments. A junior majoring in health education had this to say: "I learned how wonderful it is to work with a group with the same common goal and struggle together to achieve that goal." Another student, a senior majoring in management and journalism, added, "The spirit of the group got me out of bed at 5 a.m. I saw how effective a group can be." A third student commented that he was surprised by "how much can be accomplished when a group of motivated, sharing, and open-minded people work together."

An aspect of working together as a group is that each student may bring unique or special talents to bear on community service activities. A senior in nursing thought that a big strength of the student group was that "the people in our group all had their own special talent of relating to and helping those in need and a variety of ways to do it. There was a bond that developed among the students who volunteered."

One aspect of the power of group action is the need and opportunity to inspire one another—to rejuvenate other volunteers. "Volunteers need help too," explained one student. "We helped to refresh and inspire one another while the residents of Yonges Island taught us about love. I learned that I can do a lot to help, and they taught me that I can love more than I do." A junior majoring in psychology also alluded to the interdependence among the volunteers: "I always try to be independent, and it was beneficial for me to have to lean on others during the week. Our world has become too individualistic, and this experience has helped to remind me that community is the answer." The personal connections students made within the community of volunteers were significant to them. As one student reported, "We really have a community within our group. We're from diverse backgrounds, yet everybody really got along. We talked about all sorts of bodily functions and everything you could imagine."

Like students from the Yonges Island project, other students also talked about the importance of a group of committed volunteers as a form of community. The following comments were offered by students who participated in several other community service projects.

> There is an enormous sense of hope generated by twenty other volunteers working together for the same social cause. This hope is fuel for my own personal fire which drives me to work on behalf of those less privileged.

> The power of a small group of people to work miracles is real. The soup kitchens we worked in were all the result of someone's initiative in response to a need. This is very hopeful.

> I need to be in community with people who are interested in radical social change. Together we can work and witness all kinds of changes, and perhaps come closer to finding some answers.

> Building personal relationships with others who are involved in service is my driving force. They are the thing that provides the most significant impetus for me in my hunger for social justice and participation in social action.

> It is possible to make great changes when people with the same interests and feelings of responsibility work together.

I learned that I am just one of many and that contributing together can make a difference.

Being together as volunteers makes us very strong.

A student from the Johns Island project talked about building a porch, but she could easily have been describing how community is created: "I think doing this service project gives me a sense of how a group can work together to accomplish things. It wasn't chaotic to me like I thought it might be. It seemed effortless sometimes. The porch group . . . it just turned out so well. There was no fighting. Everyone provided input. Someone would say, 'Let's do this.' And someone else would say, 'Why do you want to do it this way?' and the first person would explain why. And we'd ask a third person. We worked together and just did it."

A Michigan State student who participated in a spring break trip in 1995 highlighted some of her experiences: "How to function in a group and get along with people in close quarters for an extended period of time was something important that I learned on the spring break project. People I went with were like an extension of myself. We could talk about the people we met and the problems we encountered. I learned from them, and I think they learned from me. We became very connected. In fact, when we came back to school I felt separated from them because we all had different lives to lead as students. I wanted to find a way to associate with them."

Other students talked about the role community plays in contributing to social change and activism in general. They pointed out how other volunteers help one another and build a larger group of people striving for social justice. For example, a first-year graduate student thought it was important to get involved with others doing community service: "I wanted to do some active social justice work and also spend time with children and God and people to get back in touch with my sense of what is important." She added, "I've learned that others have similar feelings as me about activism and that I'm not alone in the struggle to change society. I learned that people really do care and are doing some wonderful things despite many struggles they are facing." Another student also was driven by the personal connections she made through her involvement in community service and had a strong commitment to creating social change. Her name is Deborah Smith, and in the following pages I highlight her involvement in service.

A STUDENT PROFILE

Deborah Smith is a senior at Pennsylvania State University with plans to attend graduate school after she takes a year or two off to figure out exactly what she wants to do with her life. She knows that she wants to work with people in some type of educational or social service setting, but she believes she needs more work experience to clarify her career plans. Deborah is planning to work with a volunteer agency for a year or two and hopes that this will help her to get more focused. "I am considering the Peace Corps, but it's more likely I'll work somewhere in Washington, D.C., with one of the volunteer agencies there, like the Brethren Volunteer Corps. I have a friend who's in that now, and she likes it a lot. You don't make much money—I think she gets about $85 a month—but everything is pretty much paid for." (Recall from chapter 3—*Proposition 7: College students are at a time in their lives when a multitude of forces influence their sense of self; thus they often are in the midst of a period of heightened self-discovery and identity confusion.*)

Deborah participated in the second trip to Yonges Island, which primarily involved restoring a playground that had gone to waste over the years. The second trip also involved working with the children in the after-school program—the part Deborah enjoyed the most. "It was incredible to interact with the children. It made me consider being an elementary school teacher right there on the spot. I'm half kidding, but it was so enjoyable to visit with those kids—to braid their hair, to play games, to talk about the future. I'm not sure I've ever felt that kind of warmth before. They were so trusting of us, and we were so comfortable with them."

What was most fascinating about the Yonges Island project for Deborah was the uniqueness of the community and the opportunities she had to experience a different culture. "Even though we were still in the U.S., it felt like we were in another country. I mean everything was so different—the food, the spirituality, the lack of materialism. I guess it was more like what rural communities used to be like. It seemed like everybody in the entire community was related or knew each other on a personal level." Deborah had been raised in a medium-sized Pennsylvania community, and although there were some strong connections among many of the residents, there was still a certain distance that she had come to expect from people. "I have found that people rarely will open up their hearts and souls to you. That is what is so unique about the Yonges Island experience: the way they opened up to us and us to them. It was really a shared experience."

Deborah talked about the importance that community service had played throughout her collegiate career. She had become actively involved since her first year at Penn State by joining a variety of organizations, including a group of students who collected food and clothing for local shelters and needy families. She was drawn to the interactional aspects of service: "I really enjoy meeting different people—volunteers and people with different kinds of needs. There is just a great deal of warmth that springs from those kinds of interactions. I have met some of my closest friends through working together as volunteers for some project."

Deborah offers additional support about the community awareness that the experience on Yonges Island generated for students. Her discussion of her other community service experiences also calls attention to the interactional and community building aspect of service. The way Deborah relished the community-mindedness of the people of Yonges Island calls attention to a bygone era that even she wishes had not passed. She offers insights into the challenge of postmodern social life and the need we still have to connect with one another in fundamental ways.

RETHINKING COMMUNITY
AND COMMUNITY BUILDING

In chapter 5 I talked about the concept of mutuality, which bears directly on our ability to develop connections between the self and the other through service activities and thus our ability to build community. Part of what mutuality represents is the notion that we all—the doer as well as the done-to—benefit from acts of caring. Mutuality moves beyond the traditions of charity in which the rich give to the poor and instead draws on the ideals of citizenship and community. In *An Aristocracy of Everyone*, Benjamin Barber focused our attention on this point when he argued that it is dangerous to our conception of democracy for us to think of service as the rich helping the poor or students paying a debt to their society in exchange for tuition breaks, as if the community building aspect of "community" service only applies to those "doing" service. Barber went on to suggest that community implies much more than the one-directional giving associated with charity: "The language of charity drives a wedge between self-interest and altruism, leading students to believe that service is a matter of sacrificing private interests to moral virtue. The language of citizenship suggests that self-interests are always embedded in communities of action and that in serving neighbors one also serves oneself" (p. 249). Thus, for Barber, self-interest embedded in helping one's neighbors as part of a conception of citizenship contributes to the ideal of community.

But what constitutes a community? This is part of Barber's discussion and part of his critique of postmodernists and multiculturalists. Barber admits that at times he has aligned himself with progressive educators: "I have expressed a cautious solidarity with the progressives" (p. 109). Nonetheless, Barber offered extensive criticism of progressive educational views grounded in multiculturalism and postmodernism. His criticism, however, lacks any mention of some of the more recent and significant progressive educational theorists, such as Henry Giroux, bell hooks, Peter McLaren, and William Tierney. In criticizing postmodernism as part of the wave to reform education, he demonstrates a lack of knowledge of how critical postmodernists and feminists have taken aspects of postmodernism and moved beyond the nihilism inherent in some of the more radical strands of postmodern thought. It is the nihilistic strand captured most clearly in the work of Jacques Derrida that Barber latched onto as he waged his attack on what he called "hyperskepticism"—an assault on all authority and knowledge.

Barber also discussed "hyperpluralism," and here is where I partly agree with him, and perhaps many multiculturalists, feminists, and postmodernists might as well. As Barber explained, "The challenge facing modern proponents of a just and inclusive America remains how to hold the elephantine conglomeration together without surrendering the diversity of groups and liberty of individuals that define it" (p. 126). But Barber's problem is that his vision of community is still tied to traditional conceptions grounded in functionalist paradigms such as those delineated by Emile Durkheim, Talcott Parsons, and Robert Merton, discussed in chapter 3. Barber argued that a society or community can tolerate only so much diversity or difference before it bursts at the seams. For Barber, both postmodernists and multiculturalists, with their endless celebration and support of difference (as postmodernists often proclaim—_Vivá la difference!_), move society closer to this cultural explosion. (Recall from chapter 3—_Proposition 6: Postmodern identities are more fragmented and decentered, and the challenge to establish a clear sense of self is more vexing than ever before._) What Barber fails to realize is that commonality is not the sole source of a sense of connectedness. In assuming that common understandings provide the essence of solidarity, Barber follows a line of thought similar to that of Amitai Etzioni (1995) and the communitarian movement, which suggests that a person can only care about someone to whom he or she is similar. I turn to Etzioni and the notion of communitarianism to help clarify my criticism of a liberal perspective of community.

Communitarianism has created quite a divide between the radical left and their occasional liberal allies. Whereas conservatives call for a return to common values and radicals suggest a society of multiplicity, liberals have been caught in the middle of the cultural wars, at times positioning themselves with the left and at other times the right. Communitarianism can be read, in part, as an effort on the behalf of liberals to define their own agenda for society and for advancing their own vision of community.

Conservatives such as William Bennett (1984), Dinesh D'Souza (1991), and E. D. Hirsch (1987) envision a society organized around a "common culture" and see educational institutions as the vehicle for socializing youths to this culture. Intellectuals of a liberal and radical persuasion tend to reject the conservative vision of a common culture in favor of other alternatives. Etzioni (1995) and the communitarians suggest that community ought to be grounded, not in a common culture but in some essential "common values," and that schools "ought to teach those values Americans share, for example, that the dignity of all persons ought to be respected, that tolerance is a virtue and discrimination abhorrent, that peaceful resolution of conflicts is superior to violence, that generally truth-telling is morally superior to lying, that democratic government is morally superior to totalitarianism and authoritarianism" (p. 15). Barber claimed that a sense of social connectedness is dependent on a small but consistent set of common understandings, values, or cultural norms—a "cultural endowment" as Robert Bellah and colleagues describe it in *The Good Society* (1991, p. 172). This is a compromise position from the conservative stance, which seeks to achieve a common culture complete with unifying truths, values, and beliefs, and in which educational institutions instill these unifying cultural forms.

Whereas conservatives seek to build community around a common culture, and communitarians seek to build community around a few guiding principles ("cultural endowment"), other scholars typically classified as postmodernists or critical postmodernists, such as William Tierney (1993), reject altogether the idea of organizing a society around commonality of any kind for fear that such a vision of social life will silence cultural difference. Postmodernists such as Tierney, as well as Nicholas Burbules and Suzanne Rice (1991), contend that contemporary society ought to envision community building as "dialogue across difference," in which efforts to understand one another through social interaction form the basis for communal ties.

What the conservative right and liberals fail to understand is that "knowledge about" is not the only source of connection among people. We do not all need to know the same things to find common ground. This is lost in Robert Serow's discussion of schooling and diversity, as evidenced by his contention that subcultural groups need to "abandon their familiar language and customs in favor of those of the majority of Americans" (1983, p. 13). And later he argued that schools "could perhaps best serve the interests of minority students not by reinforcing minor subcultural variations, but by transmitting the academic and social skills required to enter the socioeconomic mainstream" (p. 102). One is left to ponder why conservatives and liberals see the need for so much prescription in their visions of community and the role of education. Why must we all have the same knowledge? Do they perhaps fear that the knowledge they already hold will be devalued? Ironically, of course, this is what their position does to the many in our society from culturally diverse backgrounds whose limited access to power restricts their ability to legitimize various forms of culture. (Recall from chapter 3—*Proposition 4: Power lies at the center of how culture contributes to notions of identity and the self often serving to legitimize or delegitimize various cultural identities and possible selves.*) There must be other sources for common ground than a society founded on canonical knowledge.

Processes are also involved, and the left suggests that process itself—more specifically, democratic processes characterized by inclusivity, caring, and justice—can be at the heart of a sense of community. Democracy is situated as the ties that bind. Of course, one could easily argue that democracy is one value or a value system that radicals contend ought to be embraced by all. In this regard, the radical position does not seem that far to the left of some liberals who also argue for democracy or "caring for the common good" as a core value to organizing social life, as some communitarians, in fact, suggest. An example of this more liberal argument is offered in a collection of essays entitled *Caring for the Commonweal* (Palmer, Wheeler, and Fowler, 1990), in which the concept of *paideia* is used as an organizing framework for social life: "The disciplines of *paideia* must have a creative and critical component. They not only must prepare the community's members to live according to certain precepts and values; they must also become the means by which a consensus about how we should live together may be forged, continually tested and reformed" (Wheeler, 1990, p. 3). In discussing the "means" by which a consensus about how to live might be forged, Barbara Wheeler supports a more radical perspective when she stressed "democracy" as a unifying process.

Radical educational theorists such as Giroux and Tierney situate democracy as an organizing principle because of the ability of democratic communities and societies to embrace difference and provide opportunities for the development of voice within diverse social contexts. This is not the same view of democracy stressed by liberal social theorists, who tend to emphasize hyper-individualism, often at the expense of community and connectedness. A student from Paul Loeb's book on student apathy and activism provided some insight into the idea of democratic process as the core of community when she described the multiracial efforts of students at City University of New York (CUNY) as they fought to hold down tuition increases through effective student activism. Their success was the result of "working with people of all different backgrounds. Because it doesn't matter what you are, so long as you want the same thing in your heart" (1994, p. 309).

The conservative vision of community and society grounded in a common culture clearly silences cultural diversity and situates schooling as a process designed to assimilate culturally diverse students. Serow made this vividly clear when he wrote, "The major contribution of the schools in the years ahead will not be reinforcement of students' distinctive subcultural patterns, but rather the transmission of the values, skills, and behaviors that are most characteristic of American society as a whole" (1983, p. 107). With this said, we are still left with the need to reconcile the positions of communitarianism and postmodernism if a progressive vision of community and community building is to move beyond a conservative position that tends to silence difference. I believe there is a common connection cutting across communitarianism and postmodernism, and it is revealed in part through symbolic interactionist explanations of group identity and joint action and feminist notions of caring.

Recall from chapter 3 how Herbert Blumer (1969) argued that society has great capacity to tolerate discord as individuals can exist in conflict, possess different values, and, in general, be quite diverse, and yet still be able to fit lines of action together to form joint action. Blumer maintained that forming joint action may take place for a variety of reasons and does not necessarily have to revolve around common values. Individuals may align their actions, in Blumer's words, "out of duress, because it is the sensible thing to do, or out of sheer necessity" (p. 76). For Blumer, the fitting together of lines of action is particularly likely as society grows increasingly diverse and common values become less and less unifying.

We live in a society in which difference stretches the seams that once held communities together and provided individuals with a sense of connectedness. Race, class, and cultural differences prevent many families and individuals from forging connections with others. I offered my own experience in the Farrell projects as one example of how racial tension limited the ability of my family and my neighbors to build community and make connections between the self and the other. My contention throughout this book is that connectedness is still an essential aspect of the self, which by its nature is a social self and thus directly linked to understandings of the other. If we are to maintain a sense of self bound to others, by sheer necessity we must find ways to align our actions lest community become a forgotten word, destined to the scrap heap of language along with perhaps humanity as well. Communitarians suggest that we must have a common connection, a sense of similarity, in order to care for the other. But can this happen in a society in which the other is often a diverse other, or when the other is, as Howard Radest (1993) described, "a stranger"? Robert Wuthnow offered his own answer: "When someone shows compassion to a stranger, it does set in motion a series of relationships that spreads throughout the entire society. Even if the chain is broken at some point so that no direct benefits come back to us as individuals, the whole society is affected, just as an entire lake is affected when someone pours in a bucket of water. Despite the fact that we live in a society of strangers, we can still be aware of our contribution to others by understanding how compassion spreads out through the wider society" (1991, p. 300).

Out of necessity we must develop a way, a rationale, a reason, or call it a common value if you must, but we must organize around something. Here is where feminism provides a possibility in the idea of an ethic of care. Is it possible to envision a common connection built around caring? Is it possible for caring to exist at the center of a society founded on diversity and lacking a common culture? Let us listen to the following student, who talked about his experience of working on a community service project with diverse community members: "All of the students who came on this trip and the people in the community who we worked with who we had never met came from different backgrounds. And yet we were truly connected by the same goal and it provided us a foundation to build upon." What I suggest in this book is that caring is, by necessity, the process around which we must align our actions. Caring thus may contribute to developing a sense of community despite differences. Caring enables us to embrace diversity instead of situating it as a problem to be solved or as a quality to be ignored. I argue that an ethic of care ought to form the basis of social life and that caring may be seen as both the common value and the process around which we might organize community. From such a perspective, the relationship between the self and the other is founded on an ethic of care, which helps to offset the postmodern confusion and complexity that makes community so difficult to achieve. In simplest terms, despite our multiplicitous identities, we can join in a common struggle because we care for one another.

Although I think of caring as a process, others may contend that it is a value and thus argue that at least one common value must be shared by all—that of caring. I cannot argue with such a position, for even in the work of postmodernists who espouse "dialogue across difference" the common value of caring is seemingly implied: Why else would one enter into dialogue about differences to learn from the other if one does not care? Or, as Paulo Freire argued, "If I do not love the world—if I do not love life—if I do not love men—I cannot enter into dialogue" (1970, p. 78). Communitarians also suggest that caring is an underlying value of society. For example, an ethic of care lies at the heart of many of the principles Etzioni discussed; respect for all persons and peaceful resolution are two examples. An ethic of care, with community building as the goal, thus may be seen as the bridge uniting key aspects of postmodern and communitarian thought.

My research on students' involvement in community service highlights how the development and maintenance of community is an interactive process involving giving as well as receiving. To embrace one without embracing the other does not support the ideals of community. Seen in this light, community service is an act of bridging a culture grounded in individualism. This is part of the story told by Robert Bellah (1985) and his colleagues who argued that despite a culture dominated by individualism, many Americans have sought community connections as a source of peace and contentment with life.

One of the principal goals of higher learning and education in general ought to be to foster an ethic of care among students and teachers in a way that contributes to community building. If we are to have anything in common, that commonality ought to be the ability and desire to care for one another. Obviously, we cannot *make* someone care for someone else. We can, however, create educational structures and opportunities in which caring may be fostered. As the student narratives throughout this book clearly reveal, community service is one such vehicle for encouraging an ethic of care.

SUMMARY

The challenge of a democratic society committed to cultural difference is the struggle to build community across the cultural borders that a truly democratic vision promotes. When we reject common understandings and common values as a basis for connecting with one another, what are we left with as a social bridge? Again, the difference between the radical left and the liberal position comes more into focus. Whereas the left rejects any notion of common ground and argues that dialogue across difference is what we should strive for, liberals argue that some common values are needed: Why would one enter into dialogue if there was nothing in common? Dialogue across difference seems unlikely if I do not care enough about my neighbor, countryperson, or global villager to enter into interaction. The common ground upon which we must stand in order to communicate is caring itself. Thus, it is feminism that primarily offers the connective vision bringing postmodernism and communitarianism more into focus. If one cares, then one will listen.

The challenge, then, is to elevate an ethic of care to the heart of what we teach people within our society. Community service and what we might learn from the students in this chapter and book are instructive. I paraphrase some of the comments students offered throughout this chapter as a means of highlighting the role community service might play in restructuring higher learning around an ethic of care:

• Working as a community helps resist the tendency toward individualism.
• Service work helps people learn about love and community.
• Community provides people with safety nets that support them when the system lets them down.
• Caring and respecting others help to build connections.
• Learning from each other helps to build a sense of togetherness among volunteers.
• Participating in community service is a way of being a good citizen, a way of sharing resources across society.

The preceding comments highlight the attitudes that often are fostered through community service activities. Higher education needs to bring an ethic of care to center stage, and community service and the learning that comes with it ought to be one of the cornerstone activities in such an effort. Clearly, education can foster an individual's sense of caring and concern for others.

To suggest that all forms of community service equally develop an ethic of care and advance our understanding of community is misleading. What was perhaps most rewarding for students was community service activities in which mutuality was a central component of the process. The notion of mutuality is a key concept that not only serves as a guiding light for structuring community service, but also guides other learning contexts designed to foster an ethic of care. College faculty and student affairs professionals who embrace the notion of mutuality will be more concerned with structuring a relationship between students and educators that involves both giving and receiving. Perhaps the best way of fostering an ethic of care is to embrace it ourselves: We are the taught as well as the teachers, and the education process itself mirrors the kind of caring society we hope to achieve.

In *The Thee Generation*, Tom Regan (1991) alluded to the kind of society we might hope for when he discussed an entire generation of people committed to others and to service. He highlighted what he perceived as an emerging revolution of community-minded individuals: "The Thee Generation . . . is a generation of service: of giving not taking, of commitment to principles not material possessions, of communal compassion not conspicuous consumption. If the defining question of the present generation is What can I get for me? the central question of this new generation is What can I do for thee?" (p. 3). In this chapter we heard from some members of Regan's "Thee Generation" who dispel much of the apathy expressed in another generational nickname—"Generation X." The students in this chapter and indeed depicted throughout this book are by no means a generation of slackers. They are a generation of people who care greatly about others and about the idea of community and who see themselves connected to one another. They are not separate from the homeless in Washington, D.C., the rural poor in South Carolina, or the low-income children of Lansing, Michigan. They are all part of the same community that they are striving to build.

Chapter 7

Action/Reflection

> *True reflection leads to action . . . [and] action*
> *will constitute an authentic praxis only when its*
> *consequences become the object of critical*
> *reflection. . . . Otherwise, action is pure*
> *activism.*
> —*Paulo Freire,* Pedagogy of the Oppressed

Everyone needs to slow down sometimes and simply contemplate life.
As a child, I tended to ponder life's deeper meanings right around bedtime.
Thoughts about the meaning of life are not the kind most suitable to falling
asleep. So, I did my share of tossing and turning.

A set of thoughts that always crept into my consciousness, especially at
night, was a concern for the well-being of my mother and my three younger sis-
ters. When I was about to graduate from high school, my mother was not mar-
ried and my sisters were all still in school (my older brother was on his own at
this point). It was hard for me to imagine moving away from home and not help-
ing to support them in some way. At the same time, with the state of the econ-
omy in western Pennsylvania in the mid-1970s, it was very unlikely that I
would find a good enough job to even be able to support myself. These kinds of
thoughts haunted my late-night reflections and worried me deeply.

But my worries about my family were put to rest when my mother married
for the fourth time. She had met a wonderful man and my high school girlfriend
and I stood as their witnesses at the office of the Mercer County Justice of the
Peace on that special day in April of 1977. It was special for my mom and for
John, but it was also something special for me too. A huge burden, which I had
placed on my own shoulders, was removed. No longer did I have to think about
my mom and my sisters in weighing my future and in confronting life's
choices—I simply had to do what was best for me.

Twenty years have passed and my mother and John are still together. It's funny how life turns out and although it's sad to think about the hard times that my mother endured throughout parts of her life, things have turned out fairly well for her. I am sure they have problems like other couples who have been together for twenty years, but they seem to enjoy each other's company still. I will always be indebted to John for taking so much self-imposed responsibility off of my shoulders and freeing me to pursue my somewhat scattered dreams. As I reflect back on the last twenty years, I can't help but wonder how different things might have been had it not been for John.

Reflecting on life is important. Not just our own life, but the lives of others around us, around the country, and around the world. The earth is not as big a place as it sometimes appears, and with the advanced communication and transportation systems of the 1990s, it is certainly smaller than it used to be. We are all connected in one way or another. Reflection can help us to see the connections.

My goal in this chapter is to highlight the importance of reflection as it relates to student involvement in community service. Action, such as community service work, without reflection rings a bit hollow and fails to achieve many of the ideals stressed by critical views of education and society. I use a Habitat for Humanity project conducted on Maryland's eastern shore to introduce issues related to action and reflection. However, before presenting the Habitat project, I discuss various issues related to reflections on service and others, and then highlight matters associated with action and reflection in combination.

REFLECTIONS ON SERVICE AND OTHERS

For three consecutive years, I was part of a group of students, faculty, and staff who worked in soup kitchens and homeless shelters in Washington, D.C., during the winter break. Many of our experiences were chronicled in chapter 4. What I did not capture in that chapter was the serious thought and confused feelings these trips engendered in me and the many students who participated in the project. I remember some of the thoughts I had at the culmination of the third D.C. project. Many of the faces of the homeless I had seen the first and second years no longer were visible to me. Had they changed that much, or had my memory erased their faces? Perhaps their lives had improved and they no longer called the metal grates and plastic bubbles around the Capitol building their home. I recall the comments of one student who reflected on some of the feelings she had as a return participant in the D.C. project: "I had hoped to see some of the guys I met last year. But then I thought, if they had found jobs and places to live, then I wouldn't see them. So I found myself torn between wanting to bump into them again and at the same time hoping that I didn't. I also worried that if I don't see them, then maybe something bad might have happened to them." We were both left to wonder what ever became of Frank Gardner, the homeless man introduced in chapter 4.

As part of the D.C. project, we had group discussions every evening to share our experiences and thoughts from the day. Quiet times were also a part of our evening routine as we thought it was helpful for students and staff to contemplate their day of activity and interactions with volunteers and homeless citizens. A difficulty for many of us was facing the reality that we had so much wealth and comfort and others had so little. This was one of two central themes of the discussion groups. As one student explained, "This whole experience has been a real eye opener for me. I knew there were homeless people, but I didn't realize how tough their lives really are. I have so much more by comparison. And to think that I complain back at school all the time about the food in the cafeteria." The other theme concerned what students could do to create social change and contribute in some way to eliminating the widespread economic disparities throughout our society. In fact, a central goal of the D.C. project was to challenge students to consider what role they might play in transforming society and improving the lives of the poor. A student shared her thoughts: "I know there are no easy solutions, but that's no reason not to try. We need to experiment more with a variety of social programs, like housing settlements for low-income people. We have to make housing affordable so that someone making minimum wage can at least have a roof over his head and running water. I think every society owes that to its citizens."

Many of my own reflections on the inequalities within our society turn to issues of materialism and how I might structure my life in a way that does not contribute to the materialistic frenzy that has come to characterize the middle and upper classes. However, the same stark reality always hits me: Even if I were somehow able to escape the cultural shackles of materialism, as Margaret Sanger was able to do in the brief time she witnessed her home going up in flames, what good would that do for the 18,000 homeless men, women, and children living in D.C.? Perhaps I could live on half of my income and give the rest to a homeless shelter, to be invested in skills development and job placement. That would definitely do some good. Maybe I could invest my money in helping a homeless family have their own place to live. That would certainly bring joy to their lives. I give some of my time to community service, but shouldn't I be doing more? These are some of the concerns that I toss around in my mind as I become more and more critical of the lifestyle I embrace and who I am as a person. I weigh my political choices based on candidates' stances toward the poor, and yet it seems to me that I still distance myself from their suffering. My sense of self recoils from my own self-criticisms and ineffectiveness in completely embracing the lives of others.

And, of course, I always have a rationale that I fall back on: It's all right for me to want to be financially secure and live comfortably because, after all, I had my brushes with poverty as a child. Haven't I earned the right to enjoy materialistic pleasures? My sense of self takes on a hypocritical quality as I justify the present with the struggles of my youth. Doesn't the summer my family lived in a condemned house count for something? I'll never forget that summer and how I practically stayed inside for three months for fear that someone might see me standing in the yard. I had friends next door who never knew I was their neighbor until years later, when it seemed not to matter as much anymore and so I told them. Doesn't this kind of struggle entitle me to become the richest bastard I can be? My temperature boils as I write these words—angry that I cannot succeed financially without incredible guilt, and angry that I would ever want to. In the final analysis, whatever excuse I offer for not doing more for others is just as hollow as the excuse of anyone else.

In my most rational state, I realize that I must try to find the right balance between giving to others, in both time and money, and ensuring my own physical well-being and my dream of someday having my own family. But is that a selfish dream? I wonder sometimes. I also know that my life needs to be more integrated and that efforts to change oppressive conditions for others must somehow become more of the essence of who I am and what I do, and hence be reflected in how I spend my personal as well as professional time. In part, this is one reason this book has meant so much to me; it brings together the professional and the personal and offers a greater sense of connectedness to my life and my sense of self.

Based on discussions I have had with students over the years, I know that I am not alone in giving serious thought to how service fits into my life and how I might in some way contribute to improving the lives of others. Listen to the following students reflect on their involvement in community service and what it means to them:

> I learn more through my volunteer work than I ever do in any of my classes at school. Talking to people from diverse backgrounds provides so much insight that people just can't imagine. I study all these different theories in political science and sociology, but until you get a chance to see how the social world influences people's everyday lives, it just doesn't have that much meaning.

> Community service is something that I think everybody should get involved in doing. You see a different side to our country when you

see some of the struggles the poor face. You begin to understand the barriers to their economic situation and why it is so hard to get out of poverty. I talked to this one woman, and she explained to me how expensive day care is for her children and that in order for her to take a job she needs to make at least eight to ten dollars an hour. And no one will pay her that.

Service activities are important, but we also have to help teach people how to fish. You just can't give people food or build houses for them without also helping them develop the skills to take care of their own lives and their own families. . . . Part of my goal is to help others to develop their own abilities so that they can lead productive lives.

I have been involved in volunteer work ever since I was in high school, and I'll probably continue to do stuff like Habitat until I'm old and gray. I get a lot out of working to serve others, and it's a good feeling to know that I have helped someone even if it's in some small way. It helps me to cherish people more and understand what life is all about.

There are a lot of people in this country who need help to make ends meet. You can choose to help them or you can turn your back on them. I want to help people, and I want those who choose not to help to know that there are consequences for walking away. There are children who will go hungry and people who will be living in the streets. I cannot live with that on my conscience.

One gets a sense for the serious thought these students give to their community service work, as well as their concern for others. A few of these students offer some indication of how service work connects to a larger vision they have of the world and their place in that world. These students are atypical in that, whereas the vast majority of students I have met over the past six years have demonstrated their commitment to caring for others, at the same time, most of them have not given serious consideration to the complex forces at work in people's lives. Like the above mentioned students, they are idealists, but they have not yet challenged themselves to make bigger connections between poverty and the social forces that are at work. One could classify these two groups as "idealists" and "critical idealists," with the latter group definitely the smaller of the two.

There were other students, however, who questioned the idealism that was so pervasive among the student volunteers I encountered. One student in particular offered some poignant remarks: "To be honest, and it's hard to say this around all these 'do gooders,' I'm not sure all this volunteer stuff really does a whole lot of good. I know, I'm one of those volunteers too. But I keep asking myself a bunch of questions: Am I doing this to help the homeless or am I doing this to help myself? Who really benefits? Maybe I'm being too skeptical, but I think most of the students here are like me but won't admit it. It makes them feel good to help feed someone, and that way they can go back to living their happy little lives without feeling too guilty." This student exemplifies a third group of students, who might be classified as "cynics," although they would probably identify themselves as "realists."

My own thoughts and reflections and those of the students with whom I have had contact remind me of how important action and reflection are in forcing ourselves to confront the serious challenges that lie ahead. Throughout this chapter, I want to pay significant attention to this combination—action/reflection—and its role in shaping community service and students' experiences.

THE IMPORTANCE OF ACTION AND REFLECTION

One of the group homes in Washington, D.C., with which we had extensive contact was the Olive Branch Community. The Olive Branch is an intentional community that houses many former homeless citizens, who in turn help to run a homeless shelter and Zacchaeus' Community Kitchen. Members of the Olive Branch Community are committed to serving the homeless of D.C., as well as other needy citizens of the area. They have a simple motto: "Service, resistance, and contemplation." I translate this to mean something similar to "action/reflection," in which each of these ideas exists in a reciprocal and dynamic relationship with the other. We can have no true action without reflection. And reflection without action has no sustenance. In conjunction with one another, they provide the opportunity for resistance and social transformation. Such a process has no beginning or ending and can be entered at any point. We join the oppressed in their struggle, and because we care and want to exist in communion with them, their struggle becomes *our* struggle. In turn, we reflect on our efforts and what we have accomplished or failed to accomplish and consider new options to achieve social, political, or economic change. This then leads to more action, and the process continues as we form a joint movement to transform society and alleviate oppression.

The phrase "action and reflection" implies that the two ideas are somehow separate and might exist independent of one another. The idea of "action/reflection" suggests a different possibility—that the two ought to be inseparable. Indeed, if we are to build on the multiplicity of today's postmodern communities, we must be willing to both act and reflect. As Paulo Freire posited, "One of the gravest obstacles to the achievement of liberation is that oppressive reality absorbs those within it and thereby acts to submerge men's consciousness. Functionally, oppression is domesticating. To no longer be prey to its force, one must emerge from it and turn upon it. This can be done only by means of the praxis: reflection and action upon the world in order to transform it" (1970, p. 36). Action and reflection, as Freire goes on to argue, are in such "radical interaction that if one is sacrificed—even in part—the other immediately suffers" (p. 75). For Freire, action without reflection becomes mere activism. And reflection without action is verbalism. The key to transforming social conditions is to see the two as inseparable.

Service without a reflective component fails to be forward looking, fails to be concerned with the community beyond the present, and in essence fails as community service. Community service, ideally speaking, is about community building for today and tomorrow. This means that service projects ought to have reflective components that challenge individuals to struggle to identify various forces that may contribute to homelessness, rural and urban poverty, and economic inequities in general.

But true community service does not stop with merely learning about the causes of poverty. A real commitment to community building demands that larger efforts be made to alter the social dynamics contributing to economic inequality. Jane Kendall spoke to this concern in her discussion of service learning: "Service-learning programs explicitly include features which foster participants' learning about the larger social issues behind the human needs to which they are responding. This includes understanding the historical, sociological, cultural, and political contexts of the need or issue being addressed" (1990, p. 20). Kendall described the learning component of service learning as the "reflective component," which she argued is vital to the experience being more than a charitable effort on the part of students. She explained, "A good service-learning program helps participants see their questions in the larger context of issues of social justice and social policy—rather than in the context of charity" (p. 20). Benjamin Barber also addressed the importance of the learning aspect of service: "When sited in a learning environment, the service idea promotes an understanding of how self and community, private interest and public good, are necessarily linked" (1992, p. 249). And Howard Radest reminded us that community service as "learning by doing" can be completely inadequate if serious reflection does not enter into the equation: "Learning by doing . . . is misleading advice until we specify what and who the doers are, what and who the done-to are, and what their relationships to each other are and are expected to become. We may, in other words, learn precisely the wrong lessons from community service if we forget that practice as such can serve alternative ends and values" (1993, p. 189).

When we encourage college students to do volunteer work because the needy are less fortunate and therefore deserve our handouts, a clear message of inferiority and superiority is sent, and the lessons learned only serve to reinforce the dichotomy that already exists economically between the "haves" and the "have nots." If, on the other hand, we encourage students to envision the other as part of a larger community in which we are all bound and we all share and care for one another, a different kind of message is sent. When students are challenged to connect their sense of self to their sense of the other, serious and deep reflection is encouraged. Students are confronted with the reality that if they truly care about the other and have a desire to alter social conditions, they must consider community building and community service not as a one-time endeavor but as a process demanding their continued attention. The kind of reflection I speak of here is evident in the life and work of Robert Coles.

Robert Coles is a professor at Harvard University who has given much of his life to others through his involvement in community service. I already have mentioned his life and his book—*The Call of Service*—on several occasions throughout this text. Coles reflected on his years of work with college students who have committed much of their lives to community service: "I . . . learn about the students, their hopes, their aspirations, their values, as they get worked into their lives. Not least, I am given some moral pause. How should I be living my life? That is the question I keep hearing my students put to themselves—and much more is at stake for them, obviously, than for me" (1993, p. 285). As Coles struggled to answer that very question and as he reflected back on his life and what he has committed himself to, his thoughts were not accusatory, nor critical, but instead were contemplative. He wrote, "I move back in time. I shed for a brief moment decades of accumulated thoughts, involvements, and entanglements; I hear a youth's voice wondering, asking, asserting, hesitating, insisting—and the ideas and ideals I once held to be so essential, so urgently worth advancing, are suddenly back in full force, in spite of the distractions always waiting" (p. 285). The kind of reflection highlighted by Coles captures the serious considerations many students are faced with through their participation in community service. The experiential quality of service lacks substance when questions such as the one he poses to himself are absent: "How should I be living my life?"

When we build service around a reflective component that challenges students to think about their own lives and their roles within complex social, economic, and political matrices, we challenge them to reconsider who they are as people; their sense of self faces new and sometimes conflicting values and commitments. Radest is helpful as he captured some of these challenges in his discussion of a community service-based classroom:

> The classroom acquires a more numerous cast of characters even if "class-size" remains unchanged. Some of them may always have been there, but we did not know it. Teacher and student diversify into many persons, some only variations on the familiar, others quite strange and even shocking. So, I encounter my self as biased and appreciative, as

ignorant and knowing. I am, as we say, a different person there or there or there. And I discover that these are personalities with, hopefully, a certain coherence of connections. I am not merely playing different roles but I am different actors. I am, it almost seems, a community all by myself. . . . Community service reveals myselves to myself even as it reveals others to myself and myself to others. (1993, p. 144)

For Radest, the complexities of who we are as individuals is confronted in our encounters with strangers as we are forced to reconsider what gives meaning to life. In what follows, I discuss a Habitat for Humanity project that students participated in during one of their breaks from school. In particular, I focus on the reflective aspect of this project and how such reflections were tied to student involvement in service work (the action component).

THE HABITAT FOR HUMANITY PROJECT

In the spring of 1992, a group of about twenty Pennsylvania State University students and staff traveled to Maryland's eastern shore to join volunteers from approximately fifteen other colleges and universities in a large-scale Habitat for Humanity spring break project. The students, faculty, and staff converged on the campus of Salisbury State University as we met with organizers from Habitat and received our work assignments. We were assigned to the town of Princess Anne, where we were housed in the basement of a local church.

Most people are familiar with Habitat for Humanity and the organization's work in building and restoring houses for low-income families, who qualify for the program based on economic need and typically assume a no-interest loan. A key aspect of Habitat's program is that home owners must agree either to help build their own house or to give a certain number of hours to another Habitat project.

One of the more rewarding experiences the students on the Maryland project had was being able to work alongside the families who would eventually move into the houses. At one site in Princess Anne, we worked with an African American woman named Janet and her two sons, who were set to move into the house upon its completion. Janet, who appeared to be in her late thirties or early forties, took an active role in constructing her house. She helped hang the aluminum siding and handed shingles up to a group of students working on the roof. One afternoon, I worked with Janet and a couple of college students from another school as part of the electrical team. I teased her to watch out for an electrical shock when the day finally rolled around in which she could plug in that first appliance: "This is the first time I've done any electrical work, and I have no idea about what I'm doing." She responded by teasing me back: "I'll invite you over to test the first appliance. You can have some toast."

Her sons were about eight and ten years old. I had an extended conversation with the ten year old, named Jason, who was as proud about helping to build his family's house as a schoolboy getting straight A's on his report card for the first time. He showed me around the yard and where they were going to put the swing set and the dog house, and where he and his brother were planning to lay out a kick-ball field. Jason told me about how his mother and brother were squeezed into a small apartment with his grandmother. They had moved from Washington, D.C., where his mother had worked as a secretary, but for one reason or another had lost her job and had taken a new position in the Princess Anne area. He liked his new school much better than the one in D.C. "The kids are a lot nicer here, and it's safe enough for us to walk to school. And we get to carry our lunches too." I asked him if he had a "Jetsons" lunchbox, and he looked at me kind of strangely and mentioned something about "Transformers" and that his brother had some kind of "mutilated turtles" on his.

Students in our group also talked about their experiences getting to know the families who would eventually move into the houses (there were three different work sites around Princess Anne). "That was the highlight of the entire week for me," explained one student. "Talking to Janet about her life and seeing how happy and proud she is to be able to get a new house and help to build it. I can't even put it into words. It was just so rewarding." Another student commented on her experiences: "I couldn't quit laughing. . . . Jason was so funny and excited about having his own room. He told me he was going to put a lock on his door to keep his 'nosy, annoying brother out.' I've been doing volunteer work for a number of years, but I've never had the chance to get so involved with people who I am working to serve."

Another student thought that Habitat's requirement for families to put some time in to building their houses was a great policy for fostering a sense of accomplishment among the future residents. "I think it really helps people to feel better about themselves—the idea that they helped to build it. Those kids can say to their friends for the rest of their lives that they helped to build their own house." And another student added, "I enjoyed meeting the families as much as anything else we did all week. For me it really personalized the entire experience for me. I'll never forget the faces on those two boys and the way they followed their mother around trying to help. They got in the way more than anything else, but no one seemed to mind."

A number of issues emerged from the Habitat project in Maryland. However, in keeping with the theme of this chapter, I focus on students' reflections about the experience and their thoughts on community service commitments in general.

For a senior studying political science, the Habitat project and his involvement in community service were part of his commitment to social change. "I study political science because I may become a lawyer or go into politics of some kind. I want to contribute to making this world a better place to live, and I see both my career and what I do in terms of volunteerism as connected to that goal. Like I might be a lawyer who defends low-income people—like a public defender maybe. Right now I'm having a hard time making the connections. Class seems so removed from the kinds of things I learn on community service projects like this."

Another student's parents were actively involved in community service work through their church. A commitment to service reflected her sense of spirituality and was part of her values as a Christian. "God calls us to serve others and I expect that of myself. It's not something I do as a chore or only out of a sense of responsibility. It's something I enjoy a great deal." Another student, who identified spiritually as a Hindu, also saw service as part of her religious commitment and her faith in God. "Doing good works is part of my belief system and something I was brought up to value. Giving up my spring break to help build homes for low-income families is hardly a sacrifice for me. It's one of the most rewarding experiences I've ever had, actually. I guess I shouldn't be surprised that people feel good about doing good. That seems natural to me."

Several students saw community service as more of a civic responsibility—something they believed people with the time and resources ought to do as part of their commitment to the larger social good. As one student explained, "I'm not religious like some of the students who came on this trip. For me, volunteer work is something I do for my community, for my country, because I have been given so many of the good things in life. I come from an upper-class family and have had pretty much anything I want for most of my life. Service is an opportunity for me to give back for all I've received."

Whereas some students reflected on why they thought service was important, others talked about the effects community service had on them and the fact that, for some, the experience in Maryland had forced them to think about their lives more seriously. "Seeing these families so happy over getting a tiny house that's no bigger than the living room in my dad's house, really makes me rethink how much I have and how much I actually need," commented one student. She went on, "I mean my dorm room is nearly as big as the house we're building, and yet it's plenty for them. Why do I need any more than what I already have? . . . I have some friends—I call them 'granolas' because they are always talking about simplifying their lives. Anyway, I always just shove them away as if they are crazy, but the more I get involved in working with the poor the more I question the things that I think I need to be happy. Look, this week is the happiest and most relaxed I've been in a long time, and I didn't accumulate anything. Going shopping at the mall hasn't even crossed my mind. In fact, the whole trip cost me about a hundred bucks. That ought to tell me something."

Other students also did some serious reflecting about the Maryland project: "It helped me to get some of my thoughts together and think about where I'm going in my life. I don't have any of the answers yet, but I feel like I'm getting closer to figuring them out." Another student echoed these thoughts: "This kind of thing helps me clarify who I am and what I want out of life. Do I want to chase the big money like some of my friends are doing, or do I want something different? There's just so much pressure in our society to define success by one's job, or car, or house. It's a real struggle to follow a different path. I'm struggling with these issues now, and I think somewhere down the road this kind of experience will help me."

One student who participated in this trip seemed to have already dealt with the kinds of struggles the two preceding students noted. For Samuel Frias, life was going to be about service to others in one way or another. He just had to decide what form that service might take. I highlight Samuel's life and where he was in his own personal quest to clarify his life and his sense of self.

A STUDENT PROFILE

When I met Samuel Frias in 1991, he was a junior majoring in speech communications and psychology and considering a variety of careers in social service-related fields. His plan was to find employment for a few years as a social service worker and then move on to his ultimate professional goal of going to seminary and becoming a minister. Eventually he wanted to return to Puerto Rico, where he had been born, and contribute to solving some of the social and economic problems of the Puerto Rican people.

Samuel is a very intelligent student who is well read and thoughtful about political and social issues. He articulates his beliefs in a concise and passionate manner. It seems easy for him to make strong arguments for many of the things he has come to value—such as greater economic justice and affirmative action. His commitment to these concerns relates to his conception of Christianity and his belief in what he terms "the liberatory philosophy of Christ's message." Samuel found liberation theology compatible with both his concern for social justice and his belief that Christ was committed to serving the needy. Thus, for Samuel, service is not only an act of community building, it is also something he felt called to do as part of his religious convictions. He talked about his beliefs: "I think Christianity has been perverted in the U.S. and in other parts of the Western world. People have forgotten the message of love and empowerment inherent in Christ's teachings. I try to live my life by the message of love, and that means giving a piece of myself to others through service."

Although Samuel has committed himself to community service, he firmly believes that service to others must also include involvement in the larger struggle for social justice. "Building houses for low-income people doesn't change the fact that many in our society are forced to work for wages that are inadequate to meet their needs. We can help to build houses and serve meals in soup kitchens, but we must always recognize that all we are doing is putting Band-Aids on a larger problem. The Band-Aids are important to individuals and to families, but they do not contribute to solving the disease—which for me is tied to greed and overconsumption. We cannot continue to rape our environment and marginalize people in the name of economic policy."

Samuel's spiritual journey and the role of community service and social activism in that quest played an increasingly central part in his emerging sense of self. He had always felt the need to serve others who were less fortunate economically, but only in recent years had he managed to develop the strength of his convictions to take a more active role. "I have grown a lot in recent years. I'm more sure of myself now and more confident that what I believe is right. I am able to act on these beliefs partly because I feel much stronger about them and about myself as a person."

Upon graduation, a year and a half later, Samuel took a position in New York City working with disadvantaged families. After working for two years, he moved to Mexico, where, along with a former campus minister from Penn State, he helped run a community education center for the poor of the area. I have not heard from Samuel since then, but my guess is he has entered or is about to enter seminary somewhere. Samuel was never one to let his dreams or his passions fade away without allowing them to *carry* him to fruition.

Samuel Frias highlights the role community service plays in helping students to work through critical questions about one's sense of self. Recall from chapters 1 and 2 that the self is best thought of as a process emerging from ongoing interactions with others (Mead, 1934). The other may be a particular other (as in a specific individual) or a generalized other (representing the culture or subculture to which one relates). For Samuel, his knowledge of the identity of Jesus Christ forms a set of understandings about one particular other who contributes significantly to his sense of self. Living up to Christ's vision of love and equality is of paramount importance to Samuel, and community service offers him a vehicle for enacting his interpretation of Christ's message. Also, Samuel highlights a "generalized other" in the form of fellow Puerto Ricans and the poor, who play a key role in shaping his values and commitments. One can easily see how Samuel's religious values and beliefs, along with his cultural heritage, play important roles in shaping his identity and sense of self. (Recall from chapter 3—*Proposition 3: Identities are constituted within the parameters of culture and are highly related to the concept of the self.*)

Samuel is not alone in his explorations of the self. Throughout their involvement in community service, many students sought deeper meanings and confronted personal issues relevant to identity and the self. I turn now to highlight a variety of students whom I interviewed as part of other community service projects, who also offer reflections about their sense of self.

STUDENTS' REFLECTIONS ABOUT THE SELF

Some of the students who worked with homeless citizens in the D.C. project shared their reflections about how they thought of themselves as people and where they might be heading. In general, students found their work with the homeless to challenge their sense of self on a number of fronts. For example, some students were emotionally challenged by what they experienced, as the following comments reveal: "I found that working with homeless people was much harder on me than I'd expected. I found the work somewhat difficult and a bit discouraging. I think that I was shocked emotionally and that I need to think about how I can deal with the harsh reality of their lives and where I fit in all of this." A second student also talked about the emotional nature of the D.C. project: "I found it extremely difficult to say good-bye on the last day. I wondered if I would ever see any of those people again. Maybe I shouldn't have allowed myself to get so close to some of them, but I guess that's part of why I came."

A student from Michigan State University spoke of learning that some students deal with their emotions by complaining. She described her experiences on a trip to New York City and a project working with homeless citizens: "Some of the other students on the trip didn't have experience with a lot of issues related to homelessness. They have different family backgrounds and experiences. Some aren't very tolerant. I learned how people deal with their emotions. We had to shower in a decaying basement, and some of the students reacted very negatively—'Oh, how gross!' It was hard for me to hear their complaining. My attitude is 'Just deal with it.'"

One student from the Johns Island project pondered questions regarding learning about oneself: "What did I learn? Good question. The first thing is I've learned that I'm not as afraid of heights as I thought I was [she had to climb a ladder to do roof repairs]. Second, I learned that it's okay to be fearful of major life changes. And third, I've learned more about myself. I've got another piece into my personality jigsaw puzzle. I know I like to help, and to do good for others. I like to have fun, too—to get the most out of life that I can. And the quest for knowledge of the world of fiction and the world around me is important also." A senior in wildlife management who also participated in the Johns Island project learned the following about herself: "Many of my beliefs are not like those held by the majority of the volunteers on this trip; I'm somewhat conservative, yet I had an easier time accepting these differences than they did. The experience taught me that I'm more firm in my beliefs than I thought I was and that it's hard being the one who's different, but not impossible."

A graduate student offered the following thoughts concerning his personal challenge to learn to be more patient and how working in community service settings had helped him: "I guess I have a tendency to be impatient, and I think I still need to work on it. . . . I found myself in situations when in the past I would have reacted differently. But this time I kept my thoughts to myself, and instead of ruining everybody's fun I kept quiet. I guess I was more patient and prudent with my reactions." Another student from the Johns Island project discussed what she discovered about herself: "I'm usually very shy, but on this trip I was much more open than usual and I learned that people will accept me if I'm comfortable with myself. I felt comfortable and accepted, and I think it might have something to do with the fact that we are all here for the same reason—we all have a common bond. Everyone paid to come here and help someone and for no reward other than feeling good about yourself."

Other students also seemed to be using their experience of community service to work through personal issues. One student mentioned, "I'm learning that I move more by momentum than I thought I did. . . . When I was a little kid I was a perfectionist. And it kind of got to the point that it got in the way, but now I'm getting better. . . . Now I see things on a bigger scale." Another student talked about her personal growth: "I have to distance myself because I tend to get very emotional. When I learned about the concentration camp in seventh grade, I couldn't eat. I have to work through my emotions in order to help. So I've made this conscious effort to distance myself so I can contribute. . . . I have to conquer things that prohibit me from helping; I've got to mitigate that somehow. I think these kinds of experiences are helping me to conquer my fears. I'm also learning about another culture—a lifestyle that is different from mine. And that is helping me to understand others better."

For a number of students, involvement in community service contributed to their sense of self as a spiritual person. Several students in this study saw strong connections between their faith and their commitment to serving others. A junior majoring in health education had this to say: "For me, service work always leads to a spiritual awakening. Service challenges me to face the deeper meanings of life—things that I typically try to ignore." Another student who participated in the Yonges Island project also commented on her spiritual growth: "I'm a spiritual person, but I'm not a Christian and I'm not a Catholic. I just have to look a little harder for a religion that suits me. Or maybe no religion at all. . . . These kinds of experiences help me to think about what it means to be spiritual and to ask questions about why we should care for others." Some students talked about the spirituality they experienced from those they worked to serve: "It's fascinating, the level of spirituality here [Yonges Island]. It's a neat feeling to listen to the people here and to see their relationship with God. They're so emotional. . . . I feel it too. . . . You learn a lot about yourself when you're here." Another student talked about the residents of Johns Island: "People here have a deep faith. I think that's really cool, given the hardships they live with, the way they face life. They need their faith."

Not all the learning experiences pertaining to self-understanding pleased students. For example, one student noted that she felt very uncomfortable when she was around African American homeless citizens: "I felt the gap between Black and White people. I felt very uncomfortable at times." She was not pleased with her discomfort and hoped to figure out how she could grow from it. "I have to take this feeling and see if I can't learn from it. I don't think of myself as a racist, and yet why was I so uncomfortable?" Three other students talked about things they learned about themselves from which they would like to grow:

> I learned that I am not nearly as good a person as I had thought. I learned that I still have some personal issues related to accepting others to deal with. Compared to some of the people I met, my life seems trivial and uninspired. I will resolve to do better.

> My work as a volunteer has really helped me to see that I have so much more I have to understand about myself in order to grow. I'm still on the journey and have a long ways to go.

> I think this week has helped me to recognize that I truly don't know much about myself. I've also learned that I'm not good at talking during group sharing. Everybody talks about all the things they have done this week, but I can't really explain the moments we've experienced. I guess I can't really do them justice.

The students in this section highlight how community service provides a context for extensive learning about and understanding of one's self. Sometimes their experiences helped students to find answers to their identity struggles, whereas at other times important questions arose. In both cases, the self was reconfigured through the ongoing interaction that characterizes service founded on mutuality. I turn now to another student profile as I discuss the community service experiences of Janie Dreshbach and some of the explorations of the self that she faced.

A STUDENT PROFILE

Janie Dreshbach is a sophomore majoring in international relations and has been involved in community service work since her high school days. She talked about her past involvement in community service and how it had helped her think more seriously about life. "I got involved in a lot of self-esteem work, primarily with teenagers. It helped me to think more seriously about my understanding of myself and how others think of me. I began to wonder about what kind of person I was and was going to be. I began to ask questions of myself: Am I too judgmental? Am I open to others? Am I sensitive to how other people see the world?"

Janie's involvement in self-esteem work with teenagers came about through her work at the Voluntary Action Center, where at one point during her last summer in high school she had replaced a full-time staff member who had left the organization. One of her roles was to recruit teen and preteen volunteers and place them in agencies or community service programs. Sometimes the students were less than enthusiastic about doing community service, but their parents had instigated their visit to the center. Janie was reluctant to place students who were not very interested in service, but she also knew that a degree of interest might be fostered in many of them once they experienced the satisfaction of helping others. Janie recalled one of her success stories.

David was about eleven when he was dragged into Janie's office kicking and screaming. He didn't want anything to do with community service. His mother had brought him into the center because she was worried about his being too withdrawn. David was skilled with computers and was spending more and more time alone. He was not developing social skills. The first thing Janie told him was, "I am not making you volunteer, and I am not going to place you unless you want to do something." David was reluctant at first to pick any kind of activity, so Janie asked him if he could work with her on some computer problems she was having. "He was very good and helped me quite a bit. Eventually, I mentioned this summer computer camp at a local school and how they might need older students like himself to help the kids develop computer skills. He was reluctant but agreed to do it." After a week or two, Janie called David's house to see how he was doing. "His mother told me that he hadn't come home yet. It was in the afternoon, and he should have been done around noon or so. She told me that he loved it so much he had volunteered to work extra with the afternoon program. I asked her to have him come see me, and when he did I asked him about his experience. He was very nonchalant, like it was boring him to death and he would be glad when it was over." However, after some persistent prodding on Janie's part, David finally broke down and exclaimed, "OK, I admit it. I love it!"

David is only one example. As Janie pointed out, other teenagers and preteens who had been made to volunteer seemed to get nothing out of the experience. A key for Janie was matching the youngsters' interests in some way with the type of community service activity. A sure prescription for failure was assigning a disinterested student to an area in which he or she had limited knowledge or experience. She worked hard all summer to create the best fit she could between the students and the agencies, and she had her share of successes.

Summer eventually ended, and it was time for Janie to move on to college. After such a successful experience at the Voluntary Action Center, Janie was more committed than ever to community service and got involved in volunteer work at Michigan State University. She spent her first spring break working on an Alternative Spring Break project in Louisville, Kentucky, where she helped clean transitional apartments for homeless families and worked at a group house for recovering alcoholics. She discussed her experience: "My mother wanted me to go on the typical college spring break, to Daytona or something like that, but I can't imagine myself doing nothing for a week. I'd go crazy. My mother felt I had done enough service already." But, for Janie, participating in community service work was not really work anyway. How could it be when you get so much in return? "The experience in Kentucky was fantastic. I was a site leader and had to interact with the agencies who sponsored us. I think it was Volunteers of America. I had to make all the contacts and ask all the questions. Being a spokesperson for the group was a great experience. I learned that I can be a productive and fair leader." Although the experience was rewarding for Janie, the one regret she had was not getting to spend more time with the homeless families. The biggest reward and joy for her was connecting with the people, building relationships, building a sense of community.

Janie has given serious thought to the kind of person she is and the kind of person she wants to become. For her, community service plays an integral role in her exploration of her own identity. Service work provides her with a variety of educational contexts in which she is able to learn more about others and about her self as well. (Recall from chapter 3—*Proposition 8: Education plays a critical role in fostering student learning and development and thus provides a context for student self-exploration and identity development.*) She highlights the role that community service can play in helping students clarify their own sense of self when students are challenged to ask critical questions about their own lives. Recall the interrogation Janie put herself through: "Am I too judgmental? Am I open to others? Am I sensitive to how other people see the world?" These are the critical reflections of a student engaged in the work of creating a more relational or caring sense of self.

In addition to gaining insights about themselves, as highlighted by Samuel Frias and Janie Dreshbach, students had a variety of revelations that helped clarify different aspects of their lives. (Recall from chapter 3— *Proposition 7: College students are at a time in their lives when a multitude of forces influence their sense of self; thus they often are in the midst of a period of heightened self-discovery and identity confusion.*) In what follows, I discuss students' reflections concerning leadership and values and commitments.

REFLECTIONS ON LEADERSHIP

Many students like Janie learned a great deal about leadership through their participation in community service projects. For example, a graduate student who participated in the D.C. trip talked about what she had learned in regard to leadership: "I can have a powerful influence on those around me. I can stand up for things and for the people I believe in. I also learned that loyalty is very meaningful for someone to be an effective leader." A second graduate student talked about how his experiences on an Alternative Spring Break had helped him be more confident as a leader: "My most significant learning experiences have been in the areas of being a leader of large groups. I found that by interacting with everyone on a personal level, I can learn from their strengths and special gifts. I discovered that I was better than I thought at getting people to work together." One student was beginning to see himself as a leader for the first time in his life: "I noticed that when other people were doing stuff—helping with the work, talking to the kids, painting, or helping the children with their homework—I was more willing to lend a helping hand. I know that I need to be able to initiate things everywhere, not just here in South Carolina but back home as well. I need to recognize when my help is needed and take action. I think I'm beginning to be able to do that."

A Michigan State student reflected on her experiences as a site leader for a New York City community service project: "Being a site leader was hard—trying to balance two groups that formed within the larger group: budgeting, handling the rental cars, and giving directions to the sites in and around the city, not to mention the challenge of driving the van through the city. I was so nervous. But I learned a lot about organizational skills. It was really like a mini-resident assistant job. That's exactly what it was like." A second student, despite protestations to the contrary, seemed to be setting herself up for possible leadership roles in the future: "There's so many things I need to learn . . . things I need to improve, including my motivation. I want to be more like a lot of the people on this trip [Johns Island]. I want to be more like them, not like a leader, but, yeah, like the people on this trip. I need to be more of an adult. I need to do something important that affects other people, and not just be coasting along."

A junior from Penn State University with a long history of involvement in community service attributed her leadership development to being a Big Sister, a youth leader in her church, and a participant in a variety of service organizations throughout her college career. "Through my service work I have learned so much about what motivates people. Being a Big Sister helped me to learn that there are many different ways people view the world, and if you want to serve in some kind of leadership role, you have to understand the complexity of how people view life. Things are never black and white. My work with youth groups and volunteer experiences in college have reinforced my views of the world. I am somewhat conservative religiously and I guess politically too, but I work very hard to understand the way others think. I pride myself on being accepting and tolerant. I think to truly serve as a role model for kids, which is important to me, you have to be accepting of diverse individuals."

REFLECTIONS ON VALUES AND COMMITMENTS

In addition to their thoughts about leadership and the possibility of becoming leaders themselves, students also were challenged to consider various values and commitments. For example, one student was both pleased with and excited about his new insights and motivations toward community service work. Because of his experiences working with homeless citizens, he said he planned to rethink his life and what it is he values. "I think that it's time for me to recognize that there is a role that I can play in helping others and making the world a better place, even if it's in some small way."

For a number of students, the meaning of love was one of the values they came to understand better. A sophomore in chemical engineering discussed his experience of working with low-income rural families: "Everyone is different but everyone needs love. Everyone—man or woman, Black or White—deserves love and respect, if for no other reason but their humanity. We're all in this crazy world together, and loving each other absolutely and unconditionally is the greatest way to interact with each other. I could love more and I could learn more, but the greatest thing I learned is that the love I give and the things I can teach others change them—and in so doing, change the world." A second student also talked about the value of love and how it relates to his own sense of well-being: "I learned that above the many things that I consider necessities, I need to have love as much as I need food to survive." A third student, a junior in health education, mentioned love as a key value upon which she had reflected during her community service work on Johns Island: "I got involved in volunteerism because I wanted to learn more about myself. I've learned how to love a wide range of people despite differences between us. I've learned not to be judgmental."

Some students talked about how their involvement in community service helped them understand better how important service to others is to them. For example, one student talked about how community service involvement helps him clarify his life: "Getting involved in community service helps me to get back in touch with who I really am. It reminds me that I have more to live for than merely myself." A second student offered similar sentiments: "This community service project [Yonges Island] has helped me to see how much I care for other people and how little I do back home. I think I should take the time to do more for people. Not just during spring break but in general, all the time." And a third student explained, "I'd like to be involved in community service throughout my whole life. I only hope I'm not so involved in my career and my family; I know it's easy to do that. I'll be a Girl Scout leader for sure. . . . It's important to not only be tending your own garden, but people have the responsibility to help others tend theirs."

Two students discussed community service learning experiences in the same breath as family concerns. For example, one student talked about how important it is to her to give back to her community as part of a family effort. "Lately, I've realized how lucky I've been. I need to give back. Maybe it's a selfish reason, I don't know, but I need to give something back to my community. . . . If I have a family someday, I think I'll use community service as a way to get involved together—a family thing—because of what you get out of it." Another student talked about the influence her parents had had on her values and how these values had surfaced within the context of community service: "I have skills and qualities that are valuable that I didn't know existed within me. Like working within a system and set of rules and resources, yet not alienating people who need services. I had to tell some of the homeless people that we couldn't give them seconds at the soup kitchen. That was hard, but I think I did it in a way that was kind and caring. I have a lot of values that my parents instilled in me that I thought were inconsequential. I never thought about them. But I learned that my parents had reasons and that values such as caring for others are important."

One student reflected on community service in general and the service project to Johns Island in particular. "I've learned to embrace time by myself at the end of the day. The past things I've done seem so banal right now. There's so much I can do if I set my mind to it. . . . I guess this is what it is: I can give something to the community, besides life as just waking up, sleeping, paying bills, taking exams. There's something more. If I were to explain what I learned through community service and through this trip to my friends back at school, they'd say 'Why did you go off and do that?' I'd also make them feel guilty. This is my most memorable spring break, though certainly not the wildest. Two years ago, I don't even remember what I did. I'll remember this one, though."

SOCIAL CHANGE

For the majority of the students in this study who were interviewed either formally or informally, connecting their participation in community service to larger social issues was not a primary concern. It was enough for most of them that they gave up their free time to help someone over their spring or winter break, in their free time during the semester, or during their summer vacations. In fact, several students specifically mentioned a lack of interest in getting involved in social change. For example, one student explained, "I like to help people in need, but I'm not into the politics of it all. I leave the political debates to the politicians, the lawyers. There's so much information that I don't have, that for me to get involved is idiotic." A second student offered similar comments: "Why are there so many homeless people in this country? For me, that's the $20,000 question and it's one I don't have a clue about. I'm also not sure I want to know the answers because it would probably mean I'd have to consider a lot of serious issues and where I stand on them. At this point in my life, I just want to graduate from college and get a half decent job." Certainly, these students deserve credit for their involvement in helping others, but their efforts tended to lack the critical reflection and understanding necessary to connect individual suffering to a broader vision of liberatory politics. As Samuel Frias pointed out, individuals who apply the Band-Aids are needed and deserve encouragement. But to achieve the kind of social transformation Freire and others have spoken of takes the development of a critical consciousness rooted in a concern for liberation from economic, cultural, and political oppression.

Students such as Samuel Frias and Janie Dreshbach were the exception and not the rule. In their stories we hear a deep concern for others as they struggle with some of the broader issues contributing to homelessness, poverty, and low wages. They are confused themselves, as most of us are, about where solutions lie, but they are nonetheless committed to searching for those very solutions. Both of these students also recognize the importance of *working with* the oppressed, as opposed to charitable notions of *giving to* the needy. This is a point Freire made as well, and closely resembles the ideal of mutuality discussed in chapter 5. As Freire argued, "Political action on the side of the oppressed must be pedagogical action in the authentic sense of the word, and, therefore, action *with* [my emphasis] the oppressed" (1970, p. 53). He went on to point out that those who engage in liberatory action with the oppressed must be careful not to take advantage of the emotional dependence that often accompanies their position of being dominated. We cannot provide the answers for those who are economically marginalized because they may too readily accept our solutions, which thus may serve to perpetuate a kind of learned helplessness. Reflection, as well as action, must be *mutually* engaging. Freire elaborated, "Libertarian action must recognize this dependence as a weak point and must attempt through reflection and action to transform it into independence. . . . When men are already dehumanized, due to the oppression they suffer, the process of their liberation must not employ the methods of dehumanization" (p. 53). This is why merely supplying Band-Aids, in and of itself, is not the solution to the plight of the poor. The challenge that faculty, staff, and student leaders face in structuring community service projects is to help students connect individual suffering to larger social problems and to challenge students to consider how they might contribute to social change.

Community service that is seen as part of an action/reflection dynamic that contributes to social change is dangerous in that it fosters a desire to alter the social and economic structure of our society. It is political because it questions how power is distributed and the connection between power and economics. This is not the same conception of community service that Bill Clinton or George Bush has spoken of and that has emerged as populist sentiment. Radest addressed this issue in the closing paragraph of his book:

> Ironically, the community service that emerged from the consensus around the 1990 legislation [Americorp legislation], and that emerges as schools and colleges adopt a "community service requirement," will turn out to be unexpectedly subversive of its proponents' intentions. They see it as peaceable, unthreatening and polite. It is offered as controlled activism—an activism without politics. However, a community service worth doing must lose its consensus and its innocence. At that point it becomes worthy of our support. (1993, p. 191)

The kind of community service suggested in this book—what I call "critical community service"—combines liberatory politics with the action/reflection necessary for the development of a critical consciousness. Critical community service becomes not only political action to alter social conditions, it is also a form of pedagogy capable of transforming students' and teachers' understandings of the social world. The educational implications of critical community service are the focus of chapter 8.

SUMMARY

Action and reflection are key components of the kind of liberatory pedagogy suggested in the work of Freire, and they inform how community service may be understood as both an educational and a liberatory practice. My goal in this chapter has been to point out a variety of learning experiences related to students' involvement in community service and the role reflection plays in helping students seriously consider their relationship to others and to their communities as they engage in action. As I have pointed out, students experience a variety of learning outcomes related to self-knowledge in the areas of values and commitments, and their own leadership abilities, as well as general understandings related to one's sense of self. Perhaps the most significant outcome relates to students' developing a more complex understanding of the interconnections between community service and social change. Action linked with the kind of critical reflection suggested by Freire forces students to consider their role in the lives of others and their ability to contribute to improving social conditions. This means more than serving meals to homeless citizens; it also involves confronting the larger social and economic issues that lead to homelessness in the first place. Such a view promotes a vision of democratic citizenship linked to caring and a concern for social justice. (Recall from chapter 3—*Proposition 10: Caring selves are critical to the process of democracy and the struggle to build a more just and equitable society.*)

However, the reality of my experience has been that most students do not develop a critical awareness of the mitigating factors that may contribute to rural or urban poverty, and, in fact, many do not seek such knowledge. For some students, discovering the complicated forces at work in shaping people's lives is frightening, for it might place additional demands on them (the "cynics" are an example). Janie Dreshbach and Samuel Frias are exceptions to the rule; both spend considerable time in trying to understand how they might have a broader influence on the lives of others. They may be classified as "critical idealists" in that they have a vision of a more just and caring society but also have given serious thought to how to achieve such a vision.

For many of the students introduced in this book, their excursion into service through activities such as working in soup kitchens and homeless shelters, building houses for Habitat for Humanity, doing home repairs in low-income rural areas, and tutoring educationally disadvantaged children was their first exposure to other committed students, who often challenged their views of the world. This is another reason why action and reflection in combination are so important; through activities such as small reflection groups, students have the opportunity to teach and learn from one another. Ultimately, it may be peer influence that serves to engender increased student concern for the lives of others. Therefore, simply getting students involved initially in community service through whatever means is available may be something to consider.

Even though many students in this study had not yet achieved a critical understanding of the social, political, and economic forces at work in their lives and in the lives of others, many seemed ripe for such a possibility (they may be thought of as "idealists"). One is left to wonder how continued involvement in community service activities, if structured along the lines suggested in this work, might influence their development and their views of the self, the other, and community and society. With this thought in mind, I turn now to Chapter 8 as a focus in greater detail on the notion of critical community service.

Chapter 8

Critical Community Service

> *A pedagogy which empowers students to inter-*
> *vene in the making of history is more than a lit-*
> *erary campaign. Critical education prepares stu-*
> *dents to be their own agents for social change,*
> *their own creators of democratic culture.*
> —*Ira Shor,* Critical Teaching
> and Everyday Life

    I never planned on going to college. Upon graduation from high school,
I expected to get a job at one of the local mills or join the military. The military
seemed a little more exciting than the routine of the factory, but I wasn't ready
to leave home when graduation finally rolled around. I imagined becoming
one of those mill honkies like my first stepfather: get up each morning and
carry one of those metal lunch boxes and a silver steel thermos full of coffee to
keep me awake through the morning's hangover. Get off work at three and
meet some of the guys at the local beer garden and hang out until dinnertime.
Or if I really tied one on, just stay there until bedtime. And then, as Jackson
Browne wrote in "The Pretender," "I'd get up and do it again." I'm not sure
how long I could have survived that routine, but fortunately I never had to
find out.

    The steel and coal industries in western Pennsylvania were at the front
end of a period of steep decline around 1976, when I graduated from Grove
City High School. So I got a job as a janitor at the same high school I had grad-
uated from, as part of the local job training and partnership program funded by
the federal government to help dislocated and unemployed workers. The pro-
gram also helped low-income teenagers like myself to find temporary employ-
ment. When I began my summer job, I had no idea of what I was going to do
three months later, when my employment would come to an end. To say this was
a depressing point in my life is an understatement.

Nearly all of my friends had been accepted at one college or another throughout the East, but mostly in Pennsylvania. One guy had multiple offers from Princeton and Dartmouth and other top schools. I think he ended up at Dartmouth. A couple of my other friends were set to attend some of the better schools in Pennsylvania and Ohio, such as Penn State and Oberlin. And still others selected local schools such as Grove City, Westminster, Thiel, and Allegheny Colleges. Some of the average students went to Pennsylvania's state college system and attended Clarion, Edinboro, or Slippery Rock State College. I'll never forget those awkward lunch periods when all the guys with whom I associated talked about which schools had accepted them and where they might go, and I still had no clue as to what would happen upon graduation. They had practiced for weeks for their SATs by forming study groups and buying preparation materials to help them. In the meantime, I didn't see any reason to take "that stupid test": How could someone who couldn't even afford the four dollars to sit for the exam ever think about going to college? College wasn't for me. It was for those kids with two parents and some money—at least a little bit of money.

So graduation day came, and I joined the ranks of the unemployed, at least until the janitorial job started a month or so later. I had been working at the school for three or four weeks when Mr. Schultz, one of the guidance counselors, asked me to come into his office. This was the same counselor who, three years earlier, had told me that I had scored very high on the Stanford Binet IQ test and that I should be getting better than C's for grades. Until that point in my life, no one had ever told me I was smart, or if they had, it had never sunk in. I walked into his office a C student and came out an A– student. I guess I'm one more example of how another's expectations of us sometimes dictate how well we perform. Hell, for all I know he made the whole thing up and I was really just another dummy, like most of my family believed ourselves to be.

Mr. Schultz told me about a recruiter from an electronics school in Cuyahoga Falls, Ohio. The recruiter was looking for recent graduates who had received good grades in high school but who did not have college plans for the fall. "I passed your name on to him because I didn't think you had any definite plans. This might be something to consider. There are a lot of jobs in the electronics field and your math background will be helpful." "Yea," I thought to myself, "my math background may help, but I couldn't fix anything with a tool to save my life." That was my brother Gary's talent, not mine.

The recruiter called my house, and we set up an appointment to talk. He explained what an electronics technician did—fix stereos, televisions, and computers—that was their big catch: "It's the age of computers, and electronics technicians will be in great demand. And it's only a two-year program, so you'll be out making money much quicker than if you went to college." He administered some idiotic test, which, of course, I passed because the test is only designed to make you feel like the school has academic standards. He explained how the school would help me get financial aid and that going there wouldn't cost a cent—which was good because I didn't have many cents—or much sense either, as I proceeded to waste a year of my life burning circuitry boards with my very own soldering gun.

I found the theory of electronics and electricity fascinating, but the part where I actually had to use my hands to repair something was another story. After I was finished with my practice circuitry board, it looked more like road pizza than something that would go into a computer or stereo.

I guess that was one of the first clues that I was more inclined toward academic material dealing with theory and philosophy than I was toward learning a trade. I dropped out of the electronics institute armed with new knowledge about how financial aid for college worked. For the first time in my life I realized that college was an option, so I applied to and was accepted at Slippery Rock State College. I still was not convinced that I was college material, but my high school girlfriend had been accepted to the same school and we had always been about the same caliber of student. If Lisa could make it in college, then maybe I could too. That thought is not intended as a put-down of Lisa. She was a good student. What it demonstrates, however, is the poor sense of self I had in terms of my academic abilities.

It would be hard for anyone to imagine the joy and confidence boost I experienced when I made the dean's list my first semester. I was college material? No, I was college material! Although I had some tough semesters along the way, for the most part, each year I studied brought a greater interest in learning. There was so much I didn't know, but more than anything else I wanted to shake this feeling of inferiority—this feeling of being the poor kid on the block. It was a feeling that hovered over me like a storm cloud, casting a somber note on my every accomplishment.

I have gone to great lengths to shake the feeling that I am not quite good enough, or that I do not have as much worth as the next person. Even now, as a new assistant professor at a major research university, I am dealing with feelings that I don't really belong among scholars, among academics. I'm uncomfortable with the compliments some of my senior colleagues bestow on me. I know I have accomplished a great deal already and that, according to some of my peers, I am right on track for tenure. But what it all means is that this work is really not very hard, after all, or how else could I do it? It's the same old story: If I can succeed at something, then it wasn't really worth much to begin with. It's kind of like the old Groucho Marx line: "Any club that would have me as a member I wouldn't want to join."

It's all quite confusing and daunting at times. I am the same small-town kid who was destined to be a mill honky carrying one of those metal lunch pails and a hard hat to work everyday. That was my future. That was what my father and my first stepfather did. That was what I would do, too. A college professor . . . no, that's not me. That's some other guy. That's a self I still don't know.

My fascination with philosophy and theorizing about the social world has brought me this far in life. It keeps my attention and drives much of the passion that I have for my work. But at the same time, it leaves me incomplete. Reflection without action has a hollow ring to it, and my life as a faculty member would never be satisfying if I did not make some effort to create social change through my work. This is one reason why community service has become an important aspect of my life and why I have struggled to link it to my intellectual sense of self. This is also why I am so drawn to critical social science and its attention to social transformation. I feel lucky that I am able to synthesize two important aspects of my self—the joy of theorizing and a commitment to social change—through efforts such as this book and what it represents to me.

The shadow of poverty, under which many of the students learned significant aspects about themselves and others, also provides the backdrop for my life and struggle as a student and as a scholar. Although I lived in and out of poverty for much of my childhood, I do not see it as a burden but as a blessing that has helped me understand the meaning of marginality. As a White male, I recognize the privileges that have come to me because of my race and gender. But it is my economic background that has taught me most about the "other." Growing up poor has been my greatest privilege and is what I cherish most about my past.

Not everyone has had the opportunities and the gifts that have fallen to me throughout my lifetime, and this book in part takes a look at how college students can play a role in the lives of the poor. But there is a bigger objective behind this book, which relates to the way we think about higher education and its primary mission.

Over the years, higher education has become primarily a vehicle to prepare people for their life's work. Although many students do not take positions in the areas in which they study, they nonetheless develop the sensibilities and general understandings that are helpful and necessary for assuming roles within the working world and especially the professional sphere. A college education ought to help people prepare for their life's work. I am not questioning the significance of this role. But higher learning ought to achieve much more. This is where I draw heavily from John Dewey (1916) and other educational philosophers who have argued for a broader vision of education and a view of students not only as prospective workers, but as citizens within a democratic society.

Notions of citizenship often are vague and need to be anchored in a clear understanding of what kind of society we desire. There can be no vision of citizens or citizenship without a vision of society. Feminists offer a vision of a society framed by an ethic of care. Postmodernists call attention to the cultural mosaic that is the postmodern condition. Both of these theoretical camps remind us that, more so today than perhaps at any time in our past, we need caring citizens. Having politically knowledgeable citizens is necessary for democracy to grow, but we also need people who care and are willing to seek understanding about others within their communities, their country, and around the world. What we need more than ever is a form of higher learning that fosters an ethic of care.

In this chapter, I present some ideas for advancing a more caring form of higher learning. I discuss how an ethic of care can be central to higher learning and the role community service might play in structuring a more caring context. I accomplish this first by building on the work of John Dewey. I then highlight key facets of a critical view of education and the role such a perspective plays in advancing democracy and caring. I go on to introduce what I call "critical community service" as I highlight eight basic principles of such a perspective. Finally, I conclude this chapter by offering some practical guides to elevating community service to center stage within academe.

THE WORK AND INFLUENCE OF JOHN DEWEY

One important aspect of Dewey's thinking that I build on is his view of the importance of experientially based education delineated in his discussion of progressive education. Education in the United States, for Dewey, had become the proliferation of the past. He argued that learning had simply become the passing on of static facts and information judged to be of value by society's elders. Knowledge was conveyed "as a finished product, with little regard either to the ways in which it was originally built up or to changes that will surely occur in the future. It is to a large extent the cultural product of societies that assumed the future would be much like the past, and yet it is used as educational food in a society where change is the rule, not the exception" (Dewey, 1938, p. 19). For Dewey, the solution to learning from teachers through texts about the past was "learning through experience."

Recall the thoughts echoed by Carolyn Fisher, my student friend whom I bumped into in Seattle: "There are two kinds of learning. There's academic learning that you do in school. You know, with books and professors. And there's another kind of learning that comes from traveling, from experience, from living. I needed to do some living before I could be sure about the kind of academic stuff I wanted to study and the kind of career I wanted to have." And recall the comments from a student in chapter 7: "I learn more through my volunteer work than I ever do in any of my classes at school. Talking to people from diverse backgrounds provides so much insight that people just can't imagine. I study all these different theories in political science and sociology, but until you get a chance to see how the social world influences people's everyday lives, it just doesn't have that much meaning." Other students also appreciated the experiential quality of community service, as the following two students reveal:

> The things I learned in working with poor people in the inner city have been worth more to me than anything I've learned in all my years in school. The feelings and issues you have to deal with just can't be taught in the classroom.

> This week [the Yonges Island project] has taught me so much about other people and the problems they face in life. You can read about growing up poor, but getting to share a conversation with someone who has overcome so much during their lifetime is quite a different matter. . . . It's made me much less judgmental of others and their place in life.

Dewey argued that genuine education comes about through experience, although clearly not all experiences are equally educative. "For some experiences are mis-educative. Any experience is mis-educative that has the effect of arresting or distorting the growth of further experience. An experience may be such as to engender callousness; it may produce lack of sensitivity and responsiveness. Then the possibilities of having richer experience in the future are restricted" (1938, pp. 25–26). Recall the student from chapter 4 who participated in a community service project in New York City and was so frightened by her experience that she decided never again to involve herself in the lives of homeless citizens. "I learned that I am very fortunate. It was right there in my face. I learned that I am extremely sensitive to it [homelessness and poverty]. It's not that I don't care. I just can't deal with it. I just can't deal with the first-hand experience. I need to help in some other kind of way." However, when asked to elaborate on another kind of way in which she could be helpful, this student was lost for words. Her experience may be seen as mis-educative if we take as the goal of higher learning the development of a sense of caring and commitment to others. To remove oneself from the struggle to alter the circumstances of homeless people because their realities are so stark is certainly not reflective of the kinds of caring attitudes we hope to foster through community service. A number of things might have contributed to this student's lack of genuine educational experience, as Dewey might describe it. Remember that the New York City project, unlike most others discussed in this book, did not have faculty or staff or any experienced student leaders who could lead reflective group discussions. Such discussions are important in helping students work through what sometimes can be quite traumatic experiences. Clearly, some experiences can indeed be mis-educative.

In addition to dealing with the role of experientially based education, Dewey examined the role of education in preparing democratic citizens. I contend that higher learning is not only about readying students for the world of work but ought also to involve an equally important process—helping students better understand themselves and how they fit within a democratic society (Rhoads & Valadez, 1996). As I noted in chapter 3, this idea is discussed by Dewey (1916) in his classic work *Democracy and Education,* in which he argued that democracy depends on education for a citizenry who are capable of making critical decisions about communal life. This involves the ability to reflect critically on one's own place in society, as well as the place of others. Education for democracy demands that schools help individuals see how they are linked to the public sphere.

Dewey had a specific vision of a democratic society that entailed much more than merely the right to vote. A democratic society, for Dewey, suggested a type of relational living in which one's decisions and actions must be made with regard to their effect on others. "A democracy is more than a form of government; it is primarily a mode of associated living, of conjoint communicated experience. The extension in space of the number of individuals who participate in an interest so that each has to refer his own action to that of others, and to consider the action of others to give point and direction to his own" (1916, p. 93). Dewey's version of democracy challenged all citizens to take part in a form of decision making that balances the interests of oneself with those of others. Democracy seen in this light demands that individuals understand the lives and experiences of other members of a society. How else can we weigh the effect of our actions if the other remains distant and unknown?

Implied throughout Dewey's conception of democracy is an ethic-of-care philosophy. This is expressed in his view of liberty, which is clearly grounded in a relationally based understanding of social life: "Liberty is that secure release and fulfillment of personal potentialities which take place only in rich and manifold association with others" (Dewey, 1927, p. 150). More recent political theorists such as Richard Battistoni (1985) also have recognized the importance of developing relationally based understandings of social life. For example, he supported Alexis de Tocqueville's (1945) claim that American democracy is dependent upon "the reciprocal influence of men upon one another" (p. 117). For Battistoni, reciprocal influence is fostered through participatory forms of education, which he claimed are more likely to foster citizens who see themselves as active participants in the political process.

For Dewey, Tocqueville, and Battistoni, democracy is more than an abstract ideal to be admired from a distance; it has a transformative power that demands citizens to engage in a communal struggle that is never quite complete. As Dewey explained, "Regarded as an idea, democracy is not an alternative to other principles of associated life. It is the idea of community life itself. It is an ideal in the only intelligible sense of an ideal: namely, the tendency and movement of some thing which exists carried to its final limit, viewed as completed, perfected. Since things do not attain such fulfillment but are in actuality distracted and interfered with, democracy in this sense is not a fact and never will be" (1927, p. 148).

In writing about Dewey's influence on education, Benjamin Barber stated that "public education is education for citizenship. In aristocratic nations, in elitist regimes, in technocratic societies, it may appear as a luxury. . . . But in democracies, education is the indispensable concomitant of citizenship. Where women and men would acquire the skills of freedom, it is necessary" (1992, p. 15). This is why, for Barber, the United States and the educational opportunities offered to students may be considered "an aristocracy for everyone." As Barber elaborated, "The point where democracy and education intersect is the point we call community" (p. 225). In the context of the preceding statement, and in light of Dewey's work, Barber argued that schooling must be a community-oriented process, just as democracy must be a community-minded endeavor. Thus, schooling, community, and democracy are inevitably linked: "Dewey is saying that in the absence of community there is no learning; that language itself is social, the product as well as the premise of sociability and conversation" (p. 225).

For Barber, the pathologies of our present-day society reflect the breakdown of community. The solution lies in igniting a democratic spirit that suggests we are all tied to one another in more ways than our right to vote. "We can no more learn alone than we can live alone. And if little learning is taking place in American schools and colleges it may be because there is too much solitude and too little community among the learners (and their teachers too). Schools that were once workshops of intimacy have been transformed into factories as alienating as welfare hotels and as lonely as suburban malls" (Barber, 1992, p. 225).

Where Barber and I tend to disagree is his insistence on the need for a common knowledge and shared beliefs. Like other communitarians with whom he is sometimes identified, Barber is linked to a view that parallels, but to a much lesser degree, the common culture arguments of William Bennett (1984) and Dinesh D'Souza (1991). As I pointed out in chapters 3 and 6, whereas conservatives preach the common culture rhetoric, communitarians tend to focus on a few of what they perceive as the key values and beliefs that ought to form the core of American communities, such as that all persons ought to be respected and treated with dignity regardless of inherited characteristics, that tolerance is preferred to discrimination and bigotry, that the resolution of conflict ought to be through peaceful means instead of through violence, that truth is preferred to lies, that honest work for a day's pay is desirable, that saving for one's own future is preferred to expecting a society to take care of one's needs in old age, and that democracy is superior to totalitarianism and authoritarianism (Etzioni, 1995).

Although communitarians embrace the ideals of democracy, they make a point of calling attention to the problems posed by diverse voices that, at best, should be tolerated. In implying that difference ought only to be tolerated, they fall into the conservative trap of legitimizing some cultural groups while delegitimizing others and thus contribute to the marginalization that true democracy seeks to avoid. Critical views of education such as those offered by bell hooks, Henry Giroux, and Peter McLaren have advanced the ideals of caring and democracy without resorting to a silencing of difference. I turn to these perspectives now as I advance toward a discussion of critical community service.

CRITICAL VIEWS OF EDUCATION

One of the central goals of critical education is to help students recognize their own positionality and how various forces mitigate their ability to develop a critical consciousness. Such a level of consciousness is necessary for students to write their own histories and to transform their social worlds. In dealing with students' positionality, feminist and critical theorists of education recognize the multiple and complex identities students bring to the classroom (Maher & Tetreault, 1994). Coming to terms with the positionality of students, as well as teachers, becomes part of the intellectual and reflective process involved in teaching and learning. For example, bell hooks (1994) discussed the key connection between "decolonialization" and liberatory education as the historic moment when one begins to think seriously and critically about the self and one's location in the social and political spheres of influence.

Social transformation is vital to a critical view of education. But upon what basis should liberatory work be grounded? What is the ideal held to by feminism and the feminist classroom? Here, we must return to the ethic-of-care philosophy.

In examining Carol Gilligan's work, Mary Brabek wrote that "an ethic of care is achieved through perception of one's self as connected to others" (1993, p. 36). But how does an ethic of care and fostering such an ideal get played out in the classroom? Margo Culley (1985) and colleagues argued that students bring their own "texts" to the classroom—texts reflecting views of men and women and differing conceptions of autonomy and connectedness. They described the feminist classroom as one in which we "acknowledge and welcome what everyone has always known—that more goes on in the classroom than the transmission of information. Let us welcome the intrusion/infusion of emotionality—love, rage, anxiety, eroticism—into intellect as a step toward healing the fragmentation capitalism and patriarchy have demanded from us" (p. 19). Thus, part of advancing an ethic-of-care philosophy involves limiting the fragmentation caused by competitive individualism.

One of the primary ways feminist pedagogy seeks to resist the many manifestations of patriarchy (and related capitalist hierarchies) is by rejecting traditional views of authority typically inscribed in the idea of "the teacher" (Lewis, 1992). But out of fear of embracing an authoritarian stance, some teachers may unwittingly contribute to ongoing oppression by failing to challenge some of the thoughts and assumptions of their students (Simon, 1992). As a result, the experiences that students bring to the classroom, some of which may contribute to women's lack of equality and liberty, may be perpetuated. Adrienne Rich posed a solution: "We can refuse to accept passive, obedient learning and insist upon critical thinking. We can become harder on our women students, giving them the kinds of 'cultural prodding' that men receive, but on different terms and a different style" (1979, p. 244). The different style Rich alluded to is often discussed as "nurturance," which emphasizes empowerment as a process of struggling with students in a caring and connected manner. The problem, however, often gets situated as women falling back on the traits that are socially ascribed to them, such as nurturing and caring. Jane Kenway and Helen Modra (1992) suggested a solution to the dilemma: men can also be caring and nurturing. Instead of rejecting that which has been traditionally assigned to women—nurturance—as a means of resisting patriarchy and authoritarian oppression, another tactic is to embrace an ethic of care and challenge men to do the same. This is the stance I embrace as part of my contention that community service has a place in the advancement of an ethic of care.

Although the focus of most feminist pedagogy applies directly to the marginal positions of women and how their lives are shaped by a hierarchically oriented culture formed to a large degree by patriarchal thought and action, other oppressive forces must be considered as well. Economic inequalities, racism, and heterosexism clearly come to mind. Some feminists such as bell hooks speak to a wide array of liberatory concerns. For example, hooks argued for a more inclusive vision of liberation: "Individuals who fight for the eradication of sexism without supporting struggles to end racism or classism undermine their own efforts. Individuals who fight for the eradication of racism or classism while supporting sexist oppression are helping to maintain the cultural basis of all forms of group oppression" (1984, p. 39). Hooks went on to argue that, although a certain degree of incremental change may be achieved, such efforts will not lead to a true transformation characterized by revolutionary change. "Their ambivalent relationship to oppression in general is a contradiction that must be resolved or they will daily undermine their own radical work" (p. 39).

More recently, hooks has applied her views of liberatory action to teaching and has focused on what she described as "engaged pedagogy," which for her includes a progressive and holistic strategy in which the well-being of students is central to pedagogical goals. She discussed her experiences with students and how they have contributed to an engaged pedagogy: "Currently, the students I encounter seem far more uncertain about the project of self-actualization than my peers and I were twenty years ago. They feel that there are no clear ethical guidelines shaping actions. Yet, while they despair, they are also adamant that education should be liberatory. They want and demand more from professors than my generation did" (1994, p. 19). Hooks described students living with "wounded psyches," who often seek therapists for help. What they need, from her perspective, is "an education that is healing to the uninformed, unknowing spirit. They . . . want education that is meaningful. They rightfully expect that my colleagues and I will not offer them information without addressing the connection between what they are learning and their overall life experiences" (p. 19).

An engaged pedagogy involves caring for students as whole persons and models for students the kind of moral and ethical attitudes we hope to see reflected back to us and throughout our society. As hooks stated, "To teach in a manner that respects and cares for the souls of our students is essential if we are to provide the necessary conditions where learning can most deeply and intimately begin" (1994, p. 13). We must see students "as whole human beings with complex lives and experiences rather than simply as seeking after compartmentalized bits of knowledge" (p. 15). But for hooks, an engaged pedagogy is not the end, but rather part of the road to a liberatory education that she described as "the practice of freedom," which reflects her commitment to political activism. The activism hooks embraces involves transgressing the traditional structures of the academy as well as the struggle for social change and liberation. She expresses her liberatory commitments in her discussion of Paulo Freire's influence on her work. Like Freire, she has been accused of emphasizing *conscientization* as an end and not as a means to social transformation. "This is one of the concepts in Freire's work—and in my own work—that is frequently misunderstood by readers in the United States. Many times people will say to me that I seem to suggest that it is enough for individuals to change how they think. . . . Again and again Freire has had to remind readers that he never spoke of *conscientization* as an end itself, but always as it is joined by meaningful praxis" (p. 47). Achieving meaningful praxis, for hooks, involves dismantling the oppressive forces within society that limit the freedom of individuals and groups. Such a dismantling is not limited to patriarchy, but instead includes forces such as racism, heterosexism, and ageism, as well as any other source of hatred and discrimination that situates some on the margins of society while others claim the privileged center.

Similar to hooks, proponents of "critical pedagogy" also seek liberation by battling a range of oppressive forces. For example, in *Critical Pedagogy and Predatory Culture*, Peter McLaren addressed some of the broad concerns of critical education when he described a praxis concerned with building a sense of solidarity "with all victims struggling to overcome their suffering and alienation" (1995, p. 23). For McLaren, solidarity involves students as cultural border crossers: "Students need to be able to cross over into different zones of cultural diversity . . . and form hyphenated identities in order to rethink the relationship of self to society, of self to other, and to deepen the moral vision of the social order" (p. 22). The central question, for McLaren, relates to how students might engage history as a means of reclaiming power and identity. This struggle involves examining the contradictions inherent in American society among the meaning of liberty, the idea of justice for all, and the obligations that come with citizenship in a democratic society within a social structure that often promotes silence and conformity.

McLaren (1995) advanced the idea of "resistance multiculturalism," which rejects culture as nonconflictual, harmonious, and consensual. "Democracy is understood from its perspective [resistance multiculturalism] as busy—not a seamless, smooth or always harmonious political and cultural state of affairs. Resistance multiculturalism doesn't see diversity itself as a goal but rather argues that diversity must be affirmed within a politics of cultural criticism and a commitment to social justice" (p. 126). For McLaren, difference is not something to be silenced or celebrated, it is something that exists and ought to be part of a democratic vision just as any feelings of sameness might be as well. The goal is not to organize around difference or commonality, but to organize around *social justice*. McLaren did not suggest that differences related to race, class, gender, or sexual orientation are irrelevant, but that what constitutes one's sense of identity cannot be narrowly confined to these categories alone: "Of course, a person's lived experience, race, class, gender, and history are important in the formation of his or her political identity, but we must be willing to examine our personal experiences and speaking voices in terms of the ideological and discursive complexity of their formations" (p. 125). In other words, a multiplicitous understanding of identity and the self must be sought as we seek to make sense of a whole host of complex and dynamic tensions that provide one with an ever-changing identity and sense of self. We cannot reduce people to the category of "being different" simply because they are Black or White, gay or straight, nor can we reduce an individual to sameness because he or she is Black and therefore is like all other Blacks; or because he or she is White and therefore is like all other Whites. We must reject all attempts to essentialize sameness as well as difference and challenge our students to see a multiplicitous self through a multiplicitous other and vice versa. Again, the goal is not to achieve some community or society based on common understandings, for such understandings inevitably silence difference (Tierney, 1993). The goal, instead, is to engage in a joint struggle for social justice and thus form a sense of community around concerns for democracy and caring.

The idea central to this book is that students have a sense of self that derives from their relationships with others and part of the role of education is to challenge the sense of self students bring to higher learning. In this book I am particularly concerned with the sense of self as it relates to economic injustice, although clearly a caring and liberatory education demands that we transform all forms of hierarchical structures that lead to inequality and oppression. How can we foster an ethic of care among our students? The obvious point I make in this book is that one answer is to offer more opportunities for student involvement in community service activities. However, these activities, if they are to have a liberatory effect that places others at the center of one's concerns, must be planned and conducted with serious intentions. Because my view of community service is so embedded in critical and feminist theories, I use the phrase "critical community service." In what follows, I discuss what is meant by critical community service as I offer several guiding principles that may be used to frame these kinds of service experiences.

CRITICAL COMMUNITY SERVICE

Throughout this book, I have highlighted how community service offers opportunities for students to seriously consider their sense of self in light of others and offers a context in which an ethic of care might be fostered. What I suggest here is that community service work be broadly envisioned, not as out-of-class experiences but as part of a larger restructuring of the classroom that includes "real-life" settings characteristic of community service projects.

When we think of community service activities as a form of classroom, a concern arises as to how critical and feminist pedagogies may be used to inform service and the learning that comes with it. A key question that must be addressed relates to moving from what Bill Puka calls a "do-gooder model of care to a more self-chosen, self-reflective, and self-affirming form of mature caring" (1993, p. 216). As I pointed out in chapter 7, many students who were involved in this study did not connect their involvement in community service to larger social issues, nor did they reflect the kind of mature caring discussed by Puka. Instead, students tended to see community service more in terms of charity and the "do-gooder" model. Listen to the following students discuss their motivations for getting involved in community service:

> I do community service because I want to do things for those who are less fortunate.

> It is an expectation of my religion that we give to others. And besides that, it seems like the right thing to do.

> Volunteering to help the needy is something we ought to do as good community members.

> Community service is how I meet my obligations to my community. It is incumbent on me to serve those who have less than I have.

> I am involved in volunteer work because I believe every citizen has an obligation to give back to their community. Everyone has a responsibility to help those in need. It's what makes a group of people living near one another a community.

> Volunteering is a way to do something good and meaningful. There are so many times in life where everything we do is for ourselves. For me, volunteer service is an opportunity to pay back for all we have, to show how grateful we are by helping others.

I do not want to sound too critical of these students. They gave their time and their energy out of a concern for others. Nonetheless, involvement in community service is a learning experience, and it provides many opportunities to challenge students to think in richer and deeper ways about the meaning of service and its role in shaping the self, the other, and community. For example, several students who were involved in this study hinted at having gained a more complex understanding of service, as revealed in the following comments (these were first introduced in chapter 5 as part of a discussion of mutuality):

> Rather than helping, some people view volunteering as a way to put people in their place, or as trying to save them. I believe everyone— including those in need—should help and everyone has a responsibility to help people out.

> The little bit of time and effort that I can give has a ripple effect— my time and effort is probably many times more powerful and more significant than any change from my pocket.

I think the biggest reason I participate in community service projects is the opportunity to meet and interact with real people. So often we find ourselves going through the motions and never truly experiencing people who have lives that are a lot different from ours. I love to interact with people who face struggles that I've been fortunate enough to never have to deal with. They teach me about what it means to support one another. They teach me about what a real community is.

We started working on the front of the house, but by the end of the week we were on the back porch. I think that symbolizes how quickly they opened their lives and their homes up to us. The front porch is open for all visitors, but the back porch is for your closest friends.

Whenever I get outside my own world, my community gets larger. . . . My sense of community is not defined by a certain race or population. I had a conversation with Uncle Leroy today. He started the conversation yesterday about the difference between a White man and a Black man. The way he talked was very interesting. . . . He made me think about my grandfather.

Faculty, staff, and student leaders who are concerned about fostering an ethic of care through community service projects need to be concerned about whether activities foster a "do-gooder" mentality or are truly community-building encounters with the other. This means taking into account the ideal of mutuality, as well as incorporating reflective components into the experience.

Another issue when considering community service and its educative value relates to whether the experience is situated as "academic" or "nonacademic" learning. A number of students talked about their college learning experiences and made comparisons between traditional classroom settings and community service contexts. One student explained, "I learned that I can grow and learn in incredible ways through experience rather than mere book work." Another student commented on the effect his community service work had on him: "After spending four and a half years in college, I'm beginning to feel an intense urge to commit myself towards active, practical service. Community service experiences such as working with homeless people are minimal when students must spend the majority of their time focused upon academics and course work." A third offered these comments: "Intellectual exploration has been rewarding but also suffocating at times, and so I am feeling the desire to do more experiential work. I found one way could be by working in a homeless shelter and understanding social issues from a political standpoint as well as from the perspective of those living and breathing poverty." And a fourth student contrasted community service with other kinds of learning experiences such as visiting a museum: "The community service trip was a learning vacation different from the ones my parents have taken me on where we go to museums and visit historic places. It was learning, but learning about more real life things."

What was especially interesting was how some students separated classroom learning from experiential learning. A sophomore in education who worked with low-income families on Yonges Island noted, "There is so much I have to learn. My so-called education has not really taught me anything compared to what I've learned from interacting with the families on this island." Another student, a sophomore from Michigan State University, revealed how she saw traditional learning and community service learning: "I spent the year studying and trying to figure out what I was doing spending so much time studying when there is so much that needs to be done. But then after I participated in the New York City project I realized that I need to spend my time in college doing something for myself so I can give back to the community later. If I don't educate myself, I can't contribute anything to anyone else."

For the preceding students, what goes on in the traditional classroom is clearly something apart from what goes on in the rest of their lives. This stands in opposition to the ideals of experientially based education, which seeks to link the lives of students to an active and change-oriented vision of education so that students are able to make important connections between what they learn in school and what they experience in other aspects of their lives. Although a few students who were involved in this study reported with great excitement how their community service work helped them to make sense of complex classroom discussions of such topics as economics, political science, and sociology, they were the exception and not the rule. Most students saw theoretical and practical work (or academic and nonacademic work) as largely separate. Clearly, a better effort is needed to help students integrate academic learning, life's experiences, and community service learning.

In chapters 4 through 7, I highlighted various aspects of students' experiences in community service as they relate to issues of otherness, mutuality, community building, and action/reflection. From these chapters, we can take various points that help us to think about community service as a vehicle for shaping a more caring higher learning committed to the principles of democracy. With this said, I offer eight guiding principles for structuring critical community service activities.

Principle 1: Critical community service calls attention to the notion that a commitment to working with others is fundamentally tied to an individual's sense of self and vision of others.

Educators must recognize that community service often involves a personal challenge to a student's identity and, in particular, how a student thinks about the self. Community service encounters are often, as Howard Radest (1993) explained, "an encounter with strangers" and thus pose new learning opportunities for one's sense of self and sense of otherness.

Principle 2: Critical community service demands that mutuality undergird all service activities and projects.

Two aspects of mutuality must be recognized. First, the relationship between the service worker and the community member to be served must be established on principles of equality so that each party is actively involved in deciding on the nature of the service to be rendered. This means that those being served must play a central role in determining needs. The second aspect of mutuality involves recognizing that all parties who are involved in community service benefit in different ways from such service. Thus, it is helpful to prepare students in advance for their responsibility as "receivers" and the reciprocal roles in giving and receiving. Mutuality resists the "do-gooder" model of service, for it reminds us that those involved in performing service also receive a great deal from their efforts.

Principle 3: Community building must be recognized as a central objective of critical community service.

When service is structured around the ideals of mutuality, the community service worker and the community member become associated with one another within the context of a truly caring and reciprocal relationship. The self and the other become less distant, and a common sense of connection is more likely to develop. This connective bond does not seek to silence cultural difference but instead reminds all participants that we can come together in solidarity as part of the struggle for social change and justice.

Principle 4: Critical community service seeks to build multicultural service communities and thus ought to involve a wide range of diverse students in community service work.

Just as community service may be a tool for building connections between those engaged in service and those being served, it also is an activity that builds a sense of connection among service providers. Community service offers an excellent opportunity to challenge students to learn from one another and thus every effort should be made to build diverse groups of service providers.

Principle 5: Critical community service must include reflective action linked to broader social concerns, with the goal being to foster a critical consciousness among students.

Action must be accompanied by reflection; this is a dialectical process with one informing the other. Without serious thought about the social conditions contributing to how another's life is situated, one's act of service becomes merely charity with little concern for the structural circumstances that have led others to be in need in the first place. If, on the other hand, community service participants seriously reflect on the issues underlying homelessness or rural poverty or other indicators of social inequities, they will be better equipped to make informed choices and judgments as to how their action might be guided in the future and how they might contribute to liberatory struggle.

Principle 6: Critical community service seeks to link traditional classroom learning (academic or theoretical knowledge) with the experiential learning that often accompanies service.

This principle is closely tied to the fourth principle in that reflective action must be grounded in a depth of knowledge and understanding of the larger social, political, and historical contexts. The concern here, however, relates more to the physical setting in which such knowledge may be constructed. What I suggest is that theories and issues related to the broader society need to be connected to experience. The classroom and service experience must be brought together, regardless of the physical setting: Discussions of community service need to be brought to the classroom, and classroom discussions need to take place at the sites where students engage in service. Furthermore, students need to be challenged to see how their personal lives relate to the theoretical knowledge they possess.

Principle 7: Critical community service is intended to create social change, and therefore it is expected that participants engage in the larger struggle to improve social conditions.

Action and reflection lead to a recognition that larger problems exist that contribute to the many social ills that make service necessary. If we ignore these larger issues, we are merely treating the symptom and not the source. In effect, service is the Band-Aid for the larger social disease that is inflicting serious wounds. Although reflection and action may lead to an awareness of a structural failure or the inadequacy of a social or economic policy, critical consciousness demands that such an awareness lead to participation in the larger struggle for change. If a truly caring relationship has been built and community has been fostered, then we cannot walk away from our neighbors, wherever they may be, simply because it is time to go back to school. Hence, educators must work hard to help students understand the diverse strategies and processes involved in a democracy that may lead to liberatory action.

Principle 8: Critical community service must be thought of as part of the larger struggle to create a more liberatory form of education.

Critical community service is situated within the philosophical tradition of democratic education. This tradition includes critical and feminist pedagogies, the work of John Dewey, and indeed the work of many liberal educational theorists who also understand the value of an active, educated, and concerned citizenry. As such, critical community service is part of the larger struggle to create a more caring and democratic educational process. In terms of higher learning, critical community service should be seen as a key educational vehicle for fostering an ethic of care and a commitment to democratic citizenship.

The eighth principle captures the overarching concern of this book: How can we structure higher learning in such a way that an ethic of care and a commitment to democratic citizenship are central to the educational experience? What I argue is that community service, if structured along the principles suggested here, provides one means toward accomplishing such a goal.

ADVANCING COMMUNITY SERVICE TO CENTER STAGE

I have provided eight guiding principles that frame critical community service, but I still need to describe some of the steps that may be taken to put such service programs in place or to increase their importance. With this in mind, I will focus on four groups of constituents within academe: organizational leaders, faculty members, student affairs professionals, and student leaders. I then discuss some significant structural changes that may foster greater participation and interest in community service.

Organizational Leaders

There are three areas in which college and university leaders can help move community service to a central place: by giving community service a public forum, by engaging in demonstrable community service efforts themselves, and by rewarding students and employees who participate and support others in service.

1. Give community service a public forum. Presidents and other organizational leaders have many opportunities to contribute to the vision of their institutions. They can choose to take advantage of these opportunities to elevate community service to a central place at their institution. For example, in addressing the faculty at the beginning of an academic term, a dean may raise the issue of community service and challenge faculty to involve their students to a greater degree in course-related service activities. Also, a president speaking at commencement may address community service issues and graduates' responsibilities as democratic citizens and as future leaders of this country. A vice president for student affairs can speak to the importance of community service activities throughout the year and encourage staff to do the same.

2. Engage in demonstrable community service efforts. For leaders to speak seriously about the relevance of community service, they themselves should participate in such activities. They should resist the temptation to call too much public attention to their work, for then it resembles a publicity stunt more than a true act of caring for others.

3. Reward students and employees who participate and support others in service. Organizational leaders have a variety of informal and formal opportunities through which they might foster a greater commitment to community service. For example, academic leaders may work with the faculty to make community service a formal aspect of the promotion and tenure process. Senior student affairs practitioners can develop employee performance programs that include a heavy emphasis on implementing service activities for students. In addition, there is a whole host of informal mechanisms to reward employees and students for their involvement, such as praising an individual during a staff meeting, sending a letter of appreciation, posting pictures of students who have committed themselves to community service activities on residence hall bulletin boards, or simply thanking someone in person for his or her efforts.

The Faculty

In discussing the role faculty might play in making community service more vital to an organization's identity, I focus on three areas: add service components to various academic courses, develop ways of supporting and fostering students' participation in community service beyond course requirements, and devote scholarly attention to the role of community service learning.

1. Add service components to various academic courses. Faculty must develop creative ways of incorporating community service components into their courses. It is hard to imagine a major or type of course for which some kind of service-related activity could not be developed. Faculty must use the creative abilities they often apply to their teaching and research to develop strategies for connecting academic learning to the larger social good through service options.

2. Develop ways of supporting and fostering students' participation in community service beyond course requirements. Not all faculty efforts to involve students in community service must be tied to a specific course. There are also departmental and research areas in which faculty might consider ways of involving students in service. For example, engineering students at Howard University were encouraged to devote their senior engineering projects to developing better temporary shelters for homeless people (they often use plastic tarps or cardboard boxes, which do not retain much heat). They developed an inexpensive inflatable sleeping bag that was capable of retaining a higher percentage of body heat and was also easily transported. In addition, as a means of orienting new students to a department, a group community service project could be planned as a way of helping students make connections with one another, as well as with the community.

3. Devote scholarly attention to the role of community service learning. More faculty are needed who will analyze and publish findings related to community service learning. Scholarship on teaching and learning and the role of service in helping students make connections is needed. Faculty need to share their observations and findings about how the combination of classroom instruction and community service activities contributes to students' overall progress in a course and their ability to make connections between theory and practice. Several journals will publish such scholarly work. Two that come to mind are the *Michigan Journal of Community Service Learning* and the *Journal of College Student Development*.

Student Affairs Professionals

There are several ways in which student affairs staff might also contribute to increasing community service involvement among college students. I highlight three key concerns: implement a community service learning program designed to coordinate campus information and support for service, develop service initiatives throughout the many departments of student affairs, and use community service activities as key residential programming ideas.

1. Implement a community service learning program designed to coordinate campus information and support for service. It is helpful to have an office or an individual in charge of coordinating community service options and activities. Such an office is needed to eliminate some of the duplication and repeated contacts with social agencies in surrounding communities. Agencies typically are more than willing to provide service opportunities for students, but they can become overwhelmed with multiple contacts if coordinated efforts are not in place.

2. Develop service initiatives throughout the many departments of student affairs. Each area of student affairs may be charged with developing its own service component relevant to the goals and objectives of the specific department. For example, it is conceivable that a Career Development and Placement Office might provide an opportunity for student volunteers trained in career exploration to work with a group of low-income students to help foster increased understanding of the role of schooling in career advancement.

3. Use community service activities as key residential programming ideas. The residential setting is a key area of campus life in which serious consideration needs to be given to using community service as a vehicle for student development. Resident assistants and directors should be encouraged, through their early and ongoing in-service training, to incorporate community service activities into their work with students.

Student Leaders

Students also have an important role to play in fostering a commitment to community service. There are three primary ways in which students and student leaders might participate in a campus's overall community service initiative: encourage peers to get involved in service activities, provide the necessary support for community service activities, and be role models for other students.

1. Encourage peers to get involved in service activities. Student leaders have an obligation to the campus community to promote social responsibility. One way they can do this is to encourage fellow students to become committed to community service and support them in such endeavors. These students ought to be recognized for their efforts. Student-run campus newspapers can take the lead in recognizing students' community involvement. In addition, the wide range of student volunteer activities ought to be advertised and made known to all students. Again, student newspapers should see such publicity as part of their public service responsibility. Others, such as student government leaders, can also play a role in acknowledging students' involvement in service.

2. Provide the necessary support for community service activities. Some community service projects require financial support. Activities such as Alternative Spring Breaks often have travel, food, housing, and equipment expenses. Organizations such as student government and residence hall councils ought to encourage such activities by making it known that they will provide financial support for community service efforts.

3. Be role models for other students. Student leaders across the campus can send a message to the rest of the student community through their own commitments to service. Because of their high visibility, athletes, student government officers, resident assistants, and other organizational leaders have a great opportunity to model behavior for other students. In making community service a priority in their lives, these students will challenge others to give serious consideration to such actions.

Structural Changes

In this section I discuss four areas in which structural change might be needed: the mission of the institution, the curriculum, the promotion and tenure process, and the separation between student affairs professionals and faculty.

1. Community service must be central to the mission of the institution. The institution's mission and its mission statement speak to what colleges and universities value, and they serve as guides to student, staff, and faculty behavior. Institutions that incorporate a discussion of the importance of community service specifically within the formal mission statement are likely to instill in organizational members a commitment to service.

2. Community service must be a vital component of the formal curriculum. I do not suggest that community service be part of students' graduation requirements. I am not convinced that "forced" service achieves the kinds of results that are desired. However, students ought to be encouraged to participate in a variety of courses and service learning opportunities. Perhaps a minor could be established for students who wish to pursue community service and its political, philosophical, and social connections. Such courses would be an excellent way to help students understand the link between everyday life as democratic citizens and the relevance of theory and action.

3. Formalize expectations of faculty to foster community service opportunities for students through the promotion and tenure process. Academe has come under great criticism for its lack of responsiveness to the general public (Boyer, 1990; Fairweather, 1996). Community service is one vehicle for restoring some of the sense of responsibility that colleges and universities ought to have for community, regional, and national concerns. But faculty behavior is shaped, in large measure, by the reward structure, and unless there is some formal encouragement it is highly likely that faculty commitment to community service learning will wane. Thus, one obvious solution is to consider a faculty member's contributions to community service learning as part of the promotion and tenure process. The University of Utah, for example, has recommended that the following criteria be used in evaluating a faculty member's use of service learning as part of an assessment of the individual's teaching:

- Service learning contributions must relate to the faculty member's area of scholarship.
- Service learning contributions are responsive to recognized needs of individuals and organizations within the university or local community and are seen as having lasting impact.
- Service learning contributions are carried out in partnership with the community being served (the ideal of mutuality).
- The service learning activities provide a means for students to synthesize their volunteer experiences with course content (action/reflection).
- The service learning activities demonstrate a contribution to a student's sense of civic involvement.
- The faculty member acts as a role model in demonstrating the importance of community involvement.

These are just a few suggestions for considering faculty use of community service as a learning opportunity. It is important for each college or university to develop its own criteria so that the community service learning needs of faculty and students can be met.

4. Work to bridge the gap separating faculty and student affairs professionals through joint involvement with students in community service activities. Faculty and student affairs professionals need to work together to coordinate community service options for students. A Community Service Learning Center can serve as such a bridge by coordinating course-related service options with a variety of noncourse-related activities. In creating a student affairs office (or liaison) charged with working with faculty and their community service initiatives, a step will be made toward achieving greater synergy between the academic and student side of campus. In addition, student affairs professionals should become more involved in credit-bearing community service options. A two- or three-credit course could be created that combines community service learning with career and personal exploration and might easily be taught by a member of the student affairs staff. In fact, their knowledge of student development theory might make them the best candidates for such an undertaking.

SUMMARY

In the first half of this chapter, I highlighted Dewey's contributions to thinking about a more caring and experiential form of education and its role in a democratic society. I used his work to move into a discussion of critical and feminist conceptions of education and how they might contribute to caring and the emergence of what I call "critical community service."

I used Dewey's work and the writings on critical education as a starting point for framing community service that seeks not only to improve the lives of individuals in the short term, but also to bring about fundamental and lasting change through an emphasis on mutuality and community building. Through mutuality, students are more likely to develop a complex understanding of the other, develop a more caring relationship, and thus think about the long-term enhancement of the other's life. A key aspect of challenging students to achieve such an understanding is the relevance of reflection as part of the action component of service. Community service becomes a critical form of community service only when these objectives are met. And, in this way, community service is truly community building.

In delineating the specifics of critical community service, I offered eight principles that serve as guides to thinking about service: (1) critical community service calls attention to the notion that a commitment to working with others is fundamentally tied to an individual's sense of self and vision of others; (2) critical community service demands that mutuality undergird all service activities and projects; (3) community building must be recognized as a central objective of critical community service; (4) critical community service seeks to build multicultural service communities and thus ought to involve a wide range of diverse students in community service work; (5) critical community service must include reflective action linked to broader social concerns with the goal of fostering a critical consciousness among students; (6) critical community service seeks to link traditional classroom learning (academic or theoretical knowledge) with the experiential learning that often accompanies service; (7) critical community service is intended to create social change, and therefore it is expected that participants engage in the larger struggle to improve social conditions; and (8) critical community service must be thought of as part of the larger struggle to create a more liberatory form of education.

Finally, in concluding this chapter, I offered specific ideas on advancing the relevance of community service in general within college and university settings. I discussed four constituents who might play a key role in this goal: organizational leaders, faculty, student affairs professionals, and student leaders. In addition, I suggested four structural changes relating to the institutional mission, the curriculum, the promotion and tenure process, and the chasm separating the academic and student sides to a campus.

In the concluding chapter of this book, I return to some of the larger issues that call for a more progressive view of community service. I situate the general idea of critical community service within the broad arena of utopian thought and the desire to build caring communities and advance the ideal of democracy.

Conclusion

From the earliest days of human kind, women and men have dreamed of a better world—a utopia. The Book of Genesis presents the image of a garden utopia free of fear, where everything one needs is only an outstretched arm away: "And out of the ground made the LORD God to grow every tree that is pleasant to the sight, and good for food; the tree of life also in the midst of the garden, and the tree of knowledge of good and evil" (2:9 KJV). In *The Republic*, Plato envisioned an idyllic world where people share in one another's sorrows and pains: "There is unity where there is a community of pleasures and pains." Karl Marx expressed his vision of the ideal society in the *Communist Manifesto*. He dreamed of a social world in which materialism was nonexistent and everyone shared in the work and rewards of a communal life. And in *Ideology and Utopia*, Karl Mannheim (1936) called attention to the fact that utopian visions are always the by-products of the social and historical context created by human imagination and therefore are firmly rooted in ideology and politics.

In *Island*, Aldous Huxley (1962) dramatized the very questions that men most often consider as they struggle with the ideals of what connects one to the other and what constitutes the self and community amid this "civilized" world. The journey of his fictional character Will Farnaby to the island of Pala is not unlike that of Timothy Leary, who spent much of his life engaged in a quest to unlock the doors of consciousness. For Leary, it was LSD and his psilocybin experiments at Harvard that he believed would lead him and others through the invisible door, the "historical movement that would inevitably change man at the very center of his nature, his consciousness" (Stevens, 1988, p. 150).

Whereas Timothy Leary turned on and then inward in his quest for utopia, the ideas conveyed in this book are quite the opposite. Through others, we come to know the self. Of course, we never fully comprehend the self, for it evolves with every social interaction we have. The quest is never ending. And as the quest to understand the self is never ending, so is democracy's journey.

It is a special quality of the self—the caring self—that I have addressed in this book and that is part of my utopian vision of a more democratic world. It is a world in which love is at the heart of all we do. As Thomas Wolfe wrote in *The Hills Beyond*, "Democracy through Love. Love through Democracy" (1935, p. 123).

But men are not the only ones who dream and then weave narratives about their visions, their hopes. And although history often reinforces men as the dreamers—the narrators of life, the tellers of tales of Homeric heroes, conquests, death and defeat, of white knights and whalers—women tell stories, too. But they tell different tales. Maybe men and women dream differently. Perhaps this is what Zora Neale Hurston meant in *Their Eyes Were Watching God* when she wrote, "Ships at a distance have every man's wish on board. For some they come in with the tide. For others they sail forever on the horizon, never out of sight, never landing until the Watcher turns his eyes away in resignation, his dreams mocked to death by Time. That is the life of men. . . . Now, women forget all those things they don't want to remember, and remember all those things they don't want to forget. The dream is the truth. Then they act and do things accordingly" (1937, p. 1).

Of course women dream too. And they have always dreamed. It is just that often their dreams have gone untold or were told and then silenced by "his" story.

Carol Gilligan's (1982) *In a Different Voice* offers us a modern-day account of the ways that men and women come to know their worlds. Gilligan reminds us that men and women experience the world in ways that are fundamentally different, and that women's ways of knowing often are subordinated or left out of history's account of the social world.

But Gilligan tells us something else. Something is absent from utopian theorizing about creating a more caring world: "There seems to be a line of development missing from current depictions of adult development, a failure to describe the progression of relationships toward a maturity of interdependence. Though the truth of separation is recognized in most developmental texts, the reality of continuing connection is lost or relegated to the background where the figures of women appear" (1982, p. 155). A central goal of this work has been to push developmental issues related to "a maturity of interdependence" to center stage and to highlight the role community service might play in advancing such developmental challenges. This concern is not just about women's development. This especially concerns men.

Although Gilligan's work has, in part, paved the way for serious thinking about the unique experiences of women, her use of the singular "voice" in her description of women's lives suggests a monolithic quality of women's experience when, in fact, multiple voices prevail. This is one of the central points of Cherríe Moraga and Gloria Anzaldúa's (1981) edited collection of narratives of Third World women and women of color. This book also represents a utopian vision, as Moraga reveals in the preface:

> This book is written for all the women in it and all whose lives our lives will touch. We are a family who first only knew each other in our dreams, who have come together on these pages to make faith a reality and to bring all our selves to bear down hard on that reality. It is about physical and psychic struggle. It is about intimacy, a desire for life between all of us, not settling for less than freedom even in the most private aspects of our lives. A total vision. For the women in this book, I will lay my body down for that vision. *This Bridge Called My Back.* (p. xix)

Men and women speak in different voices, and they are by no means monolithic voices. Gender plays a major role in shaping our experiences, but clearly, as Moraga and Anzaldúa point out, so do a variety of other factors such as race, class, and sexual orientation. Multiplicity prevails in this world that is the postmodern condition.

The challenge, as I have pointed out throughout this book, is to acknowledge a plurality of voices—a multiplicity of identities—and to work with multiplicity to forge caring relations and fashion a dream of true democracy. Democracy in its truest form does not seek to silence, but instead seeks to listen.

Early in this book I argued that personhood is constituted by a sense of self that is dynamic and multiplicitous. The self is a social self. It develops out of the social context, and therefore the other plays a key role in how the self is formed. The social self, highlighted by interactionists such as George Herbert Mead, is further advanced theoretically by feminist theories of the relational self. Because the self is tied to a social and relational context, social life plays a central role in contributing to the self. Furthermore, the overwhelming complexity and ambiguity of a postmodern world creates a dilemma for the self: Because the other is often the diverse other, understanding the self through the other becomes a far greater challenge than in the past, when commonality once characterized community. The cultural diversity of postmodern social life thus makes forming community and understanding the self that much more difficult, but it does not end the desire we have for community and to develop a sense of self. The challenge of contemporary life is to build community, not despite our differences, but in spite of our lack of common identity.

Dialogue across difference is the phrase we often hear, but such expressions beg the real question: Why should anyone enter into such dialogues? I have suggested in this book that the answer is: "Because I care." I have argued that caring for one another must be the driving concern of our society and indeed of our educational system, and I have suggested that community service informed by a critical view of education offers opportunities for us to foster an ethic of care among our students as well as within ourselves.

So the last piece of the puzzle is in place, and it is not an overly complex puzzle at that. We live in a changing world in which community escapes us. More so today than ever before, we need to foster a sense of self committed to others if we are to traverse the complex and multiplicitous nature of postmodern life. Critical community service may be seen as a key component of a broad feminist and critical vision to create more caring individuals and thus build community despite a lack of common identity. Clearly, education in general and higher education in particular have roles to play in this process.

HIGHER LEARNING AND AN ETHIC OF CARE

Placing the development of caring citizens at the core of higher education requires a fundamental rethinking of what colleges and universities most often do and poses a challenge to the traditions of the academic profession itself. In *Exiles from Eden*, Mark Schwehn (1993) argues that a rethinking of higher education hinges on the question of who we are as a group of people engaged in academic work: "The answers to the basic human questions, such as, What can we know? or How should we live? or In what or whom shall we place our hope? have come to depend, for a large number of intellectuals, upon the answer to a prior question, Who are we?" (1993, p. 23). For Schwehn, "ways of knowing are not morally neutral but morally directive" (p. 94). By "morally directive," Schwehn refers to a spiritual dimension of life which he describes as a search for meaning and purpose (spirituality in a broad sense). Schwehn maintains that the American university is caught within the constraints of modernity, an idea expressed most vividly, for Schwehn, in Max Weber's *The Protestant Ethic and the Spirit of Capitalism* and his essay "Science as a Vocation." The constraints revolve around a hollow intellectualism characterized by overspecialization. The result is disenchantment and alienation stemming in part from the pursuit of knowledge for the sake of power as opposed to the use of knowledge to build relations and community.

The quest for knowledge, for Schwehn, involves something more than the interpretation and reinterpretation of "webs of meaning" as highlighted first by Weber and then by Clifford Geertz. Education must foster a spiritual self: "Spiritually grounded education in and for thoughtfulness seeks cultivation of those virtues that make the communal quest for the truth of matters possible, an undertaking that is in every sense prior to both the explication of various systems of meaning and the project of *Wissenschaft*" (pp. 135–36). Schwehn represents the belief that as a society, as academic institutions, we need some binding truths to frame our lives and conversations as we engage in making sense of life. In the communitarian tradition, he calls for common ground.

Spiritual questions often are absent from academic conversations. Whether grounded in specific religious traditions, such as Schwehn's rootedness in Christianity, or more representative of a very personal spiritual self-exploration, these matters lie under the surface of most faculty interactions. Colleagues reject my work on lesbian, gay, and bisexual lives because they have religious objections rooted in their Christian faith, and yet they must create other excuses for their criticism. And I, on the other hand, continue such research because of my religious views, which, ironically enough, are also rooted in the Christian tradition but clearly are from a different interpretation. Rarely do we truly get the chance to integrate these selves that are so important to who we are as scholars, as people.

Although I disagree with communitarians on many points, especially their predilection for the common culture argument, I do agree with their basic premise that some sense of common ground is needed from which to build community. The postmodern call for dialogue across difference rings hollow if we have no common ground from which to start. And although I accept a piece of the communitarian argument, the size of the common ground we speak of is perhaps much smaller from my perspective and should remain open to criticism and ought to accommodate the inclusive dialogue stressed by critical postmodernists and feminists.

Throughout this book, I have argued that caring ought to be that common ground. In so arguing, I suggest two simple assertions: Caring is good. Love is good. And both are needed for the survival of this utopian dream we call democracy.

References

Astin, Alexander W. (1979). *Four Critical Years: Effects of College on Beliefs, Attitudes and Knowledge*. San Francisco: Jossey-Bass.

Astin, Alexander W. (1993). *What Matters in College?: Four Critical Years Revisited*. San Francisco: Jossey-Bass.

Barber, Benjamin R. (1992). *An Aristocracy of Everyone: The Politics of Education and the Future of America*. New York: Oxford University Press.

Battistoni, Richard (1985). *Public Schooling and the Education of Democratic Citizens*. Jackson, Miss.: University Press of Mississippi.

Baudrillard, Jean (1994). *Simulacra and Simulation*. Translated by Sheila Faria Glaser. Ann Arbor: University of Michigan Press.

Baxter Magolda, Marcia B. (1992). *Knowing and Reasoning in College: Gender-Related Patterns in Students' Intellectual Development*. San Francisco: Jossey-Bass.

Belenky, Mary F., Blythe M. Clinchy, Nancy R. Goldberger & Jill M. Tarule (1986). *Women's Ways of Knowing: The Development of Self, Voice, and Mind*. New York: Basic Books.

Bellah, Robert N., Richard Madsen, William M. Sullivan, Ann Swidler & Steven M. Tipton (1985). *Habits of the Heart: Individualism and Commitment in American Life*. New York: Harper & Row.

Bellah, Robert N., Richard Madsen, William M. Sullivan, Ann Swidler & Steven M. Tipton (1991). *The Good Society*. New York: Vintage Books.

Benhabib, Seyla (1992). *Situating the Self: Gender, Community, and Postmodernism in Contemporary Ethics*. New York: Routledge.

Bennett, William J. (1984). *To Reclaim a Legacy: A Report on the Humanities in Higher Education*. Washington, D.C.: National Endowment for the Humanities.

Bloom, Allan (1987). *The Closing of the American Mind*. New York: Simon & Schuster.

Blumer, Herbert (1962). Society as symbolic interaction. In Arnold M. Rose (ed.), *Human Behavior and Social Processes*, pp. 179–92. Boston: Houghton Mifflin.

Blumer, Herbert (1969). *Symbolic Interactionism: Perspective and Method*. Berkeley: University of California Press.

Boyer, Ernest (1990). *Scholarship Reconsidered: Priorities of the Professorate*. Princeton, N.J.: The Carnegie Foundation for the Advancement of Teaching.

Brabek, Mary (1993). Moral judgement: Theory and research on differences between males and females. In Mary Jeanne Larrabee (ed.), *An Ethic of Care: Feminist and Interdisciplinary Perspectives*, pp. 33–48. New York: Routledge.

Brown, Robert M. (1984). *Unexpected News*. Philadelphia: Westminster Press.

Bulger, Stephanie (November 1995). "Strategies to Increase Participation by African American Students in Campus-based Community Service Programs at the University of Michigan. (Paper presented at the annual meeting of the American Association for the Study of Higher Education, Orlando, Florida.)

Burbules, Nicolas & Suzanne Rice (1991). Dialogue across differences: Continuing the conversation. *Harvard Educational Review*, 61(4), pp. 393–416.

Burke, Kenneth (1989). *On Symbols and Society*. Edited by Joseph R. Gusfield. Chicago: The University of Chicago Press.

Cain, Maureen (1993). Foucault, feminism, and feeling what Foucault can and cannot contribute to feminist epistemology. In Caroline Ramazanoğlu (ed.), *Up Against Foucault: Explorations of Some Tensions between Foucault and Feminism*, pp. 73–96. London: Routledge.

Chickering, Arthur W. (1969). *Education and Identity*. San Francisco: Jossey-Bass.

Chodorow, Nancy (1974). Family structure and feminine personality. In Michelle Rosaldo & Louise Lamphere (Eds.), *Women, Culture and Society*, pp. 43–66. Stanford: Stanford University Press.

Chodorow, Nancy (1978). *The Reproduction of Mothering: Psychoanalysis and the Sociology of Gender*. Berkeley: University of California Press.

Coles, Robert (1993). *The Call of Service: A Witness to Idealism*. Boston: Houghton Mifflin.

Cooley, Charles Horton (1902). *Human Nature and the Social Order*. New York: Charles Scribner's Sons.

Conroy, Pat (1972). *The Water is Wide*. New York: Bantam Books.

Crapanzano, Vincent (1985). A reporter at large. *The New Yorker* (March 18), pp. 50–99.

Culley, Margo, Arlyn Diamond, Lee Edwards, Sara Lennox & Catherine Portuges (1985). The politics of nurturance. In Margo Culley & Catherine Portuges (eds.), *Gendered Subjects: The Dynamics of Feminist Teaching*, pp. 11–20. Boston: Routledge & Kegan Paul.

D'Augelli, Anthony R. (1991). Gay men in college: Identity processes and adaptations. *Journal of College Student Development* 32, pp. 140–46.

Davis, Angela (1974). *Angela Davis—An Autobiography*. New York: Random House.

Denzin, Norman (1977). *Childhood Socialization*. San Francisco: Jossey-Bass.

Denzin, Norman (1985). Emotion as lived experience. *Symbolic Interaction* 8(2), pp. 223–40.

Denzin, Norman (1987). A phenomenology of the emotionally divided self. In Krysia Yardley & Terry Honess (eds.), *Self and Identity: Psychosocial Perspectives*, pp. 287–96. New York: John Wiley & Sons.

Denzin, Norman (1989). *The Research Act* (3rd edition). New York: Prentice-Hall.

de Tocqueville, Alexis (1945). *Democracy in America*. New York: Alfred A. Knopf.

Dewey, John (1916). *Democracy and Education*. Carbondale, Ill.: Southern Illinois University.

Dewey, John (1927). *The Public and its Problems*. New York: Henry Holt & Company.

Dewey, John (1938). *Experience and Education*. New York: Macmillan Publishing.

D'Souza, Dinesh (1991). *Illiberal Education: The Politics of Race and Sex on Campus*. New York: The Free Press.

Durkheim, Emile (1933). *The Division of Labor in Society*. New York: Macmillan.

Eckert, Penelope (1989). *Jocks & Burnouts: Social Categories and Identity in the High School*. New York: Teachers College Press.

Erikson, Erik H. (1950). *Childhood and Society*. New York: W. W. Norton & Company.

Erikson, Erik H. (1968). *Identity: Youth and Crisis*. New York: W. W. Norton & Company.

Etzioni, Amitai (ed.) (1995). *Rights and the Common Good: The Communitarian Perspective*. New York: St. Martin's Press.

Fairweather, James (1996). *Faculty Work and Public Trust: Restoring the Value of Teaching and Public Service in American Academic Life*. Boston: Allyn and Bacon.

Feldman, Kenneth A. (ed.) (1972). *College and Student: Selected Readings in the Social Psychology of Higher Education*. New York: Pergamon Press.

Feldman, Kenneth A. & Theodore M. Newcomb (1970). *The Impact of College on Students*. San Francisco: Jossey-Bass.

Ferguson, Kathy E. (1984). *The Feminist Case Against Bureaucracy*. Philadelphia: Temple University Press.

Fine, Michelle (1991). *Framing Dropouts: Notes on the Politics of an Urban High School*. Albany: State University of New York Press.

Foucault, Michel (1977). *Discipline and Punish*. Translated by Alan Sheridan. New York: Vintage Books.

Foucault, Michel (1978). *The History of Sexuality: An Introduction*, vol. 1. Translated by Robert Hurley. New York: Random House.

Foucault, Michel (1980). *Power/Knowledge*. New York: Pantheon.

Freire, Paulo (1970). *Pedagogy of the Oppressed*. Translated by M. B. Ramos. New York: Continuum.

Freud, Sigmund (1923/1961). The ego and the id. In J. Strachey (ed., trans.), *The Standard Edition of the Complete Psychological Works of Sigmund Freud* (vol. 19), pp. 3–66. London: Hogarth Press.

Geertz, Clifford (1973). *The Interpretation of Cultures*. New York: Basic Books.

Geertz, Clifford (1983). *Local Knowledge: Further Essays in Interpretive Anthropology*. New York: Basic Books.

Gergen, Kenneth (1991). *The Saturated Self: Dilemmas of Identity in Contemporary Life*. New York: Basic Books.

Gilligan, Carol (1979). Woman's place in man's life cycle. *Harvard Educational Review* 49(4), pp. 431–46.

Gilligan, Carol (1982). *In a Different Voice: Psychological Theory and Women's Development*. Cambridge, Mass.: Harvard University Press.

Gilligan, Carol & Jane Attanucci (1988). Two moral orientations. In Carol Gilligan, Janie Victoria Ward & Jill McLean Taylor (eds.), *Mapping the Moral Domain*, pp. 73–86. Cambridge: Harvard University Press.

Giroux, Henry A. (1992). *Border Crossings: Cultural Workers and the Politics of Education*. New York: Routledge.

Giroux, Henry A. (1993). *Living Dangerously: Multiculturalism and the Politics of Difference*. New York: Peter Lang.

Gleason, Philip (1983). Identifying identity: A semantic history. *The Journal of American History* 69(4), pp. 910–31.

Goffman, Erving (1959). *The Presentation of Self in Everyday Life.* New York: Anchor Books.

Gore, Jennifer M. (1993). *The Struggle for Pedagogies: Critical and Feminist Discourses as Regimes of Truth.* New York: Routledge.

Hall, Stuart (1990). Cultural identity and diaspora. In Jonathan Rutherford (Ed.), *Identity: Community, Culture, Difference*, pp. 222–37. London: Lawrence & Wishart.

Harding, Sandra (1986). *The Science Question in Feminism.* Ithaca, N.Y.: Cornell University Press.

Harding, Sandra (ed.) (1987). *Feminism and Methodology.* Bloomington: Indiana University Press.

Harding, Sandra (1991). *Whose Science? Whose Knowledge?: Thinking from Women's Lives.* Ithaca, N.Y.: Cornell University Press.

Hartsock, Nancy C. M. (1987). The feminist standpoint: Developing the ground for a specifically feminist historical materialism. In Sandra Harding (Ed.), *Feminist Methodology*, pp. 157–80. Bloomington: Indiana University Press.

Heath, Shirley Brice (1983). *Ways with Words: Language, Life, and Work in Communities and Classrooms.* Cambridge: Cambridge University Press.

Hirsch, E. D., Jr. (1987). *Cultural Literacy: What Every American Needs to Know.* New York: Vintage Books.

Hoare, Carol H. (1991). Psychosocial identity development and cultural others. *Journal of Counseling and Development* 70(1), pp. 45–53.

Holland, Dorothy C. & Margaret A. Eisenhart (1990). *Educated in Romance: Women, Achievement, and College.* Chicago: University of Chicago Press.

hooks, bell (1984). *Feminist Theory: From Margin to Center.* Boston: South End Press.

hooks, bell (1992). *Black Looks: Race and Representation.* Boston: South End Press.

hooks, bell (1994). *Teaching to Transgress: Education as the Practice of Freedom.* New York: Routledge.

House, James S. (1977). The three faces of social psychology. *Sociometry* 40(2), pp. 161–77.

Hurston, Zora Neale (1937). *Their Eyes were Watching God.* New York: Harper & Row.

Huxley, Aldous (1962). *Island.* New York: Harper & Row.

Iannello, Kathleen P. (1992). *Decisions without Hierarchy: Feminist Interventions in Organization Theory and Practice.* New York: Routledge.

James, William (1890). *Principles of Psychology* (vol. 1). New York: Holt.

Kendall, Jane C. (1990). Combining service and learning: An introduction. In Jane C. Kendall (ed.), *Combining Service and Learning: A Resource Book for Community and Public Service*, pp. 1–33. Raleigh, N.C.: National Society for Internships and Experiential Education.

Kenway, Jane & Helen Modra (1992). Feminist pedagogy and emancipatory possibilities. In Carmen Lake & Jennifer Gore (eds.), *Feminisms and Critical Pedagogy*, pp. 138–66. New York: Routledge.

King, Patricia M. & Marcia B. Baxter Magolda (1996). A developmental perspective on learning. *Journal of College Student Development* 37(2), pp. 163–73.

Kohlberg, Lawrence (1975). The cognitive-developmental approach to moral education. *Phi Delta Kappan* 56, pp. 670–77.

Kohlberg, Lawrence (1980). The future of liberalism as the dominant ideology of the West. In Richard W. Wilson & Gordon J. Schochet (eds.), *Moral Development and Politics*, pp. 55–68. Westport, Conn.: Praeger.

Kolb, David A. (1984). *Experiential Learning: Experience as the Source of Learning and Development*. Englewood Cliffs, N.J.: Prentice-Hall.

Krieger, Susan (1983). *The Mirror Dance: Identity in a Women's Community*. Philadelphia: Temple University Press.

Krieger, Susan (1991). *Social Science and the Self: Personal Essays on an Art Form*. New Brunswick: Rutgers University Press.

Kuhn, Manfred (1964). Self and self-conception. In J. Gould and W. L. Kolb (eds.), *A Dictionary of the Social Sciences*. New York: Free Press of Glencoe.

Lever, Janet (1976). Sex differences in the games children play. *Social Problems* 23, pp. 478–87.

Lewis, Magda (1992). Interrupting patriarchy: Politics, resistance and transformation in the feminist classroom. In Carmen Lake & Jennifer Gore (eds.), *Feminisms and Critical Pedagogy*, pp. 167–91. New York: Routledge.

Liebow, Elliot (1993). *Tell Them Who I Am: The Lives of Homeless Women*. New York: Penguin Books.

Lincoln, Yvonna S. & Egon Guba (1985). *Naturalistic Inquiry*. Beverly Hills: Sage.

Lincoln, Yvonna S. & Egon Guba (1986). But is it rigorous? Trustworthiness and authenticity in naturalistic evaluation. In David D. Williams (ed.), "Naturalistic Evaluation," pp. 73–84. *New Directions for Program Evaluation*, 30. San Francisco: Jossey-Bass.

Lipsitz, Joan (1995). Prologue: Why we should care about caring. *Phi Delta Kappan* 76(9), pp. 665–66.

Lock, Andrew (1981). Universals in human cognition. In Paul Heelas & Andrew Lock (eds.), *Indigenous Psychologies*, pp. 19–36. London: Academic Press.

Loeb, Paul Rogat (1994). *Generation at the Crossroads: Apathy and Action on the American Campus*. New Brunswick, N.J.: Rutgers University Press.

Logan, Richard D. (1987). Historical change in prevailing sense of self. In Krysia Yardley & Terry Honess (eds.), *Self and Identity: Psychosocial Perspectives*, pp. 13–26. New York: John Wiley & Sons.

London, Howard B. (1978). *The Culture of a Community College*. New York: Praeger.

Lukács, Georg (1968). *History and Class Consciousness*. Translated by Rodney Livingston. Cambridge: The MIT Press.

Lyons, Nona Plessner (1988). Two perspectives: On self, relationships, and morality. In Carol Gilligan, Janie Victoria Ward & Jill McLean Taylor (eds.), *Mapping the Moral Domain: A Contribution of Women's Thinking to Psychological Theory and Education*, pp. 21–48. Cambridge: Harvard University Press.

Lyotard, Jean-François (1984). *The Postmodern Condition: A Report on Knowledge*. Minneapolis: University of Minnesota Press.

MacLeod, Jay (1987). *Ain't No Makin' It*. Boulder, Colo.: Westview.

Maher, Frances A. & Mary Kay Thompson Tetreault (1994). *The Feminist Classroom*. New York: Basic Books.

Mannheim, Karl (1936). *Ideology & Utopia*. San Diego: Harcourt Brace Jovanovich.

Markus, Hazel & Paula Nurius (1986). Possible selves. *American Psychologist* 41(9), pp. 954–69.

Marx, Karl (1844/1983). *Private Property and Communism*. Sections reprinted in Eugene Kamenka (ed.), *The Portable Marx*, pp. 146–52. New York: Penguin Books.

McAdams, Don P. (1990). Unity and purpose in human lives: The emergence of identity as a life story. In A. I. Rabin, Robert A. Zucker, Robert A. Emmons & Susan Frank (eds.), *Studying Persons and Lives*, pp. 148–200.

McAdams, Don P. (1995). What do we know when we know a person? *Journal of Personality* 63(3), pp. 365–96.

McLaren, Peter (1986). *Schooling as a Ritual Performance*. London: Routledge.

McLaren, Peter (1989). *Life in Schools*. New York: Longman.

McLaren, Peter (1995). *Critical Pedagogy and Predatory Culture*. New York: Routledge.

McRobbie, Angela (1978). Working-class girls and the culture of femininity. In Centre for Contemporary Cultural Studies (ed.), *Women Take Issue*, pp. 96–108. London: Routledge & Kegan Paul.

Mead, George Herbert (1934). *Mind, Self, & Society*. Edited by Charles W. Morris. Chicago: University of Chicago Press.

Mead, George Herbert (1982). *The Individual and the Social Self*. Edited by David L. Miller. Chicago: University of Chicago Press.

Merton, Robert K. (1949). *On Theoretical Sociology*. New York: The Free Press.

Messer-Davidow, Ellen (1985). Knowers, knowing, knowledge: Feminist theory and education. *Journal of Thought* 20(3), pp. 8–24.

Minh-ha, Trinh T. (1989). *Women, Native, Other: Writing Postcoloniality and Feminism*. Bloomington: Indiana University Press.

Minh-ha, Trinh T. (1991). *When the Moon Waxes Red: Representation, Gender and Cultural Politics*. New York: Routledge.

Minnich, Elizabeth Kamarck (1990). *Transforming Knowledge*. Philadelphia: Temple University Press.

Moffatt, Michael (1989). *Coming of Age in New Jersey: College and American Culture*. New Brunswick: Rutgers University Press.

Moraga, Cherríe & Gloria Anzaldúa (eds.) (1981). *This Bridge Called My Back: Writings By Radical Women of Color*. New York: Kitchen Table Press.

Morgan, Kathryn Pauly (1987). The perils and paradoxes of feminist pedagogy. *Resources for Feminist Teaching* 16, pp. 49–52.

Morris, Brian (1994). *Anthropology of the Self: The Individual in Cultural Perspective*. London: Pluto Press.

Morrison, Toni (1970). *The Bluest Eye*. New York: Holt, Rinehart, and Winston.

Murdoch, Iris (1970). *The Sovereignty of Good*. London: Routledge & Kegan Paul.

Naylor, Gloria (1988). *Mama Day*. New York: Vintage Books.

Nicholson, Linda (ed.) (1990). *Feminism/Postmodernism*. New York: Routledge.

Noddings, Nel (1984). *Caring: A feminine Approach to Ethics and Moral Education*. Berkeley: University of California Press.

Noddings, Nel (1992). *The Challenge to Care in Schools: An Alternative Approach to Education*. New York: Teachers College Press.

Noddings, Nel (1995). Teaching themes of care. *Phi Delta Kappan* 76(9), pp. 675–79.

Oliner, Pearl M. & Samuel P. Oliner (1995). *Toward a Caring Society: Ideas into Action.* Westport, Conn.: Praeger.

Palmer, Parker J. (1993). *To Know As We Are Known: Education As a Spiritual Journey.* San Francisco: Harper.

Palmer, Parker J. (1987). Community, conflict, and ways of knowing: Ways to deepen our educational agenda. *Change* 19(5), pp. 20–25.

Palmer, Parker J., Barbara G. Wheeler & James W. Fowler (eds.) (1990). *Caring for the Commonweal: Education for Religious and Public Life.* Macon, Ga.: Mercer University Press.

Parks, Sharon (1986). *The Critical Years: The Young Adult Search for a Faith to Live By.* San Francisco: Harper & Row.

Parsons, Talcott (1961). *Theories of Society.* New York: The Free Press. Sections reprinted in Leon H. Mayhew (ed.), *Talcott Parsons, On Institutions and Social Evolution*, pp. 157–72. Chicago: The University of Chicago Press, 1982.

Pascarella, Ernest T. & Patrick T. Terenzini (1991). *How College Affects Students: Findings and Insights from Twenty Years of Research.* San Francisco: Jossey-Bass.

Paulson, Karen, Robert A. Rhoads, Susan Campbell & Susan B. Millar (1994). *Tracking Progress & Envisioning the Future* (research report sponsored by the National Science Foundation). Pennsylvania State University, University Park, Pa.: Center for the Study of Higher Education.

Perry, William (1970). *Forms of Intellectual and Ethical Development in the College Years: A Scheme.* New York: Holt, Rinehart, & Winston.

Puka, Bill (1993). The liberation of caring: A different voice for Gilligan's "different voice." In Mary Jeanne Larrabee (ed.), *An Ethic of Care: Feminist and Interdisciplinary Perspectives*, pp. 215–39. New York: Routledge.

Radest, Howard (1993). *Community Service: Encounter with Strangers.* Westport, Conn.: Praeger.

Ramazanoğlu, Caroline (ed.) (1993). *Up against Foucault: Explorations of Some Tensions between Foucault and Feminism.* London: Routledge.

Regan, Tom (1991). *The Thee Generation: Reflections on the Coming Revolution.* Philadelphia: Temple University Press.

Rhoads, Robert A. (1994). *Coming Out in College: The Struggle for a Queer Identity.* Westport, Conn.: Bergin & Garvey.

Rhoads, Robert A. (1995a). The cultural politics of coming out in college: Experiences of male college students. *The Review of Higher Education* 19(1), pp. 1–22.

Rhoads, Robert A. (1995b). Learning from the coming-out experiences of college males. *Journal of College Student Development* 36(1), pp. 67–74.

Rhoads, Robert A. (1995c). Whales tales, dog piles, and beer goggles: An ethnographic case study of fraternity life. *Anthropology & Education Quarterly* 26(3), pp. 306–23.

Rhoads, Robert A. (1997). Crossing sexual orientation borders. *International Journal of Qualitative Studies in Education* 10(1), pp. 7–23.

Rhoads, Robert A. & James R. Valadez (1996). *Democracy, Multiculturalism, and the Community College: A Critical Perspective.* New York: Routledge.

Rich, Adrienne (1979). Taking women students seriously. In Adrienne Rich *On Lies, Secrets, and Silence: Selected Prose, 1966–1978,* pp. 237–46. New York: W. W. Norton & Company.

Riesman, David, Nathan Glazer & Reuel Denney (1950). *The Lonely Crowd: A Study of the Changing American Character.* New Haven, Conn.: Yale University Press.

Rosaldo, Renato (1989). *Culture and Truth: The Remaking of Social Analysis.* Boston: Beacon Press.

Ryff, Carol D. (1991). Possible selves in adulthood and old age: A tale of shifting horizons. *Psychology and Aging* 6(2), pp. 286–95.

Sampson, Edward E. (1985). The decentralization of identity: Toward a revised concept of personal and social order. *American Psychologist* 40(11), pp. 1203–11.

Sampson, Edward E. (1989). The challenge of social change for psychology: Globalization and psychology's theory of the person. *American Psychologist* 44(6), pp. 914–21.

Sanford, Nevitt (1956). Personality development during the college years. *Personnel and Guidance Journal* 35, pp. 74–80.

Sanford, Nevitt (1967). *Where Colleges Fail: A Study of the Student as a Person.* San Francisco: Jossey-Bass.

Sanger, Margaret (1971). *Margaret Sanger, an Autobiography.* New York: Dover Publications.

Savage, Mary C. (1988). Can ethnographic narrative be a neighborly act? *Anthropology & Education Quarterly* 19(1), pp. 3–19.

Schultz, Steven K. (1990). Learning by heart: The role of action in civic education. In Jane C. Kendall & Associates (eds.), *Combining Service and Learning: A Resource Book for Community and Public Service,* pp. 210–24. Raleigh, N.C.: National Society for Internships and Experiential Education.

Schwalbe, Michael L. (1991). Social structure and the moral self. In Judith A. Howard & Peter L. Callero (eds.), *The Self-Society Dynamic: Cognition, Emotion, and Action*. Cambridge: Cambridge University Press.

Schwehn, Mark R. (1993). *Exiles from Eden: Religion and the Academic Vocation*. New York: Oxford University Press.

Serow, Robert C. (1983). *Schooling for Diversity: An Analysis of Policy and Practice*. New York: Teachers College Press.

Shor, Ira (1987). *Critical Teaching & Everyday Life*. Chicago: University of Chicago Press.

Simon, Roger (1992). *Teaching Against the Grain: Texts for a Pedagogy of Possibility*. New York: Bergin & Garvey.

Stevens, Jay (1988). *Storming Heaven: LSD and the American Dream*. New York: Harper & Row.

Stone, Gregory P. (1962). Appearance and the self. In Arnold Rose (Ed.), *Human Behavior and Social Processes*, pp. 86–118. Boston: Houghton-Mifflin.

Strange, Carney (1994). Student development: The evolution and status of an essential idea. *Journal of College Student Development* 35(6), pp. 399–412.

Stryker, Sheldon (1991). Exploring the relevance of social cognition for the relationship of self and society: Linking the cognitive perspective and identity theory. In Judith A. Howard & Peter L. Callero (eds.), *The Self-Society Dynamic: Cognition, Emotion, and Action*, pp. 19–41. Cambridge: Cambridge University Press.

Taylor, Charles (1989). *Sources of the Self: The Making of the Modern Identity*. Cambridge: Harvard University Press.

Thomas, William I. & Dorothy Swaine Thomas (1928). *The Child in America*. New York: Alfred A. Knopf.

Tierney, William G. (1992). *Official Encouragement, Institutional Discouragement: Minorities in Academe—The Native American Experience*. Norwood, N.J.: Ablex.

Tierney, William G. (1993). *Building Communities of Difference: Higher Education in the Twenty-First Century*. Westport, Conn.: Bergin & Garvey.

Tierney, William G. & Robert A. Rhoads (1993). Postmodernism and critical theory in higher education: Implications for research and practice. In J. C. Smart (ed.), *Higher Education: Handbook of Theory and Research*, pp. 308–43. New York: Agathon.

Tönnies, Ferdinand (1957). *Community and Society:* Gemeinschaft und gesellschaft. Translated by Charles P. Loomis. New York: Harper & Row.

Turkle, Sherry (1995). *Life on Screen: Identity in the Age of the Internet.* New York: Simon & Schuster.

Turner, Ralph (1987). Articulating self and social structure. In Krysia Yardley & Terry Honess (eds.), *Self and Identity: Psychosocial Perspectives*, pp. 119–32. New York: John Wiley & Sons.

Upcraft, M. Lee & Leila V. Moore (1990). Evolving theoretical perspectives of student development. In Margaret J. Barr, M. Lee Upcraft, & Associates (eds.), *New Futures for Student Affairs*, pp. 41–68. San Francisco: Jossey-Bass.

Weber, Max (1904/1958). *The Protestant Ethic and the Spirit of Capitalism.* New York: Charles Scribner's Sons.

Weber, Max (1919/1946). Science as a vocation. In Hans H. Gerth & C. Wright Mills (eds.), *From Max Weber: Essays in Sociology*, pp. 129–56. New York: Oxford University Press.

Weis, Lois (1985). *Between Two Worlds.* Boston: Routledge.

Welch, Sharon D. (1990). *A Feminist Ethic of Risk.* Minneapolis: Fortress Press.

West, Cornel (1993). *Race Matters.* New York: Vintage Books.

Wheeler, Barbara G. (1990). Introduction: A forum on paideia. In Parker J. Palmer, Barbara G. Wheeler & James W. Fowler (eds.), *Caring for the Commonweal: Education for Religious and Public Life*, pp. 1–7. Macon, Ga.: Mercer University Press.

Willis, Paul E. (1977). *Learning to Labor.* Aldershot: Gower.

Wolfe, Thomas (1935). *The Hills Beyond.* New York: New American Library.

Wuthnow, Robert (1991). *Acts of Compassion: Caring for Others and Helping Ourselves.* Princeton, N.J.: Princeton University Press.

Wuthnow, Robert (1995). *Learning to Care: Elementary Kindness in an Age of Indifference.* New York: Oxford University Press.

Young, Iris Marion (1990). The ideal of community and the politics of difference. In Linda J. Nicholson (Ed.), *Feminism/Postmodernism*, pp. 300–23. New York: Routledge.

Index

A

administration (university), 60
African Americans: identity, 56–58
agape, 87
agency, 43, 60
Aids Project, 21
Akre, Brian, 100
Alternative Spring Break, 133–134, 143, 156, 196–197, 225
An Aristocracy of Everyone, 171
Anna Karenina, 100
Anzaldúa, Gloria, 231
Appalachia, 136
As You Like It, 26
Astin, Alexander, 34
atomistic formalism, 47
Attanucci, Jane, 50

B

Baldwin, James, 117
Barber, Benjamin, 9–10, 122, 171–173, 185, 211
Battistoni, Richard, 210–211
Baudrillard, Jean, 1, 61
Baxter Magolda, Marcia, 48, 93

Belenky, Mary, 48, 50, 53, 92
Bellah, Robert, 71, 73–75, 123, 173, 176
Benhabib, Seyla, 1
Bennett, William, 172, 211
Bloom, Allan, 37
Bluest Eye, The, 7, 57
Blumer, Herbert, 6, 24, 28, 76, 82–84, 175
border crossings, 124–125
bourgeoisie, 79
Boyer, Ernest, 226
Brabek, Mary, 50, 212
Brethren Volunteer Corps, 170
Brown, Robert, 19
Bulger, Stephanie, 32
Burbules, Nicholas, 2, 87, 173
Burke, Kenneth, 59, 76, 82–84
Bush, George, 119, 122, 201

C

Cain, Maureen, 21
Call of Service, The, 100, 186
Campaign for Economic Democracy, 73–74
Campbell, Susan, 48
Campus Opportunity Outreach League, 37

capitalism, 76
Caring: A Feminine Approach to Ethics
    and Moral Education, 50
Caring for the Commonweal, 174
Cartesian dualism, 123
Challenge to Care in Schools, The, 90
charity, 128, 149, 163, 171
Charleston, South Carolina, 132, 141,
    157–158, 160–162
Charleston Sea Islands, South Carolina,
    89, 130
Chicago School. See symbolic interac-
    tionism
Chickering, Arthur, 35
Child in America, The, 25
child-mother relationship, 45
Chodorow, Nancy, 6, 29, 45–46
Christianity. See spirituality
Church of the Brethren (Washington,
    D.C.), 103–104
citizenship, 5, 171, 208, 222
City College of New York, 37
City University of New York, 174
Civil Rights movement, 167
class consciousness, 79–80
Clinton, Bill, 122, 201
cognitive development, 49
Coles, Robert, 2, 38, 100, 138–139, 144,
    185
collaboration: mutuality, 146–149
collegial model, 87
communism, 74, 79
Communist Manifesto, 229
communitarianism, 8, 10, 172–177,
    211–212, 233
community: community building,
    171–176, 220; community service,
    90–94; community service learning,
    165; conflict perspectives, 79–82;
    individualism, 71–76, 81; postmod-
    ern conceptions, 85–90; student
    experiences, 163–169; symbolic per-
    spectives, 82–84; traditional concep-
    tions, 76–84
community service: community, 90–94;
    critical community service, 216–222;

education, 90–94; faculty, 223–224;
    mutuality, 136–139; organizational
    leaders, 222–223; others, 90–94; self,
    90–94; structural changes, 225–227;
    student affairs, 224–225; student
    leaders, 225
conflict theory, 84
connected knowing, 92
connectedness, 46–47, 119, 155, 172,
    175, 212
Conroy, Pat, 134, 157
conscientization, 214
conservatives, 173, 211
Cooley, Charles Horton, 26
Crapanzano, Vincent, 11
critical community service, 216–222;
    eight guiding principles, 219–222
critical consciousness, 9, 93–94
critical education, 9, 91, 94
critical idealists, 183
critical pedagogy, 9, 94, 215–216, 221
Critical Pedagogy and Predatory
    Culture, 215
critical theory, 5, 9, 10, 17, 66, 87, 95,
    212, 216; education, 212–216
Culley, Margo, 48, 91, 212–213
culture: collegiate culture, 63–67; diver-
    sity, 7, 85, 90, 172, 175, 177; dynam-
    ic and dialectical view, 55, 95, 124;
    endowment, 173; identity and
    schooling, 55–61
curriculum, 2, 35, 60, 165, 226

D

D'Augelli, Anthony, 36
Darwin, Charles, 61; Darwinism, 78
Daufuskie, South Carolina, 158
Davis, Angela, 117
Day, Dorothy, 100
decolonization, 212
democracy, 35, 95, 146, 174, 208, 210;
    democratic education, 9, 49; democ-
    ratic society, 10, 16, 34, 94
Democracy and Education, 210

Democracy in America, 74
Denney, Reuel, 77, 90
Denzin, Norman, 6, 24, 29–31
Derrida, Jacques, 172
deterministic theory, 77
de Tocqueville, Alexis, 74–75, 210–211
Detroit, Michigan, 99
Dewey, John, 4, 9, 34, 93–94, 207–212, 221, 227
dialectical view, 56
Diamond, Arlyn, 91
Discipline and Punish, 85
diversity, 10, 109, 154, 172, 176; culture, 7, 85, 90, 172, 175, 177; difference, 85, 87, 173
dramaturgy, 28, 83
D'Souza, Dinesh, 37, 172, 211
Durkheim, Emile, 7, 76–78, 172

E

Eckert, Penelope, 55
Edisto Island, South Carolina, 156
education: community service, 90–94; critical views, 212–216; culture and identity, 55–61; democratic education, 9, 49; elementary education, 90; higher education, 176–177, 207; identity, 61–63
Edwards, Lee, 91
ego, 3, 28
Eisenhart, Margaret, 55
Emancipation Proclamation, 158
emancipation theory, 60
engrossment, 51–53
epigenetic principle, 43
Erikson, Erik, 35–36, 43–45, 59, 61
essentialize, 137, 154
ethic-of-care, 2, 4–5, 7–10, 43, 47, 49–54, 63, 94, 100, 138, 148, 175–177, 208, 212–213, 216, 232–233
ethic of risk, 89
ethnography, 106–107
Etzioni, Amitai, 172, 176, 212

Eye of Power, The, 85
Exiles from Eden, 232
experiential learning, 208–212, 219, 221
extracurriculum, 165

F

faculty, 4, 6, 34–35, 48, 60, 87, 218, 226; community service, 223–224
Fairweather, James, 226
Feldman, Kenneth, 34
feminism, 4–7, 9–10, 17–22, 29, 39, 43, 50–51, 54–55, 63, 66, 88, 148, 172, 175, 177, 208; caring, 175–176; feminist classroom, 212; gendered identities, 45–49; historical materialism, 19; pedagogies, 91, 94, 213, 216, 221; theory, 95, 212, 216
Ferguson, Kathy, 48
Fine, Michelle, 55
Foucault, Michel, 55, 82, 85–86, 88
Fowler, James, 174
fraternities, 64
Freire, Paulo, 4, 9, 93–94, 176, 179, 184–185, 200–202, 214
Freud, Sigmund, 3, 28, 61
functionalism, 7, 78, 84, 88, 172

G

gay/lesbian/bisexual: identity, 57
Geertz, Clifford, 32, 55–56, 61, 81, 232
gemeinschaft, 76, 80, 90
gender, 29, 148; feminism, 45–49; research, 49
Generation at the Crossroads, 37, 72
Genesis, 229
Gergen, Kenneth, 1, 86
gesellschaft, 76
Gilligan, Carol, 4, 6, 29, 39, 45–47, 50–51, 53–54, 148, 212, 230; relational self, 4, 6
Giroux, Henry, 4, 55, 93, 123–124, 171, 174, 212

Glazer, Nathan, 77, 90
Gleason, Philip, 3
God. *See* spirituality
Goffman, Erving, 26–28, 83
Good Society, The, 173
Gore, Jennifer, 91
Greeks for Peace Movement, 37
Guatemala, 115
Guba, Egon, 31, 33, 107
Gullah, 134, 159

H

Habitat for Humanity, 9, 14, 16, 89, 155,
    180, 183, 187–190, 202
Habits of the Heart, 71, 74
Hall, Stuart, 55, 59
Harding, Sandra, 18–19
Hartsock, Nancy, 19
Harvard University, 186
Heath, Shirley Brice, 130
higher education. *See* education
Hills Beyond, The, 230
Hilton Head, South Carolina, 157–158,
    160
Hirsch, E. D., 37, 172
Hoare, Carol, 41, 55–57, 59, 62
Holland, Dorothy, 55
Honduras, 115
hooks, bell, 4, 60, 93, 171, 212–214
House, James, 24
Howard University, 223
Hughes, Everett, 24
Hurston, Zora Neale, 230
Huxley, Aldous, 229
hyperindividualism, 174
hyperpluralism, 172
hyperskepticism, 172

I

Iannello, Kathleen, 48
id, 3
idealism, 38

idealists, 183
identity: African Americans, 56–58; cri-
    sis, 44; culture and schooling, 55–61;
    educational practices, 61–63; gay/les-
    bian/bisexual, 57; technology, 61, 63,
    75, 88, 90
Ideology and Utopia, 229
In a Different Voice, 230
individualism: community, 71–76,
    81
individuation. *See* self
instrumentalism, 88–89
interdependence, 10, 107
internet community, 75
internet identity, 75
interpretive analysis, 32–33
Island, 229

J

James, William, 26
Jefferson Community Center (South
    Carolina), 161
Jesus. *See* spirituality
Johns Island, South Carolina, 8, 27,
    128–134, 136, 140, 142–144,
    149–150, 156, 162, 192–193, 199;
    Johns Island Project, 129–136,
    138–139, 145, 147, 165–166, 169
*Journal of College Student
    Development*, 224

K

Kendall, Jane, 130, 137, 164, 185
Kenway, Jane, 213
Kiawah Island, South Carolina,
    130–131, 157
King, Patricia, 93
Kohlberg, Lawrence, 35, 49–50
Kolb, David, 93
Krieger, Susan, 17–19, 106–107
Kuhn, Manfred, 57

L

Lansing, Michigan, 15, 101, 166, 178
Lansing State Journal, 99
Leary, Timothy, 229
Lennox, Sara, 91
Lesbian, Gay, and Bisexual Student
    Alliance, 65
Lever, Janet, 29
Lewis, Magda, 213
liberation theology, 89
Liebow, Elliot, 102, 117–118, 124
Life on the Screen, 61
Lincoln, Yvonna, 31, 33, 107
Lipsitz, Joan, 2
Lock, Andrew, 69
Loeb, Paul, 20, 37–38, 72, 167, 174
Logan, Richard, 3
London, Howard, 55
Lonely Crowd, The, 77, 90
looking glass self, 26
Louisville, Kentucky, 15, 111, 121, 196
Lukács, George, 76, 79–81
Lyons, Nona Plessner, 45
Lyotard, Jean-François, 1, 55, 61

M

MacLeod, Jay, 55
Madsen, Richard, 71
Magolda, Marcia Baxter, 48, 93
Maher, Frances, 212
Mama Day, 132, 134, 157
Mannheim, Karl, 229
Marine Corp, 73–74
Markus, Hazel, 62
Marx, Karl, 7, 19, 76, 79–81, 229
Marxian imperative, 23
Marxism, 23
materialism, 79, 81, 181
McAdams, Don, 57
McLaren, Peter, 4, 55, 93, 119, 122–124,
    171, 212, 215
McRobbie, Angela, 55

Mead, George Herbert, 4, 6–7, 17,
    23–30, 39, 63, 66, 76, 82–84, 191,
    231; social self, 4, 23–30, 39
mechanical solidarity, 76
member checks, 107
Merton, Robert, 76–79, 172
Messer-Davidow, Ellen, 18
Mexico, 14, 115, 191
*Michigan Journal of Community Service
    Learning*, 165, 224
Michigan State University, 3–4, 30, 92,
    110, 166, 192, 196–197, 219
Millar, Susan, 48
Minh-ha, Trinh, 45, 51, 55–56, 85–86,
    97, 106–107
Minnich, Elizabeth, 21
Miriam's Kitchen, 102–104
Mirror Dance, The, 106
modernism, 1, 3, 10, 75–76, 85, 90, 95,
    155
Modra, Helen, 213
Moffatt, Michael, 35
Moore, Leila, 35
Moraga, Cherríe, 231
moral philosophy, 51
moral reasoning, 49–50
morality, 45, 52, 74–75
Morgan, Kathryn Pauly, 91
Morris, Brian, 3, 148
Morrison, Toni, 7, 57–59
Mother Teresa, 72
Multi-User Domains (MUDs), 75
multiculturalism, 85, 171–172, 220;
    resistance multiculturalism, 215
multiplicity, 1, 60, 86, 90, 106, 176
Murdoch, Iris, 51
mutuality, 7–8, 107, 154–155, 167, 171,
    177–178, 217–218, 220; community
    service, 136–139; receiving,
    139–145; collaboration, 146–149

N

National Science Foundation, 48
naturalistic inquiry, 17, 22, 31, 39

naturalistic interactionism, 31
Navy, 118
Naylor, Gloria, 132, 134, 157–158
New Orleans, Louisiana, 15
Newcomb, Theodore, 34
New York City, 15, 73, 111–112,
    191–192, 197, 209, 219
Nicaragua, 115
Nicholson, Linda, 55
nihilism, 172
Noddings, Nel, 2, 50–52, 90–91, 138
nonequilibrium theory of identity, 86
normalization, 85
Nurius, Paula, 62
nurturer, 91

O

oedipal identification, 46
Oliner, Pearl, 34, 47
Oliner, Samuel, 34, 47
Olive Branch Community, 184
organic solidarity, 76
organizational leaders: community ser-
    vice, 222–223
others: community service, 90–94; oth-
    erness, 2, 5, 7; understanding the
    other, 105–108

P

paideia, 174
Palmer, Parker, 2, 16, 174
Palo Alto, California, 117
Panopticon, 85
Parks, Sharon, 36
Parsons, Talcott, 76–78, 172
Pascarella, Ernest, 34
paternalism, 137
Paulson, Karen, 48
Peace Corps, 170
pedagogy, 54; critical pedagogy, 9, 94,
    215–216, 221; engaged pedagogy,
    214; feminism, 91, 94, 213, 216, 221

Pennsylvania State University, 3, 7–8,
    21, 30, 65, 92, 100, 103, 114,
    160–161, 163, 167, 169–170, 187,
    191, 197
Perry, William, 35–36
Phi Delta Kappan, 2
Plato, 229
politics of difference, 55
politics of identity, 40, 43, 55, 59–61, 63
Portuges, Catherine, 91
positionality, 6, 17–23, 107, 212
Postmodern Condition, The, 61
postmodernism, 1, 2, 5, 8, 10, 17, 39,
    60, 62, 66, 68, 71, 75–76, 82, 84,
    89–90, 95, 118, 154, 171–177, 184,
    208, 233; community, 85–90; critical
    postmodernism, 55, 172–173, 233;
    culture, 43; power, 85, 107, 137, 173;
    praxis, 33, 87, 179, 185, 214; pre-
    modern, 3
*Presentation of Self in Everyday Life,
    The*, 27
Princess Anne, Maryland, 187–190
proletariate, 79–80
*Protestant Ethic and the Spirit of
    Capitalism, The*, 232
Puerto Rico, 14, 190
Puget Sound, 114
Puka, Bill, 216–217

Q

qualitative methods, 30–34, 39

R

race, 32, 153, 167, 175, 194; racial iden-
    tities, 122; racism, 120, 161; stereo-
    types, 120–124
Radest, Howard, 2, 4, 8, 87, 108,
    118–119, 136–137, 146–147, 149,
    175, 185–187, 201, 220
Ramazanoğlu, Caroline, 55
reciprocity, 137

reflection, 5, 8–9, 112; action, 184–187, 207; leadership, 197–198; self, 192–197; service, 180–184; social change, 200–201; values, 198–200
Regan, Tom, 152, 178
religion, 14, 177, 147, 191. *See also* spirituality
Republic, The, 229
representation, 106
resistance multiculturalism, 215
Rhoads, Robert, 36, 48, 55, 57, 65, 210
Rice, Suzanne, 2, 87, 173
Rich, Adrienne, 213
Riesman, David, 77, 90
Rosaldo, Renato, 32
Rural Mission (South Carolina), 131–134, 142, 144
Rutgers University, 36
Ryff, Carol, 90

S

Salisbury State University, 187
Sampson, Edward, 3, 54, 86
Sanday, Peggy, 65
Sanford, Nevitt, 35
Sanger, Margaret, 81, 112, 181
Savage, Mary, 33
Savannah, Georgia, 157
schooling: culture and identity, 55–61
Schultz, Steven, 92
Schwalbe, Michael, 26
Schwehn, Mark, 232–233
Sea Islands of Charleston, South Carolina, 89, 156
Seabrook Island, South Carolina, 130–133, 157
Seattle, Washington, 114–115, 208
self: community service, 90–94; constitutive, 62; educational practices, 61–63; individualism, 29, 46; looking glass self, 26; Mead and the social self, 23–30; possible self, 62; reflection, 192–197
Serow, Robert, 78, 173–174

service: reflection, 184–187
service learning, 4–5, 164–165, 185
Service Learning Center (Michigan State University), 127
sexual identity, 65
Shakespeare, William, 26
Shor, Ira, 204
social change, 9; reflection, 200–201
social construction of knowledge, 18
social Darwinism, 78
social interaction, 3–4, 52, 55
social justice, 5, 112–113, 115–116, 147, 168, 215–216
social life. *See* community
social policy, 112–113
social psychology, 5, 24
social saturation, 86
Social Science and the Self, 17
socialism, 74
socialization, 54
sociological theory, 95
SOME (So Others May Eat), 103–104, 109
Special Olympics, 93
spirituality, 16, 36, 158, 193; Christian, 189, 233; Christianity, 135, 158, 189–190, 233; God, 72, 132, 135–136, 169, 189, 229; Hindu, 189; Jesus Christ, 14, 147, 190–191; religion, 14, 77, 147, 191, 193–194, 217
St. Helena, South Carolina, 158
St. Johns, South Carolina, 158
standpoint theory, 18
Stanford University, 35
State College, Pennsylvania, 114, 161
stereotypes, 110, 124
Stevens, Jay, 229
Stone, Gregory, 6, 28, 57
Strange, Carney, 35
Stryker, Sheldon, 57
student affairs, 4, 9, 35; community service, 224–225
student leaders: community service, 225
Sullivan, William, 71
superego, 3
Swidler, Ann, 71

symbolic interactionism, 4, 6, 17, 23, 39, 46, 51, 53, 59, 63, 66, 138, 175, 214; Mead's social self, 23–30

T

Taylor, Charles, 3
technology: identity, 61, 63, 75, 88, 90
Tell Them Who I Am, 102
Terenzini, Patrick, 34
Tetreault, Mary Kay Thompson, 212
Thee Generation, The, 178
Their Eyes Were Watching God, 230
This Bridge Called My Back, 231
Thomas, Dorothy Swain, 25
Thomas, Theorem, 25
Thomas, William I., 24–25
Thousand Points of Light, 119
Tierney, William, 2, 4, 10, 55, 87, 93, 171, 173–174, 216
Tipton, Steven, 71
Tolstoy, Lev, 100
Tönnies, Ferdinand, 75–78, 90
Toward a Caring Society, 34
Turkle, Sherry, 61, 63, 75, 86
Turner, Ralph, 57
Tutu, Desmond, 19

U

Upcraft, M. Lee, 35
University of California at Berkeley, 115
University of Chicago, 24
University of Michigan, 37
University of South Carolina, 3, 8, 30, 129–130, 133–134, 145
University of Utah, 226
University of Washington, 114

V

Valadez, James, 55, 210
values: reflection, 198–200
Vietnam War, 73
Voluntary Action Center, 195–196

W

Washington, D.C., 7, 14–15, 52, 88, 92, 100, 109, 111–112, 115, 117–118, 125, 170, 178, 184, 188; D.C. Project, 101–105, 116, 118, 155, 164–165, 180–181, 192, 197
Water is Wide, The, 134, 157
Watson, Lila, 126
Weber, Max, 56, 232
Weis, Lois, 55
Welch, Sharon, 88–89
West, Cornell, 55, 59–60
Wheeler, Barbara, 174
whiteness, 122
Whose Science? Whose Knowledge?, 18
Willis, Paul, 55
Wolfe, Thomas, 230
World War II, 102
worldviews, 3
Wuthnow, Robert, 2, 72, 88, 92, 112, 143, 175

Y

Yonges Island, South Carolina, 8, 123, 154, 165, 167–168, 170–171, 194, 199, 209, 219; Yonges Island Project, 156–163
Young, Iris Marion, 47, 55

Z

Zacchaeus' Community Kitchen (Washington, D.C.), 102–105, 184